W. M. L. Jay

**My Winter in Cuba**

W. M. L. Jay

**My Winter in Cuba**

ISBN/EAN: 9783337253516

Printed in Europe, USA, Canada, Australia, Japan

Cover: Foto ©Thomas Meinert / pixelio.de

More available books at **www.hansebooks.com**

## BY W. M. L. JAY,

*Author of "Shiloh."*

This country excels all others, as far as the day surpasses the night in brightness and splendor.—COLUMBUS.

> A land of leaf and bloom,
> Of shining palm and drooping coco-tree,
> Of spiced mimosa, tremulous bamboo,
> And giant ceiba, *in an air of balm.*
> LUTO.

---

NEW YORK:
E. P. DUTTON & CO., 713 BROADWAY.
HARTFORD: CHURCH PRESS.
1871.

Entered, according to Act of Congress, in the year 1871, by
E. P. DUTTON & CO.,
In the Office of the Librarian of Congress, at Washington.

M. H. MALLORY & CO.,
PRINTERS AND ELECTROTYPERS,
HARTFORD, CONN.

TO THE

## *HOME-CIRCLE,*

For whose Dear Eyes it was First Written,

### This Chronicle

IS RIGHTFULLY DEDICATED.

# PREFACE.

The personal pronoun "my" in the title of the present work is explanatory, not egotistical. The "Winter" herein described is mine, and not another's, in that it deals so largely with that domestic side of Cuban life, which few travellers ever see, and whereof none, to my knowledge, have ever written. The reader may find elsewhere more graphic descriptions of Cuba's scenery; combined with accurate tables of her statistics, and profound views of her politics; but he will find no work that opens to him so frankly the doors of Cuban homes, and allows him to watch the inner currents of Cuban life. Nor could the present narrative have flowed thus freely across private thresholds, except by the use of fictitious names. There may have been SÁMANOS in Cuba, but I never saw them there. The real names of my kind entertainers are stereotyped only on my heart. But, with this slight exception, the narrative may be relied upon as strictly true.

If it be found to touch but lightly upon matters of policy and government, it is because their present aspect is felt to be so transitory. Enough has been said to show that the Cubans had cause for revolt; more might cease to be pertinent between the pen and the press. Whether the present rebellion succeed or no, its ultimate effect can scarcely fail to be beneficial to the Cubans. Whether that benefit is to come through amelioration of the Spanish rule, independence, or annexation, it is not worth while to predict. But all those who have felt the fascination of the beautiful island, and keep her fair memory in their hearts, will most devoutly pray that it come soon, and bring with it social, political, and religious regeneration.

Hudson, N. Y., July, 1871.

# CONTENTS.

|  |  | PAGE |
|---|---|---|
| I. | WHEREFORE, | 9 |
| II. | THE VOYAGE, | 12 |
| III. | LANDING AND HOTEL, | 16 |
| IV. | AT THE RETRETA, | 26 |
| V. | THE PALACE AND PLAZA, | 33 |
| VI. | WITHIN AND WITHOUT THE WALLS, | 39 |
| VII. | COLUMBUS.—THE CATHEDRAL, | 49 |
| VIII. | THE FISH-MARKET, | 61 |
| IX. | SHOPPING.—STREET SIGHTS.—LA FUERZA, | 69 |
| X. | FROM HAVANA TO MATANZAS, | 80 |
| XI. | EVERY MORNING, | 92 |
| XII. | DURING THE DAY, | 103 |
| XIII. | EVERY EVENING, | 117 |
| XIV. | THE VALLEY OF YUMURÍ, | 131 |
| XV. | LAS CUEVAS DE BELLAMAR, | 140 |
| XVI. | A PROCESSION, | 155 |
| XVII. | A TE DEUM, | 162 |
| XVIII. | SUNDAY SEEINGS AND DOINGS, | 169 |
| XIX. | THE ENTRANCE AND EXIT OF LENT, | 184 |
| XX. | COSAS DE CUBA, | 195 |
| XXI. | TO SANTA SOFÍA, | 211 |
| XXII. | THE INGENIO, | 217 |
| XXIII. | PLANTATION PICTURES, | 227 |
| XXIV. | FIRE IN THE CANE! | 247 |
| XXV. | A CAFETAL, | 252 |
| XXVI. | BEMBA AND LIMONAR, | 264 |
| XXVII. | SHADOW, | 270 |
| XXVIII. | WAITING IN HAVANA, | 278 |
| XXIX. | DEPARTURE, | 293 |

# MY WINTER IN CUBA.

## CHAPTER I.

### WHEREFORE.

"CHANGE of climate," prescribed the doctor, at the end of his wits and the *materia medica*.

I only looked into the fire, and smiled. But the doctor quickly diagnosed the smile, and detected satire.

"Well?" said he, in his crisp, no-time-to-waste, professional tone.

"I was reminded," said I, "of a ludicrous little incident that I witnessed last summer. A frightened ox-team ran away with an empty cart and a drunken driver. After the clumsy vehicle had been violently whisked over logs and rocks, and through bushes and briars, and the unhappy occupant, clutching at the air, alternately rolled from side to side and end to end thereof, the one was upset and the other pitched into a wayside ditch. 'Why didn't you jump out?' chorused the bystanders, as they picked him up. 'I sh-should just like to know,' hiccoughed he, angrily, 'h-how I could jump out, when I c-couldn't stay in!'"

"Oh! the jumping out can be managed for you," said *le curé*, benignantly.

"Certainly," quoth the doctor, with a twinkle in his eye. "Was not the story intended to point the moral that people who can neither stay in nor jump out, must be pitched out? How would you like to be pitched into —— Florida, for instance?"

I shrugged my shoulders ungraciously. I had all an invalid's reluctance to move out of the narrow orbit wherein he has swung so long as to be at once tired of it and wedded to it.

"There is Juan's invitation," suggested *le curé*.

"Eh! what?" said the doctor, discovering a gleam of something like interest in my face.

"Juan," briefly explained *le curé*, "is a youth who was consigned to us by a mutual friend, three years ago, with the handsomest of Spanish faces, and the most stubborn of Spanish tongues, to be taught English. He stayed with us two years, became to us as a brother, went hence to Cuba, and is continually entreating one or all of us to visit him there."

"The very thing!" said the doctor, rising. "Pack up your fig leaves, and be off at once!"

"Pray," asked I, "can you tell me whether said leaves should be plucked from a flax plant or a sheep's back?"

He hesitated, with his hand upon the door-knob.

"Write to *la Clarita*," said *le curé*. "She visited Cuba, you remember."

The doctor nodded approvingly and shut the door.

This was what *la Clarita* wrote back:

"Fig leaves, did you ask? Those which you shed in the hottest part of last summer—if they are not too faded. The Cubans, when they outgrow their Eden garment of innocence (which is not so early as sophisticated foreigners could wish!), get the summer fashions from Paris, and wear them throughout the year. *Y porqué no?* Have they not summer all the time?"

And thus it came to pass that I spent a winter in Cuba, and wrote thereof as follows:—

## CHAPTER II.

**THE VOYAGE.**

HEAVY clouds brooded above, and the air was thick with snow. It was the dreariest of drear December days. From the deck of the "Eagle," I watched the forms of friends on shore merge and fade in the distance, and their waving handkerchiefs flicker and go out like spent lamps. After them glided the snow-whitened shores of the harbor, the islands, the Narrows; over me settled a sense of isolation and exile chiller than the snowflakes, and grayer than the gathering twilight. Only those who have tasted this one great drop of bitterness in the pleasant cup of foreign travel, can realize how completely, for the time, it neutralizes every sweetness which Hope and Imagination present to the lips. It seems as if no land, however bright with tropical sunshine, however mossed and garlanded with legend, song, or story, can ever be so fair as that which is fast becoming only a blue line upon the horizon; and which, when it sinks beneath the wave, seems to have left you homeless in the world.

For change of scene, temperature, and mood, I went below. A forlorn circle of passengers was drawn round a huge, red stove, which toasted their faces, without in the least mitigating the chill at their backs. My stateroom was like an icehouse. Fig leaves, indeed! I wished that mine had been of sable and otter, six deep! Fortunately, the good ship "Eagle" had foreseen the want, and provided ample store of blankets. In these I wrapped myself, and wondered how *she* stood it, with full dress of naught but ropes and spars, and for *robe de nuit* a wet sheet and a flowing sea!

It would seem that every pain turns to something like pleasure in the retrospect. Else, why should sea-voyagers invariably linger so lovingly, in print, over those pangs of sea-sickness that were so irksome, in fact! I shall not follow their example further than to state that I spent the two following days under the aforenamed blankets, testing the virtues of various remedies for *mal de mer*, provided by kind and credulous friends; and that I left a goodly collection of half-emptied phials on the shelf of my berth, for the behoof of any future occupant disposed to try such experiments. May he find the study more pleasing and profitable than I did!

During the third night out, there was a rapid increase of temperature; and the morning was like a morning in mid-June. Through my narrow window I beheld a cloudless sky, a golden shimmer of sunshine, a sea blue and tranquil as an inland lake. The stateroom grew insufferably hot and stuffy; I was fain to take a pillow and drag myself to the upper deck, which was roofed with an awning, furnished with chairs, and so transformed into a kind of sky-parlor. Here were grouped many of the passengers,—the ladies enjoying chat, books, and fancy-work, the gentlemen, political discussions and cigars; with here and there a pale and spiritless individual, like myself, caring to do nothing but gaze at sea and sky and far-off glimpses of shore.

Nearly all day, we were in sight of the Florida coast, studded with islands, and broken by such deep indentations that, at times, it seemed to be coming out to meet us, showing distinctly a low sweep of sand-beach, and a thick fringe of evergreen oaks; and anon receding to only a faint line in the distance. The rising of clouds from the ocean is a singular and interesting sight; they seem both nearer and denser than on land. I watched a number of dark cloud-peaks come slowly into view, solid enough, in appearance, to deceive one into the belief that they belonged to a veritable mountain range,—only that, after a little, they broke, scattered, and vanished, in unmistakable cloud fashion.

After a time, I fell into conversation with some of my fellow-passengers, and was amazed to learn what an amount of gossip was current among them,—yes, positively, gossip!—on a steamer only three days out, with a crowd of passengers gathered from the four quarters of the globe, not a dozen of whom had ever met before, or would ever meet again! The histories of one deserted wife, and one heart-broken one, of a runaway couple, a defaulter fleeing from justice, a Mexican Crœsus, a bewitching flirt, et cætera, et cætera, were told me with a clearness of outline and a breadth of color that defied criticism. I listened and marvelled, admiring the ingenuity that had invented all these concurrent details, or the detective skill that had wormed them out. It might be that the talent was here running to waste!

At sunset, there was a lavish outpouring of brilliant color, and some wonderful sky-scenery. At early dusk we made the southernmost Florida light, and then quickly left it behind. At the rising of the moon, we looked out over an unbroken extent of shining, murmuring semi-tropical sea. I say *semi*, to be geographically correct, the Tropic of Cancer not yet being passed. But for artistic and atmospheric accuracy the qualification is not needed.

Now, finally, it was necessary to face the horrors of my stateroom. Like many anticipated evils, they shrank to nothingness in the reality. The demon of sea-sickness had flown. Over the moonlit ocean, I sailed softly into Dreamland.

One more day of smooth gliding through balmiest sunshine and gentlest trade-winds, of quiet enjoyment of pleasant ocean pictures and curious contrasts of faces, characters, and languages; of growing strength and spirits; of eating and drinking, chatting, gossiping, musing, and yawning;—one more night of moonlight splendor and peace;—and the voyage was over.

## CHAPTER III.

#### THE LANDING AND HOTEL.

ONLY four days and a half from New York to Havana!—that is to say, from snow to verdure, from frost to flowers, from bare, gray boughs to clustering fruits, from winter to summer! There is a touch of enchantment—of Aladdin's lamp and the Emir's carpet—about it!

The first land made by south-going steamers is the *Monte del Pan*, or Bread Mountain, of Matanzas; which we saw with the earliest sunbeams on its top. Thereafter, we skirted the Cuban coast for two or three hours, near enough to see that the island's surface was green and undulating, on the ocean, and that it rose into mountain and table-land, in the interior. By and by, palms and other forms of tropical vegetation were dimly distinguishable. Thereupon the whole land became picture and poem, and I slid into delicious reverie, and took but vague note of time or scene, till roused by the report of a gun to see that Havana was full in view.

To the left, was the far-famed Morro Castle, with little of the grimness of a fortress about it, but much of the dreamy and delicate beauty of an enchanted palace.

So it seemed to me, at least; but I suspect that I saw everything *couleur-de-rose*, at that moment. Its walls of a light golden brown, seemed to grow out of, rather than to be built upon, a ridge of rocks curiously worn and seamed by the action of the water; from the midst of which rose a single, lofty, slender tower, with a graceful balcony and beacon at top; the whole looking so slight and aerial, in the shimmering sunshine, that I should scarcely have marvelled to see it melt slowly, and vanish in thin wreaths of mist. That this fair vision had *teeth* was made plain, however, by a long line of embrasures for cannon; nor did the sharp hail of a sentry from its walls, demanding the steamer's name and port of departure, sound wholly amiable. The position of the castle gives it entire control of the entrance to the harbor, which is a kind of channel, scarcely more than three hundred yards wide, and about a thousand long. On the point opposite the Morro, is a smaller, older, and less striking fortification, known as "El Castillo de la Punta," built in 1589, by Philip II.; in the rear of which are seen the white walls of the city prison. Back from the Punta, in either direction, stretches the city; the old, historic portion, with its grim walls and bastions, following the channel and the bay, while the new part, with long lines of green trees marking the course of its pleasant *paseos*, extends along the ocean.

Passing between the Morro and the Punta, and entering the channel, we came in sight of the "Cabañas," a huge, strong fort behind the Morro, commanding both that and the city, as well as the greater part of the bay. It is built of the same stone that forms the steep bluff on which it stands, and so difficult is it to discover the exact line where rock and masonry meet that one is almost driven to conclude that its walls and bastions are the result of some strange freak of nature. Soon the channel widened into the open harbor—an irregular sheet of water, in shape somewhat resembling a trefoil, and not far from three miles long, but considerably less than half as wide. Very beautiful it looked from our steamer's deck, set in the midst of low green hills, gilded by the morning sun, and with a multitude of ships of all nations lying on its bosom and reflected—every hulk, every spar, every rope—in its still depths. Some of these reflections were broken into wavering, indistinct fragments as we steamed past and, turning to the right, dropped anchor about half a mile from the custom house, to await the coming of the Health Officer, before whose visit nobody could be permitted to leave the vessel or to come on board. It was out of the kindest consideration, doubtless, that this official kept us waiting for an hour or two. It gave us time to observe the odd architecture and colors of Havana, and to make ourselves familiar with the relative positions of harbor, fortifications, city, and suburbs—knowledge that would be of service by and by; also, to realize that our weary souls had arrived off a land where life was not lived in a perpetual hurry, nor a whole people bent on getting ahead of time, being once fully persuaded of which, we should be better fitted for life on its shores.

For further pastime, we could watch the movements of a fleet of small, awning-covered boats, by which the steamer was surrounded immediately on casting anchor. The swarthy boatmen in charge thereof demeaned themselves much like a crowd of New York hackmen, shouting, swearing, crowding, and trying to bargain with such of the passengers as were within hail, for the debarkation of themselves and luggage. Some of them, too, held up great bunches of bananas and other fruits for sale.

At last, Mr. Health Officer appeared, inspected the ship's papers and condition, pronounced " all right," and lifted his hat politely to captain and passengers as he went over the side; whereupon, the decks of the steamer immediately swarmed with a crowd of boatmen, hucksters, idlers, and expectant friends, comparable only to the miraculous gathering of the locusts in Egypt. Amid this vociferous crowd, my friend Juan's smiling face soon beamed out like a veritable beacon-light to one sailing on unknown waters; and a few moments later, I found myself in one of the afore-mentioned boats, being rowed toward the custom house landing. It is impossible to describe the exceeding charm of that moment! Glad to escape from the confinement and discomforts of the steamer, interested by the novelty and beauty of the scene, lulled by the soft gliding motion of the boat and the musical plashing of the oars, and refreshed by the cool breeze which just rippled the surface of the sparkling water, I thought that the very essence of enjoyment had been distilled for my tasting!

After snow-banks and frost-rime, brown, bare boughs, and winds straight from polar ice-fields, these green banks! these waving palms! these caressing breezes! I felt as if I had landed in another planet!

At the custom house, there was another delay of half-an-hour, ere my trunks took their turn at being examined—not a formidable operation, when the keys are readily and good-humoredly produced. A courteous official, in a light and becoming uniform of linen, thrust a remarkably white hand down a corner of each of my trunks, without anywise displacing the contents; and immediately signified, by a polite bow and gesture, that his business with them was over.

From the custom house I stepped into what I thought the oddest vehicle conceivable, until the sight of a "volante," thereafter, convicted me of a mistake. This affair was in size and shape much like one of our barouches, but mounted on two wheels only, with shafts of an absurd length; at the farther extremity of which, with much superfluous expenditure of leather and metal, was harnessed a little, stout pony, who shook his square head, and trotted off with the clumsy vehicle as if it were the easiest thing in the world. Indeed, I am fast verging to the opinion that a native Cuban horse is the strongest, toughest specimen of the equine race that trots on the face of the globe. I have little to say for his beauty, however.

I was unprepared to find Havana so thoroughly Oriental—perhaps I should say, Moorish—in its aspect. The same narrow streets, roofed with awnings—the same one-storied houses, built around a court—the same shallow shops, on a level with the pavement, and all open in front, exposing their entire contents to view—the same long files of cumbrously laden mules, tied together, and with a gayly-dressed muleteer in charge—and the same bright-turbaned, stately-stepping negresses, with heavy burdens poised on their heads. Many of the cross streets are so narrow that only a single vehicle can pass through, and it becomes a matter of wonderment how awkward meetings and hindrances are avoided. The pavements, too, are only designed for the accommodation of one foot-passenger. Parties must go in single file; while passing is accomplished by a turning sideways, and a nice calculation of distances and adjustment of angles; unless, as is most usual, one of the parties prefers to step down into the street.

Arrived at the "Hotel del Telégrafo," I was conducted to my room by so circuitous a route, that I begged Juan to come for me at the dinner-hour, much doubting my ability to find my way out of the labyrinth. First up stairs, then down—then across a court—then up again—then through somebody's private parlor—then across a portion of the roof—and so on, until I grew confused, and gave up trying to take any "bearings." At length, I reached a room, opening on a court, threw myself into a rocking chair, and looked around me with some curiosity as to what my first lodging in Cuba might be.

Certainly, it had the merit of novelty! A doorway, lofty and ample enough to admit a coach and six; two doors, sufficiently heavy to stand a siege, and with such an accumulation of odd and uncouth bolts and hasps and padlocks as would have been unpleasantly suggestive of midnight assault, if the thick coat of rust thereon had not saved them from any suspicion of ever being used. Two windows, one so high that I was forced to climb upon a chair to look out; both iron-grated, like a prison, and with heavy, wooden, inside shutters, into one of which was inserted a single pane of glass, for the admission of light on rainy days, probably,—from which, heaven preserve us! A lofty ceiling of huge beams and boards, painted blue, by way of pleasant contrast with the deep green of the window frames and the red and yellow tiles of the floor! Carpet? No, friend; carpets are almost unknown in Cuba. I *have* seen one, about the size of a table-cloth, spread in the middle of the floor of the *salon*, on state occasions; but neither carpets nor matting are in common use, and would only be hiding-places for vermin, if they were.

By way of furniture, my room owned a dressing-table and chairs of unmistakably Yankee origin; but there, all familiar forms ceased. The bedstead was of iron, narrow and high, with ample provision of lace-edged mosquito-netting, indicative of unpleasant nocturnal visitants. Upon examination, it proved to be destitute of either mattress or bed, nothing in the world to sleep on except a sacking bottom, with a sheet spread over! This is the universal custom of the Cubans; they hold it to be more comfortable, in their climate, than anything softer. I do not quarrel with the theory, but I am bound to say that I found it extremely hard to conform to the practice. A pair of pillows stuffed with moss, not much harder than a log, and a perfect nightmare of a flowered counterpane, completed the bed-furniture. Add to the above, a pair of large water-jars, of Pompeian pattern, a queer carved centre-table, of Venetian pattern, a wash-stand absolutely *sui generis*, and a row of brass hooks, and you have my room and its furnishings complete. Nevertheless, it was golden with sunshine, and fresh with breeze, and had a foreign flavor about it very pleasing to a traveller.

At four o'clock, Juan came with an invitation to dine with certain American friends of his, recent arrivals at the hotel. After the usual number of twistings and turnings, ascents and descents, we reached their pleasant parlor, and I was welcomed as cordially as if I had always been known to them. "All Americans are friends in a foreign country," said Mrs. R——; and I was quite ready to accept the doctrine, as my new acquaintances were cultured and agreeable, and a seat at their table much more to my taste than one in the public dining-room. Nor was it too retired, as you will divine, when you are informed, that a *private* parlor in the "Hotel del Telégrafo," means nothing more nor less than a sort of hall or ante-chamber, surrounded by bedrooms whose doors open upon it, and whose occupants must needs be constantly passing in and out. The present specimen was large and lofty, furnished with American rockers and large antique vases, and floored with marble, in alternate blocks of black and white. At one end was the wide doorway, opening upon a portion of the roof, by which we had gained admittance; at the other, a broad, balconied window overlooking the military parade ground, known as "El Campo de Marte," and giving an almost unlimited view of the quaint, tiled roofs of the city,—the hotels being among the very few buildings that can boast of more than one story.

The dinner was really good and well-served, although the dishes were mostly new acquaintances, or so disguised by strange sauces and modes of cookery as to defy recognition. "Will you take some of this queer-looking compound?" questioned my hostess, as each dish made its appearance; "I haven't the slightest idea what it is, nor if it is good,—you must taste and see, as we do!" In general, the tasting was not disagreeable, though now and then, it resulted in irrepressibly wry faces; which, however, only added to the mirth of the party. The attendant showed a most unusual and praiseworthy readiness to supply whatever was desired. On one occasion, being asked, if "chicken" formed any part of our bill of fare, he replied, "No, but I will *make* one!" which soon appeared, in verification of the statement, and did credit to his powers of creation, being in no wise inferior to the article produced in ordinary process of hatching and growth.

And such fruits as came on for dessert! Oranges, of which only the most remote of kin ever enters the United States; bananas that seem to repeat to the taste all that a summer sunset gives to the eye; and *melaos*, unfamiliar to you by name, but which you can conceive of as a sort of sweet, rose-colored cream, eaten with a spoon from a thick, brown rind or skin, about the size of a musk-melon, but of a more oblong shape. Unhappy dwellers in a frozen clime, what would you not give for a share in such luxuries as these!

Afterward, there was a visit to the roof, to watch the large, tropical moon sailing gloriously through the heavens; mellowing into soft lines and harmonious tints the angular forms and incongruous colors of the city, and touching the distant harbor with a shimmer of silver light. Here, I saw plainly what I had before suspected, that the hotel was an odd jumble of buildings of different heights and ages, connected together by a new and imposing front; and my after wanderings through its mazes, the utter confusion of mind that seized upon me whenever I lost sight of my own door, the odd mistakes that I made, the awkward intrusions of which I was guilty, would form an amusing and voluminous chapter of my Cuban experiences. Seldom did I reach my destination without stirring up some lazy *mozo* from a stolen nap in a dusky corner, and putting myself under his guidance.

Yet, notwithstanding this and other drawbacks, the "Hotel del Telégrafo" is the best of the Spanish hotels, in Havana. And who would go thither to stop at an "American Hotel?" Are there not enough of them and to spare, at home!

## CHAPTER IV.

### AT THE RETRETA.

A SORT of open air concert is given, every evening, from eight to nine o'clock, by the Government of Havana, in two of the public squares of the city, the music being furnished by the regimental bands. This is called the "*retreta*," and thither flock foreigners and natives, in crowds. The former behold there many striking features of Cuban life, and to the latter it is the place where friends meet, and lovers woo, and flirtations go on, and toilets are displayed,—the music seeming to be only a secondary consideration. To the *retreta*, therefore, went our small party of four,—which, nevertheless, represented three nationalities, Spain, England, and the United States,—in a large barouche, such vehicles being kept on hire, for the convenience of parties; the native *volante* admitting of but two—or at most, three—occupants.

The *plaza* was crowded when we arrived, the music already begun, and the *volantes* standing in double and triple rows all around the enclosure. In these odd equipages sat the dark-eyed *Cubanas*, in that minimum of attire which "Society" absurdly terms "full dress." Their *coiffures* were elaborate, but, as far as I could see, they were without bonnet, veil, shawl, or any wrap whatsoever. I looked eagerly for the black lace mantilla, always a graceful and indispensable accessory to the ideal picture of Spanish beauty, drawn from books, and hung in a sunny corner of Memory's-gallery; but I am told it is now discarded, except for wearing to Mass on Sundays. The full, flowing skirts of these ladies were spread carefully out at each side of the volante, hanging nearly to the ground, and giving to the vehicle, when viewed from the rear, the appearance of being furnished with wings. This is the prevailing style; no Cuban lady thinks it necessary or expedient to tuck her skirts into her carriage. Such an arrangement would not sufficiently display their length and showy trimmings; and her opportunities for exhibiting them elsewhere are extremely limited. The practice is not so utterly ruinous as it would seem, the wheels of the vehicle being so far in the rear as to preclude any danger of contact.

But the volantes themselves—or the *quitrins*, as the more modern and stylish variety is called—attracted my attention at first even more than their occupants. I wished that one could be transferred bodily—horses, harness, postilion, inmates, and all—to the Central Park, some fine day. Not Cleopatra's chariot, with the beautiful Egyptian Queen therein, would create a greater sensation.

Fancy a pair of enormous wheels, not less than six feet in diameter, with an axle of corresponding size, to which is fastened a pair of long, curved shafts;—add to these a phaeton-shaped body, whereof top and dashboard nearly meet, hung entirely forward of the wheels and between the shafts, by leathern straps depending from the axle behind and a cross-bar in front;—harness a single horse into these shafts, not less than three or four feet from the dashboard, and using as much leather and plate as possible in the process;—put a heavy saddle on his back, to enable him to support the cumbrous structure, which the much burdened animal is also expected to draw;—fasten another horse to the whiffletree, at the left side, by a pair of traces long enough to allow him to keep about half his length in advance of the other;—on this latter mount a negro "calesero," with richly-laced and bright-colored jacket, broad laced "sombrero," enormous jack-boots reaching nearly to the hips, large silver-plated spurs, and heavy leathern whip, whose duty it is to lead the working horse by a short rein, shout at him vociferously, crack his whip at him with a report like a small pistol, and thrash him unmercifully whenever he slackens his trot;—imagine postilion, horse, harness, and vehicle to be glistening with gold lace or silver plate, and between shouting, jingling, creaking, and rattling, making more noise than a half-dozen of our carriages;—and *then* you may have some faint conception of a Cuban volante! But the thing must be seen to be duly appreciated. It is an unique article of its kind, striking the unaccustomed gaze even more oddly than a French *diligence* or an Irish jaunting-car, yet possessing a certain barbaric splendor, and a graceful, easy, swinging motion, to which those vehicles have no claim.

I have omitted one small, but ludicrous detail. The long tails of both horses are tightly braided, and tied to the harness or the saddle with bright-colored cords or ribbons, in such wise as to prevent any movement of those useful members. I am at a loss for the reason, since the arrangement gives an absurdly rat-like look to the small native pony; and in a climate where gnats and mosquitos do so abound, it seems a positive cruelty.

Ordinarily, neither volante nor quitrin has more than one seat and two occupants; but a third seat, called *la niña bonita* (the pretty child), is sometimes attached to the other, whereon, slightly in advance, sits the youngest of a dazzling party of three. Thus enthroned, and with the top of the volante flung back, the fair *Cubanas* sit out the *retreta*, flirting their fans, and acknowledging the bows and salutations of passing acquaintances; but never, for one moment touching their dainty satin slippers to the pavement, or seeming to care to do so. But we, being *forasteros*, privileged to "do in Rome as the Romans do *not*," alighted from our carriage, made our way through the masculine crowd in the square, hired chairs from an enormous pile, fearfully and wonderfully reared on a negro's back, and established ourselves at the foot of the statue of "*Isabel la Católica*," in a position favorable for the hearing of the music. Here, I contrived to squeeze myself into a space between the base of the statue and the nearest bench, leaving Miss R. to take the brunt of the staring consequent upon our unusual procedure; where I was able to listen undisturbed to the concord of sweet sounds, study the statue above and the faces around by the soft transfiguring moonlight, inhale rich wafts of fragrance from neighboring orange and lemon trees, and try to realize that only five days ago I looked upon a scene where Winter reigned supreme. Harder still was it to realize the transition from the four walls of an invalid's chamber, where existence dragged wearily between couch and easy-chair, and no moment was free from pain, to this brilliant out-door scene, with nothing between me and the stars, and, save some slight remnant of weakness, the serenest sense of physical well-being. Life had

> " Suffered a sea-change
> Into something rich and strange."

The music consisted chiefly of selections from favorite operas, and was exquisitely rendered. It ended with a "Quickstep," to the lively measure of which the band marched off, followed by the crowd; such part of it as did not resort forthwith to the "Café Dominica," to enjoy ices, or cooling drinks known as *refrescos*. Thither went we,—not to enter, however, though foreign ladies may do it when accompanied by gentlemen, and prepared to endure any amount of eyeshot. But the moonlight was far too lovely to leave outside; so we summoned a waiter, and were served, Cuban fashion, in our carriage. The ices, flavored with a fruit called *guanabana*, were delicious; and we ate them by the help of certain delicate tubes of sweet paste, known as *barquillos*, experiencing the novel sensation of devouring our spoons and our ices simultaneously, and leaving not a vestige of either behind!

So we chatted and ate, under the magical radiance of the tropical moon, with a soft, india-ink view of the *plaza* in the distance, and in our ears the ever fainter and fainter harmonies of the receding band. And thus ended my first day in Cuba—a day crowded with new scenes and sensations, a day whereof the greenness and goldenness, the novelty and quaintness, the grace and the grotesqueness, will be a joy forever!

But after the day, the night cometh! And of my first night in Cuba, the chronicle runneth briefly thus:—

On returning from the *retreta*, I summoned the chambermaid, or *man* (for the post was filled by a handsome Cuban youth of eighteen or twenty), and asked for a mattress,—having been informed that the article was sometimes supplied to foreign demand. Whereupon, he presently brought in a dingy affair, not more than two feet wide and two inches thick, which he threw upon the middle of the bedstead and proceeded to unroll with a grand, this-is-precisely-what-you-want air,—when, lo! a sudden glancing and scampering of innumerable cockroaches!

"*Caramba!*" said he, with a decided change of countenance.

"*Que hueste invencible!*" exclaimed I, beating a quick retreat.

The dark legions vanished in the twinkling of an eye, however, as is their amiable habit when suddenly brought to light, and my *mozo's* discomfiture went with them. Pouring out a voluble and confident assurance that they had all retreated to the crevices of the walls and would appear no more, he quickly made the bed, bade me a courteous "*Buenas noches,*" and withdrew.

I cannot speak enthusiastically of my night's rest upon that mattress. It was as hard as the Irishman's three feathers, it had an odor strongly suggestive of stables, and the fleas did not decamp with the cockroaches!

Besides, there were the *serenos*—not a species of vermin, but a peculiarly Cuban species of watchmen. Seeing one for the first time, you think he has walked out of the Middle Ages to meet you. He is habited in a queer, gown-like coat; he has a clumsy pistol stuck in his belt; and he carries a long pike, a whistle, a lantern, and a rope. It is his business to cry the time and the state of the weather every half-hour during the night; prefacing the cry with a vigorous knocking of his pike-staff on the pavement. As the nights are almost invariably clear and fine, his usual cry is "*sereno,*" from whence he derives his name. To the eye, he is a sufficiently picturesque institution; to the ear, an execrable one. Not more effectually did Macbeth "murder sleep" than he does, until one becomes accustomed to his nocturnal din.

## CHAPTER V.

#### THE PALACE AND PLAZA.

TEN o'clock is the breakfast-hour for all Cuba, at least, for that portion of it which does not belong to the "hewers of wood and drawers of water;" and at that hour I was again enjoying Mrs. R.'s cordial hospitality, and drinking the very best cup of coffee that ever I tasted. Whoever desires to enjoy that beverage in perfection, may be very sure of doing so in Cuba, if he puts himself under wise guidance. But the tea is only fit to fling after the German diplomatist's salad, "out of a *very* wide open window!" It is a comfort to be assured that no one drinks it "unless he is sick."

The day was devoted to sight-seeing. First, we took a look at the Palace of the Captain General, which I regarded with some interest, knowing it to be the centre of a system of military despotism; which, although somewhat lighter than formerly, has still certain features calculated to rouse the indignation, or secure the contempt, of any free-born American. For was not I—*I*, the most harmless and insignificant little woman in the world!—obliged to procure a certain six-by-eight, dingy, ill-printed paper, called a "permit," before I was allowed to stir in Cuba; which seemed far less worth the eight dollars paid for it, than the wildest auction purchase, or "damaged-goods" bargain, in which I ever indulged! The face of this precious document declares to all whom it may concern that,—

"THE GOVERNOR OF THIS JURISDICTION
Grants a ticket of disembarkation in favor of Doña W. M. L. Jay, a native of the United States, of no profession; who arrived at Havana in the Steamer Eagle," etc. etc.

On the left, in a square, are the "particular signs," by which the said "Doña" may be identified; the blanks calling for a description of height, age, complexion, hair, eyebrows, forehead, eyes, nose, mouth, and *beard* (*!*); but as only the items of age and height are filled out, the permit might serve as well for half the foreign females in the Island; showing conclusively that its true object is a species of legalized plunder. Then follow the signature of the Chief of Police, with a *fac-simile* of that of the Governor, and the seals proper to each. Underneath are the following "notices":

"The present document shall be null and void whenever it loses the seal or crest of the Government here affixed.

"Foreigners should notice particularly the third paragraph of the regulations to be found on the back."

Turning to the back, therefore, we find a number of petty rules, printed in French, Spanish, and English, some few of which I copy from the English column, *verbatim, et literatim, et punctuatim.*

"WARNING.

"This permit must be presented to obtain the baggages, which can be landed every day, Sundays & holidays included, from sunsete till sunrise provided the consignee of the vessel has obtained the necessary permit from the collector.

"This permit must likewise be presented to owners of the house or establishment where the passenger goes to stop, so that he may give the necessary advice to the police.

"This permit will enable newly arrived foreigners to transit in all directions during one month from its date. It will also enable to fixe residence in every place in the Island: according to it, its presentation is always necessary before the *Capitan de partido, Comisario ó Celador* respective. After that period a *pase de tránsito* is required to travel over the Island.

"The want of the compliance to these regulations implicates a fine of ten dollars.

"No passenger will be allowed to enter the city without subjecting to these requisites, and will be obliged to justify its fulfilment, by presenting the permit and the mark or sign which the Custom house agents put to the respective packages after inspection.

"No foreigner is allowed to reside more than three months in the Island without procuring a *carta de domicilio*, which he will obtain by a petition backed by the Consul of his nation."

Even long residents of Cuba, born in Old Spain, are not exempted from these restrictions. Each year they are obliged to procure the aforementioned "*carta de domicilio*," which they are liable to be called upon to show at any railway, or police-station, or even at their houses; and any infraction of the rule is punishable with a fine.

With this document in my pocket, in token of the

extreme solicitude which the Spanish Government feels for its guests, I examined the Vice Royal Palace on a certain footing of equality, conscious of having duly paid eight dollars for its support, and bought the privilege of saying and thinking what I pleased about it. I soon decided that it had but a moderate claim to architectural grandeur or beauty. It fronts on the "Plaza de Armas," is built of a yellowish-colored stone, in the form of a hollow square, and is two stories in height, of which the upper one only is the residence of the Captain General. This projects far over the lower one, and is supported by a row of stone pillars, making a pleasant colonnade along the front. The ground floor is devoted to various public offices. An arched way leads into a *patio*, or court, upon which open the interior windows. On either side of the principal entrance is a guardroom; and across the colonnade, from door-posts to pillars, two sentinels are marching stolidly all day, and doubtless, all night. At least, I see no reason why they should not keep up the same monotonous, indolent performance throughout the night, and sleep like dormouses at the same time.

The "Plaza de Armas" is very handsomely laid out with walks, and ornamented with shrubbery, a few palm and cocoa trees, and a statue of one of the numerous Ferdinands,—whose images adorn, or disfigure (according to taste), nearly every *plaza* and *paseo* in the Island. The enclosure is surrounded by a thick row of extremely old and luxuriant *laureles de India*, a species of banyan tree; whose dark, glossy foliage is so close as to seem almost solid, and furnishes the densest shade to be found in all Cuba. It affords shelter to numerous bright-plumaged birds, whose name I forget, but the story of whose introduction into the Island found a firmer lodgment in my memory. They were brought hither by a sailor from Spain, in the days when Havana was a walled city, at whose gates all comers were stopped, and cross-questioned, and when custom-house regulations were even more strict than now. The old, weather-beaten "salt" was desired to pay an exorbitant duty on his pets. After some altercation, irate and rebellious, he opened the cage-door, saying, "They *shall* enter, and they *shall not* pay duty." The birds immediately flew over the walls to the nearest trees, where they settled, made themselves at home, increased and multiplied, and have sent out colonies into all parts of the Island. And still the traveller sees their bright wings glancing in and out amid the thick boughs of the old laurels, while he listens to this story of their naturalization, told by some grave, courteous Don; and takes their cheery warblings for a confirmation of the tale, or a sarcastic comment thereon, according to temperament.

These ancient laurel-trees are the pride of the "Habanero," but no tree will so charm a stranger's gaze, or win such a place in his affections, as the *palma real*, or royal palm. The straight, smooth, slender trunk shoots up some fifty feet, or more, into the air, with the perfect finish and lofty aspiration of a Corinthian column; and then crowns itself with a spreading cluster of graceful, plumy leaves, whose deep, vivid green shines like satin in the sunlight. These look so delicate and feathery at their dizzy height that I marvelled, when I had opportunity to examine one fallen to the ground, to find it ten or twelve feet in length, with a stem much thicker than my arm; while those apparently tender, tapering rays of green, of which it is composed, seemed like swordblades in my hand. This discovery increased my respect without lessening my admiration. Indeed, whether seen in stately colonnades and long avenues, or standing singly or in groups on the plain, the palm-tree grows constantly in my esteem, and I am ready to render it my deepest homage as the King of trees. And what wealth of association gathers around its name! What troops of images, sacred, historic, poetical, throng on the mind with every bend of its kingly crest, with every whisper of its rustling plumes! Soft, faint echoes of gray, quaint fable and purple Eastern poesy,—visions of wide reaches of sandy desert—slow, winding marches of stately caravans—bright oases by crystal fountains—mazy dances of flushed Almes—mystic rites of wild dervishes—grand, silent ruins and dethroned statues—holy labors and sorrows of apostle and martyr—the calm, sad, benignant face of the SON OF MAN going about Jerusalem or to and fro across the hills of Galilee,—these, all, drenched my soul, and left me breathless and awe-struck before the majestic marvel! Like Dana, "I was glad that they had strewn palm-leaves in the path of the Saviour,—I was glad that the saints in Heaven carry palm-leaves in their hands!"

# CHAPTER VI.

### WITHIN AND WITHOUT THE WALLS.

GOING up Obispo street from the Plaza de Armas, we were confronted with one of Havana's most noticeable and interesting features—the remaining portion of the old city wall, with the gateways and bastions thereto pertaining. This ancient barrier overtops the nearest houses, and is solidly built of hewn stone, about twenty feet thick at bottom, with a smooth perpendicular face, but with two or three terrace-like projections on the inner side, whereon troops were originally stationed for its defence. Outside there is, or was, a moat, now dry, and filled as full of weeds and creepers as it formerly was of water.

It is a novel experience to find these grim, hoary relics of bygone days and modes of life bursting up through the quiet, prosaic flow of our modern existence; and a single sight of them gives vastly greater vividness to our mental pictures of that ancient time, than is attainable by the closest study of books and pictures. The man who might read Cervantes or look on the masterpieces of Velasquez without once feeling his fancy stirred, or his imagination quickened, would find these gray towers bristling even more with quaint suggestions than ever they did with guns; and as many flowers of fancy and creeping, ramifying lines of thought, would start forth from the time-worn, weather-stained surface of the old wall, as there are blooming plants rooted in its corners and projections, and vines climbing and tangling along its sides. However, this curious relic is even now in process of removal, as an useless cumberer of the ground; the town having long ago overleaped it and spread itself over the adjacent country to an extent exceeding its former area. But it will be years ere the venerable landmark disappears from the city vocabulary; the terms *estramuros* and *entremuros* being still in constant use, even where no vestige of the wall remains, to denote that boundary line between the historic and the modern city which it once defined so clearly. And it seems a pity to demolish it altogether. One of the gateways, at least, should be spared, to help us to realize an age and a manner of life otherwise very dim and unreal to our modern vision.

Looking up at this gray wall, or standing under the gateway's frowning arch, one sighs to see how notably the picturesque has dropped out of the onward march of invention. Utility leads the way, comfort and convenience swell the ranks, and the spirit of beauty is not altogether absent; but the sweet, coy, vagrant charm of the picturesque seems left behind. Let him who thinks otherwise, confront a modern cooking-stove with an ancient fire-place, or a silver ice-pitcher with the earthen water-jars in my Cuban bed-chamber, or set down his newly-built villa (" with all the modern conveniences") by the side of this time-incrusted gateway, and see which has the best of it artistically—of which he would choose to make a picture for his parlor wall.

Our next visit—for we were "doing" Havana thoroughly, though not systematically—was to "La Honradez," otherwise "Honesty," otherwise an immense cigarette manufactory. This institution is in such favor with foreigners that one day in each week is set apart for their reception and entertainment; when the whole establishment puts on a gala-day air, and gentlemanly ushers, speaking English, French, and German, are in waiting to attend upon its guests. Having entered our names in the register (which would turn an autograph collector yellow with envy), we proceeded to the inspection of the building. It consists of several departments, with telegraphic connections, that no time may be wasted in running to and fro. Chief among them are the offices and counting-rooms,—the carpenter's shop, for the construction of packing boxes and barrels,—the machine room, with cutting and pressing machines,—the printing office, printing daily millions of labels, circulars, fancy-wrappers, etc.,—the designing, engraving, and lithographic room,—and, what is most interesting of all, the vast room where the Chinese workmen twist up those little rolls of paper and scented tobacco with an ease and celerity that seems little short of miraculous; producing an average of over two millions of cigarettes per day. The courtesy of the attendants is a most pleasing feature to a visitor; everything is shown and explained with the most minute, unflagging attention and politeness; and if a lady guest expresses any admiration for the pretty boxes or fancy pictures scattered about, she is immediately prayed to accept of such as she most fancies. Finally, when the hour of leave-taking arrives, each visitor is presented with a package of cigarettes, prettily tied with gay ribbon, and with his or her name printed in full on the ornamental wrapper, having been copied from the register during the inspection of the premises. One of our party, who has an utter detestation of tobacco in all shapes and modes of use, and was with difficulty induced to enter the building, accepted hers with a somewhat embarrassed grace; while her companions shook with ill-suppressed merriment at the incongruity between the donation and the tastes of the donee. Nevertheless, she heartily endorsed the general opinion that the generosity and courtesy of the proprietors of "La Honradez" deserve honorable mention, and might fitly be imitated by manufacturers of wares that have a better title to the interest of the public.

We now left the narrow streets of the old city behind, and drove through the "Gates of Monserrate," the "Prado," and the "Paseo Tacon," to the gardens of the Captain-General,—a large extent of ornamental grounds, surrounding a pretty, villa-like residence known as "Los Molinos;" where that dignitary seeks repose from the cares of state, and where his family resides for the greater part of the time, reserving the sombre Palace for state occasions. The gardens are very handsomely laid out with walks, avenues, thickets, flower-beds, and arbors, and contain a fine collection of foreign and native plants. There was a dazzling profusion of gorgeous, tropical flowers,—cacti of every hue of blossom and every sort of prickly development— tall, shapely oleanders—shivering mimosas—coral flowered pomegranates—jessamines that seemed to have laughed themselves into their exuberance of sunny blossom—water-lilies that it took away one's breath to look at—aloes, whose stately candelabra of gorgeous blooms were worthy of a place on Nature's highest altar —and vines whose prodigality of leaf and flower gave one an almost painful sense of beauty running to waste. Beside these, there was a lovely wilderness of blossoms, unknown to me by name.

Among the trees I noticed several fine specimens of the date palm, apparently perfectly at home; and I see no reason why that species should not flourish anywhere in the Island, if the people had enterprise enough to introduce it. But never was there a race more wedded to the policy of "letting well-enough alone." I suggested the idea to Juan, to see what he would make of it.

"What need?" said he, with the ever ready shrug; "we have fruits for every month in the year, and vegetables all the year round. Why desire more?"

This garden owns one of the finest avenues of the royal palm to be seen in all Cuba. Its grand perspective seems like that of a vast and lofty temple. The smooth, straight trunks of the trees are the most stately and shapely of columns; and the intertwining leaves of green, shimmering and gleaming in the sunshine, form the loveliest of traceries and illuminated roofs. Looking through it, I seemed to discover whence came the inspiration of Grecian architecture, as he who wanders through long aisles of arching elms may believe that he sees whence sprang the graceful outlines of the Gothic temple. And as the latter clearly breathes of aspiration,—embodying its yearnings, its struggles, and even its vagaries,—so the former is full of the repose of attainment, and symbolizes the completeness, the simplicity, and the majesty of law.

There is a little canal running through the grounds, for purposes of irrigation, as well as to lend a bright sparkle of water to their attractions, and as I was resting on the bank two bright boys of the Captain-General's came out, and embarked in a gayly-painted boat anchored near; and while the younger was wholly intent on raising a small Spanish flag in the stern, the elder deferentially doffed his hat to my foreign face as they floated past me. What a charm there is in ease and grace of manner! I believe that my countrymen are, in the main, more intelligent and large-hearted and sincere, than these courtly foreigners; but I do wish that some of the fair flowers of courtesy, which spring so naturally from a Spaniard, might be ingrafted on the sturdy stock of their solid virtues!

Having been forced to observe how far the tropics surpass us in luxuriant foliage and brilliant flowers, my national pride was soothed to notice that Cuba can produce nothing like the vivid green of our velvet turf.

There is an attempt at it in the Captain-General's garden, but the grass is thin and sickly; evidently it is an exile, thrusting no willing root into the soil, and having left all heart and energy behind. I felt drawn toward it by a certain dreary sympathy, and I pressed a forlorn sprig thereof in my note-book, beside a dainty spray of a lovely, wandering vine and a flower whose ruby coronal might have been cut from the very heart of the sunset that was glorifying the western sky as we left the grounds. All honor to the Captain-General for throwing them so generously open to the public. There is a sentinel at the gate, to be sure, and two others are pacing before the house; but neither interferes with any quietly-behaved visitor, and the walks, the avenues, the flowers, and the arbors, are free to all who come.

We finished the day on the *paseo*, a mixture of street and pleasure-ground, whose use is peculiarly a Cuban institution. Society, as we understand it, does not seem to exist here. *La retreta* takes the place of our evening visits, and the *paseo* serves for our morning calls. Beside these, there are calls of ceremony, set balls, "*il teatro*," an occasional dinner, and—nothing more!—or if there is, I have failed, as yet, to discover it.

The Paseo de Ysabel Segunda crosses the city in a straight line from bay to ocean, just outside the walls. It is between three or four hundred feet wide, and about a mile long; different parts of it being known by different names, as the "Prado," the "Parque de Isabel," etc. It is ornamented with fine trees, shrubbery, flowers, *glorietas*, statues, and fountains,—the finest of the latter being of Carrara marble, the gift of a patriotic citizen, and known as *La fuente de la India.* Furthermore, it has two broad drives for carriages, between which there are seats for loiterers and walks for promenaders; and along its course are some of the finest public and private buildings of the city. But the favorite drive and promenade is the "Paseo de Tacon,"—a noble double avenue, lined with trees and villas, and beautified with fountains and statuary, leading from the Prado to El Cerro,—a small hill-village three miles from Havana, commanding a magnificent view of city, suburbs, and ocean. This *paseo* is named in honor of a former Captain-General, to whom, though he seems to have been an unmitigated despot (or perhaps for that very reason), Havana owes more improvements than to any of his predecessors.

Up and down this *paseo* go long lines of volantes and carriages, in which one sees all the beauty and fashion of the city, all its civil and military dignitaries, all its visitors, and as large a delegation of its plebeians as are fortunate enough to own or can hire a shabby volante for the purpose. Now and then a mounted guardsman, in a pretty and seasonable uniform of striped linen, with collar and cuffs of scarlet or green cloth, and sword and pistols flashing in the sunlight, rides by, to show that the government takes as kindly an oversight of the pleasures of its children, as it does of their business and journeyings.

Up and down, up and down, in long flashing lines, go the jingling volantes, with a pair, or it may be a triad, of gayly-dressed ladies in each; and gentlemen crowd the footpaths, and stare and smile and bow, with a cigar in each mustachioed mouth, to sustain them under the exertion. It is rare to see a gentleman occupying the seat with a lady. Occasionally an unmistakable *paterfamilias*, with wife and children, exhibits himself thus; but in general, the masculine sex takes a volante to itself, or lounges on the sidewalks. The ladies, according to their wont, are bareheaded and *decolletées*, with their long, showy skirts hanging out of their volantes; and one look at the combinations of colors in their toilets would go far to make a French *modiste* a candidate for the mad-house. Yellow and scarlet, blue and purple, green and orange, seemed to be favorite combinations; and though the dark eyes and complexions of the *Cubanas* carry off these astounding contrasts with a far better grace than their fairer sisters of the North could do, still they give them a look undeniably "dowdy"—not to say vulgar—to eyes unaccustomed to such gaudiness of attire. Perhaps this was the reason why so very few of them seemed anywise pretty to me. After a little, I came unwillingly to the decision that my cherished ideal of Cuban beauty could never stoop to incarnate itself in any of those fat, fussy, overdressed matrons, nor those thin, sallow, lifeless, and likewise overdressed maidens. In all that vast crowd of the *élite* of Havana, I saw only two or three that it gave me any pleasure to look at; and not one that I should ask to play Juliet to my Romeo, from a vine-wreathed balcony on a moonlit night, if I were the gay gallant that I am not. It must be admitted that most of them had bright black eyes, but these could not redeem an otherwise utterly heavy, characterless physiognomy.

The carriage of the Captain-General passed us several times, wherein sat that official, with one or two of his staff, all smoking and staring like their brethren on foot. He was a stout man, with a stolid face, and an *ennuyé* air; and I could not help a sad wonder, as I encountered his dull gaze, if those two bright, rollicking boys of his that I had seen just before, could ever grow up into so many pounds of heavy, inert flesh, and take on such a burnt-out, inanimate cast of countenance. I hope it was not wicked to think it were better for them to go down in their painted skiff to the bottom of the tranquil water, and leave their images pure beside the water-lilies on its banks!

## CHAPTER VII.

### COLUMBUS.—THE CATHEDRAL.

NEAR one corner of the Plaza de Armas is a small Grecian chapel, standing, tradition affirms, on the spot where Mass was first celebrated in Cuba, under the direction of Columbus. A comparison of dates and records shows the statement to be hypothetical, as far as regards the presence of Columbus,—which is probably a bit of that green, mossy growth wherewith Time loves to deck the hard, gray outlines of Fact,—but there seems to be no reasonable doubt that this is the site of the performance of the first Mass. The interior of the chapel is nowise remarkable; it contains a bust of Columbus and three historical paintings, all of very moderate merit; and is opened to the public but once a year, on the feast of San Cristobal, which is made an occasion of much solemnity. In front of the chapel is a courtyard, with a handsome iron gateway bearing aloft the royal arms of Spain, encircled by the ever-recurring motto, "*La siempre fielisima isla de Cuba*"; and about half-way between the gate and chapel stands a monumental column, which bears on one side, in Spanish, the following inscription:—

"The city of Havana was founded in 1515, and when it was removed from its first site to the shores of this harbor, in 1519, there stood on this spot a luxuriant Ceiba tree, under which, it is said, was celebrated the first Mass, and the first Council. It survived until 1753, when it became sterile; and in order to perpetuate its memory, our Catholic Sovereign, Ferdinand VII., then governing Spain, caused this monument to be erected. Field Marshal Don Francisco Cajigal de la Vega, Knight of Santiago, being Governor and Captain-General of this Island, and Doctor Don Manuel Philip de Arango, LL.D., being Attorney-General. A.D. 1754."

It will be observed that the above mentioned Ceiba tree must have been more than three centuries old when it "became sterile;" as Cuba was discovered in 1492, and the first Mass could not have taken place many years later. Not less than fifty years could have sufficed to make it the "luxuriant" tree it is stated to have been, as the Ceiba is slow of growth, though it attains to an enormous size, and is one of the most striking trees in Cuba. It is often a hundred feet in height, sending up a strong, massive, sinewy trunk to more than half that distance, when it divides into brawny, wide-spreading branches, and covers their delicate sprays with a thick green canopy of velvety leaves,—the whole bearing a striking resemblance to a mighty umbrella.

The inscription, quoted above, is repeated in Latin on another face of the monument; and on a third is still another, of the following import:—

"D. O. M.

"The most illustrious and august hero, Christopher Columbus, famed for his nautical skill, after having discovered a New World and given it to the crown of Castile, died at Valladolid, May 20th, 1506. His body, being given in charge of the Spanish Carthusians, was transferred, at his own request, to the Church of the Metropolis of Hispaniola.* When peace was concluded with the French Republic, his remains were removed from thence to the Cathedral of the Virgin Mary of the Conception; the principal religious orders assisting at the solemnities, Jan. 19th, 1795. The city of Havana, honoring the memory of so great a benefactor, treasures his remains unto the last great day.

"The illustrious Señor Don Philip Joseph Trespalacios being Bishop, and His Excellency Don Louis de las Casas, Governor and Captain-General."

Few stories have so deeply stirred the world's heart as that of Columbus; few pictures are so clear to our mental vision as the calm, noble figure of the great Genoese, standing on the prow of his miserable, leaky vessel, with a background of dark, mutinous faces, and straining his eager, confident gaze over the unknown seas, for a first glimpse of that New World which had so long limned itself upon his imagination, or beckoned to him in his dreams. I turned my steps toward the Cathedral, therefore, with something of the spirit in which devout pilgrims, in Catholic countries, seek out the tombs of saints and martyrs.

The "Cathedral de la Virgen Maria de la Concepcion" (to give its name in full) is a large, quaint struc-

---

* Hayti was named Hispaniola, or New Spain, by Columbus; its "metropolis" was St. Domingo. It is curious to note how successfully these islands have resisted all foreign christening. Cuba was successively named Juana, Fernandina, Santiago, and Ave Maria, but still clings to its first Indian name of Cuba.

ture of stone, with a pillared front, a tower at each angle, and a hoary, crumbly, moss-grown surface. It is not beautiful; it would scarcely be imposing but for its age and the spiritual grandeur which invests and transfigures it. For the edifice that contains the ashes of Columbus must needs have a moral sublimity far more impressive than any mere majesty of architecture; they honor the walls where they lie more than the grandest mausoleum could honor them. And in truth, no building repays long study, unless its walls contain some ideal structure or shadow forth some Divine truth, vastly more grand and beautiful than aught which meets the outward gaze; and whenever this sentiment, or *soul*, of the structure is lost sight of, and you feel yourself compassed about and overborne by barren facts of stone and mortar, height and depth, color and finish, better turn your back upon it and go your way, ere the hard, unyielding details of the Actual have conquered and cast out the richer, nobler, lovelier vision of the Ideal.

Mass was being celebrated as we entered the shadowy portal, and the nave was partly filled with kneeling figures of women. I but half noted these things, however, in the first, quick glance that I sent round the building, in search of its chief object of interest; and having found that, I saw nothing further. A mural tablet, in the choir, on the left of the high altar, shows where the remains of the Great Discoverer rest finally, after their several sojourns at Valladolid, Seville, and San Domingo, before they were brought hither and inurned in the chancel wall. The tablet is of white marble, and presents in alto-relievo a bust of Columbus, with nautical instruments grouped underneath, and the following inscription:

> "O Restos é Imagen del grande Colon!
> Mil siglos durad guardados en la Urna,
> Y en la remembranza de nuestra Nacion." *

This seems rather meagre, but it suffices to bring the whole familiar story of that marvellous life before the spectator; and leaning against a convenient column, I gave myself up to the contemplation thereof, and the reflections inseparable therefrom. I thought of his long, patient struggle, his short, brilliant triumph, his sudden, unmerited disgrace; I remembered his unflinching courage, his high-souled devotion, his patience under provocation, his generosity in success, his dignity in misfortune; until, at last, bowed and broken—far less by the toils of an adventurous life, the long sickness of hope deferred, or the persecutions of enemies, than by the coldness and treachery of friends, and the "serpent's tooth" of ingratitude—he gave up the long struggle, and died with the pathetic request that his chains (those chains wherein he had been brought back from the hemisphere which he had discovered, to the country which he had enriched by the magnificent gift!) might be buried with him in the Island of his love. Poor, proud, broken

---

\* A literal translation of which is,—

> "O remains and image of the great Colon!
> Endure for a thousand ages, guarded in this urn,
> And in the remembrance of our nation."

heart! its long ache over, its indignant throbbings stilled, it rests tranquilly in the bosom of the beautiful "Queen of the Antilles," the fairest jewel in the crown of that realm which repaid the donor with coldness, ingratitude, imprisonment, and neglect. Yet thus has the world ever treated its benefactors, even as it crucified its Christ! O hearts that toil and yearn for the good of your race!—O eyes straining your gaze across the ocean of discovery for some yet unfound help or consolation or beauty!—look for no reward *here* but the iron that enters into the soul and the crown that lacerates the brow. Yet be not discouraged! but so labor and so pray that ye may receive your reward hereafter from the hand of Him, whose sweet words float down to us through the wrong and the discord of nineteen centuries, "*Not as the world gives, give I unto you.*"

The thread of my meditations was broken by a light touch on my shoulder, and a priest at my elbow said, very politely, and in good English, "Will you please to kneel?" I heard him make the same request of other visitors standing near, but, as far as I could see, without producing any effect, except that one or two drew back into a somewhat less conspicuous position, near the wall. However, it seems to me both discourteous and irreverent, to listen to any religious service without paying some token of respect to its intent, or to the proportion of truth which it contains; and as a pleasant-faced Spanish girl close at my feet, with a courteous gesture, made room for me on her bit of carpet, I sank down beside her in the desired posture. It was beautiful and fitting, I thought, in that vast, old temple, with the tomb of Columbus preaching solemnly of earth's mutations and disappointments, that I should join my foreign sisters in a fervent prayer that, as Christ was lifted up on the cross for the whole race of man, so we, and all who believe on Him, might be lifted above the ambitions, the temptations, and the cares of the world, into a purity of life and a charity of temper becoming His followers. But it was impossible to preserve a devotional frame of mind long; thoughts of Columbus, of Romish dogmas and corruptions, recollections of a simpler and more helpful ritual in the home-tongue and the home-land, chased each other swiftly through my brain: and I was glad when the service allowed a change of posture, and I could sit comfortably (*squat* were the more descriptive, though less elegant, term) on my carpet, and gaze around me like my neighbors,—only without the pretence, or the mechanical habit, of devotion, which kept the beads of their rosaries sliding through their slender fingers, and their lips moving with inaudible "Pater Nosters" and "Ave Marias."

There was a number of priests at the altar, twelve or fifteen, at least,—all dignified of mien, and reverent of manner. The intoning of the service was unpleasantly loud and harsh, and the echo from the marble walls was like the blare of a trumpet. There was no choir but the priestly one, which was accompanied by an extremely fine, sweet-toned organ. There was somewhat more of ceremony in the lighting, placing, and carrying of wax candles, and the swinging of censers and burning of incense, than I have observed in the service of the Romish Church in the United States; and at one time an altar-boy offered a small golden vessel—probably containing a relic—to the lips of the devotees nearest the altar, who kissed it with great apparent reverence and eagerness.

The interior of the Cathedral is far finer than its outside warrants. The lofty dome and vaulted roof are supported by tall pillars of marble; there is some very fine masonry of stones of divers colors, whereof the dominant hue is a sunny yellow; and the walls are richly frescoed, though the colors are somewhat dimmed by time. The high altar is a magnificent affair, consisting of a base of various kinds of marble supporting a dome and pillars of porphyry, under which is a statue of the Immaculate Conception; but it is covered with such a medley of images, candlesticks, artificial flowers, and tinsel, that all idea of sacredness is quite lost in its irresistible suggestion of a toy-shop. Behind it is the bishop's throne; and around are the stalls for the priests, of richly wrought mahogany, with carved heads of the apostles over them. Various smaller altars and shrines are ranged along the side-walls, each with its appropriate pictures, doll-like images dressed in tinsel and tawdriness, artificial flowers, and bones of saints preserved in alcohol like diseased specimens in a surgeon's office; but I brought none of these things away in my memory, except a hideous, distorted image of the *Mater Dolorosa*, which, having once seen, it is not easy to forget.

The floor was of variegated marble, unincumbered by seats, except a few benches running from pillar to pillar up the nave, for the accommodation of foreign visitors. In the body of the church knelt the dark-eyed *Habaneras*, telling their beads with a graceful, piquant turn of their small hands, and taking calm note of all that was going on around them, at the same time. Every few moments, a new-comer appeared, followed by a servant bearing her square of carpet; and when that was duly spread for the mistress in the most eligible vacancy, the servant knelt behind on the marble, with a manifest expectation of sailing smoothly to heaven in her wake. The ladies were nearly all dressed in black— the prescribed costume for church-going,—with the graceful Spanish mantilla of black lace covering their heads and falling around their shoulders. I was surprised to see how much prettier, more delicate and more womanly, they looked thus than as I had seen them on the *paseo;* and I remembered half-remorsefully the sweeping criticism on their personal appearance that I there registered against them. The young girl who had made room for me looked positively lovely, with her eyes cast down, their long lashes sweeping her cheek, and her face partly shaded by her mantilla; and just opposite was a lady of regal beauty, whose large, black, steadfast eyes, and statue-like grace and stillness of *pose*, held me spellbound with admiration. It was melancholy to think that such loveliness should be disguised, degraded, utterly lost, in those tawdry fineries of the paseo!

Near the altar I saw a Franciscan monk in dark blue

gown with rope-girdle; farther down was a Carmelite in brown; and an old negro, wrinkled, white-haired, and bent, knelt in the shadow of one of the pillars, with a touchingly devout and absorbed face—the only males that I saw joining in the service. Several gentlemen, mostly foreigners, lounged in the aisles outside the columns, scanning, and commenting upon, the kneeling women; and many more were gathered at the door, waiting to hand them to their volantes, as they came forth. This service may be rendered to a lady by any gentleman who is at hand; and, if he be so minded, he can add a compliment to her beauty, and it will be received with smiles and thanks. Let him not presume upon this graciousness, however, to accost her elsewhere; she will probably ignore any previous knowledge of him, and her nearest male relative will be prompt to avenge the insult with pistol or stiletto. It is almost the only thing in which you can expect a Spaniard to be in a hurry. For every other hasty impulse, in business or pleasure, he has a convenient, salutary proverb, "*El que se apresura, se muere, y el que no tambien,*" (he who hurries, dies, and he who hurries not, dies also); but in the matter of resentment, it is not even a "word and a blow," but the blow comes first and renders word unnecessary.

Mass being over, we commenced a systematic tour of the building. Beginning with the side altars, we found them to be mostly of solid mahogany, richly carved and gilt; with now and then a really fine old painting by way of altar-piece. One of these is said to be a Murillo, but the evidence of its genuineness is scarcely conclusive. Opposite to the tomb of Columbus is a painting on glass, more curious and venerable than beautiful, having been painted in Italy, and blessed by the Pope, in 1478, some years before the discovery of America.

Seeing us hesitate between two doors, a handsome young deacon, or neophyte of some sort, came forward and offered to guide us. Under his auspices, we took a closer view of the high altar and the choir; and were especially delighted with the glorious vista of the interior church as seen from thence, with yellow rays of sunshine and deep shadows of massive pillars and arches intermingling on its marble floor. We also beheld the rear of the tomb of Columbus, and glanced into the little chapel of the "Virgin of Loretto," where two or three penitents were kneeling, not so absorbed in their devotions but that they returned our glance with interest. In the *vestuario*, we were shown the robes of the priests, of rich velvet, satin, lace, and gold and silver tissue, often richly embroidered and adorned with precious stones; also the altar linens and laces, of exquisite fineness and beauty; also divers silver crucifixes, candlesticks, censers, chalices, sprinklers, etc., etc. Our young guide tossed these things about in a way that would have made his superiors stare, I am certain; he threw a chasuble over Juan's broad shoulders, to give better effect to its embroidery, put the incense boxes to my nose, and hospitably offered us a bumper of the sacramental wine. He then led the way to the parish chapel alongside of the Cathedral, showed the large font containing the holy water (of such capacity that it needs to be filled and blessed but once a year), and offered to fill me a bottle with the sacred fluid, if I desired. Next, he led us through the shadowy cloisters,—worn smooth by the footsteps of more than a hundred years!—to the sunny inner court-yard, where flowers were blooming and ancient fountains dripping; and upon which looked the windows of the ecclesiastical dormitories and offices, and the galleries of the theological seminary of San Carlos. On our way, we saw priests praying, hearing confessions, reading, smoking, chatting, and promenading, and the sweet echoes of the organ and the deep voices of the priestly choir followed us throughout,—a second service being now in progress in the Cathedral.

Finally, our obliging guide showed us out through a side-entrance at the right of the chapel. Here, I thought I should have sunk through the floor, to see Juan take out his purse and offer him a gratuity for his pains! But my mortification was wasted, inasmuch as he accepted it without surprise or difficulty. I have since learned that no one need scruple to hold out a *real* or a *peseta* to anybody in Cuba from whom he has occasion to receive the smallest service.

## CHAPTER VIII.

### THE FISH-MARKET.

"WE will just look into *la pescaderia*," said Juan, as we left the Cathedral. "It is close by."

"I would rather be excused," said I. "Fish have no charms for me, at any point between the water and the dinner-table. And as for a fish-market—faugh!"

"But everybody goes," persisted Juan.

"I will be nobody, then, and stay away."

Nevertheless, Juan's native Spanish obstinacy carried the day. The fish-market being reached, in we went.

Nor was the visit ill-repaid. *La pescaderia* is built of stone, with an arcaded front. The forms for the reception of the fish are permanent structures of stone or marble, with tiled tops; and upon them is perhaps the finest piscatorial display to be seen in the world; for the waters hereabout have a multifarious finny population, some portion of which makes part of every breakfast and dinner served in Havana or its vicinity. In my tour of the market, I saw sharks, large and small, whole and in fractions,—huge porpoises, waiting to be turned into oil, *tasajo*, and canes,—rays, armed with wicked-looking spines,—beautifully striped bass and parrotfish, — immense flounders, — fish blue, green, silver, golden, spotted, and rainbow-hued, — to say nothing of snake-like eels, and shell-fish of every known and unknown variety. It was impossible to avoid becoming interested; some of the monsters were fascinatingly ugly, some of the smaller fry exquisitely beautiful; and I hung over the stands till Juan sarcastically observed that the difficulty of getting me in was likely to be more than equalled by the difficulty of getting me out!

"What a fine building it is!" I rejoined, somewhat irrelevantly, looking up at the massive stone pillars and arches, and comparing them mentally with the dinginess and dilapidation of the larger New York markets.

"Oh!" said Juan, "the market is a government institution and monopoly, you know."

"But I don't know," returned I. "How should I?"

Thereupon Juan told me a story. To the best of my recollection and belief, it ran as follows:

In the days when Tacon was Captain-General of Cuba, — that is to say, between 1834 and 1838, — a certain daring and skilful adventurer, half-smuggler, half-pirate, named Marti, at the head of a number of lawless men like himself, haunted and harassed the coast; making the neighboring Isle of Pines, of which he styled himself the "King," his chief stronghold and base of operations. With characteristic energy and determination, Tacon at once set to work to capture the leader and break up the band; but after some months of ceaseless activity and vigilance, was mortified to see that he had accomplished literally nothing. The light, fleet vessels of the rovers, guided by men who were familiar with every rock, shoal, channel, and inlet, of the waters which they frequented, had laughed to scorn his whole maritime force; while his coast-guard had been alternately beaten and outwitted.

Tacon now set another and more powerful agent at work—gold. He offered a large reward and a free pardon to any one of the band who would desert and turn informer; and double the sum for any information that should lead to the capture of Marti, dead or alive. The utmost publicity was given to these offers; they were carefully posted wherever they would be likely to meet the eyes of the rovers, but for a time without apparent effect,—the band of Marti held no traitor.

However, late one night, as Tacon was writing in his room alone, with a sentinel marching up and down the corridor, a tall, dark man, wrapped in a military cloak, quietly walked in from the antechamber.

Tacon sprang to his feet. "Who are you?" he demanded, haughtily. "And how came you here, at this hour, unannounced? What do you want?"

"One question at a time, *Excelencia*," answered the stranger, composedly. "It does not matter, at present, who I am. I came by the door, as you saw. And I am here to give information of great value to the government. But it is for your ear alone. Therefore, speak not so loud; the entrance of yonder guard would seal my lips, and tortures would not open them. Is your Excellency willing to listen to what I have to say?"

"Speak on," replied Tacon.

"You desire information of the island-rovers. You have offered a princely reward for the capture of Marti, their captain."

"Yes, yes!" exclaimed Tacon, eagerly,—"what do you know of him?"

"*Excelencia*," replied the stranger, "I must needs be cautious; I would not criminate myself."

"Be easy on that point," returned Tacon, "a free pardon is guaranteed to the informant."

"Suppose he were himself a leader among the rovers?"

"It makes no difference," said Tacon, impatiently.

"A distinct understanding at first saves trouble at last," replied his visitor, coolly. "Have I your Excellency's word of honor that I shall receive the promised reward, and an unconditional pardon for all past violations of the laws,—no matter what is my name and character,—if I guide you to the secret haunts of the rovers, and deliver Marti into your hands?"

"You have."

"*Excelencia*, the Captain-General Tacon has been called ambitious, despotic, even cruel; but no one has ever yet accused him of breaking his plighted word—"

"Nor ever will," interrupted the general, haughtily.

The dark stranger folded his arms with dignity.

"*Señor*, one half of my part of our compact is fulfilled. I am Marti—and in your hands."

Tacon started, and almost involuntarily extended his hand toward a brace of pistols lying on the table.

The rover stood unmoved and motionless. Instantly recovering himself, the general drew back his hand, eyed his visitor keenly, mused for a moment, resumed his chair, and began a low, business-like conversation, which we need not follow.

Early on the next morning, a man-of-war in the harbor was ordered to prepare for an immediate cruise. At noon, Marti was sent on board, under guard. His directions were to be obeyed strictly, as long as he seemed to be acting in good faith; but he was to be shot down without delay at the first indication of treachery. The rover, however, had not the least intention of turning back in the path upon which he had entered. One by one, the hiding-places of the rovers were visited, their stores seized, their vessels captured, and themselves made prisoners, by the help of the chief whom they had refused to betray!

When the work was complete, Marti returned to the general to claim his reward. "You have kept your word," said the latter, "I keep mine. Here is your pardon; and here is an order on the treasury for the sum of ——"

"*Excelencia*, I have thought better of it," interrupted Marti. "The treasury is low, the payment of so large a sum will be inconvenient. I propose an exchange. No man on the island knows the fishing-grounds so well as myself. Give me the exclusive right to the fishing, and the fishing trade, in the vicinity of Havana, for the next twenty years, and you may keep the order: I will build a public market that shall be an ornament to the city; and at the end of the twenty years, both the market and the right shall revert to the government."

"Agreed," said Tacon, after a moment's consideration.

At the expiration of the time specified, Marti was the richest man in Cuba. The market and the right then reverted to the government, which has since retained it.

"And how did Marti end finally?" I asked, when the story was done.

"Died in his bed, with the consolations of the Church. Beyond that—one doesn't care to follow him!" replied Juan, with an expressive shrug of the shoulders, as he turned away to examine the writhing, flouncing load of a newly-arrived fisherman.

Seeing me leaning somewhat wearily against one of the pillars, a good-natured fish-wife wiped the end of a bench and pushed it toward me.

"Thank you," said I, sitting down. And I added, by way of explanation,—"I have spent the whole morning in the cathedral."

"Ah! no wonder *la pobre niña* is tired," said the woman, compassionately. "But isn't it a beautiful church!" And she brought the tips of thumb and fingers to a focus and kissed them ecstatically, which is the *ne plus ultra* of Cuban encomium.

"It is very fine," said I, somewhat less enthusiastically. "But the tomb of Columbus interested me most."

She looked puzzled.

"Of Colon," I repeated. "You have heard of Cristobal Colon."

"Oh, yes," she replied, smiling. "But he is not dead; he still lives."

"Lives?—ah, yes—I suppose so," responded I, wondering if she meant "*en la remembranza de nuestra nacion,*" and thinking that she didn't look quite like it.

"*Si, señora,*" she replied, calmly, "he keeps a cigar-shop just below here."

Shade of Columbus, didst thou hear her!

I repeated the dialogue to Juan. "What would you have!" said he, laughing. "Columbus has nine thousand nine hundred and ninety-nine namesakes on the island; you may find them in worse places than cigar-shops. And as for history!—if you should ask that woman who is the present Captain-General, she would tell you 'Tacon!' I think I heard, in the United States, that there were people who regularly voted for Jackson, at every presidential election."

The ground being thus taken from under my feet, nothing remained but to thank "that woman" for her courtesy, and depart. I had already discovered that she was not a mulatto, as I first thought, but a native, with an extremely limited acquaintance with soap and water. In truth, it is astonishing to see how small a supply of those articles suffices for the daintiest *Cubana* of them all. Instead thereof, she keeps a bottle of *aguardiente* (a kind of rum) on her toilet-table, with which she moistens the corner of a napkin, and rubs her face, neck, and hands; beyond which she seldom goes. Water, she assures you, is "very bad for the skin;" and is dangerous in the extreme if you happen to have a cold. And if any one gets more than a daily allowance of a pint of water and a twenty-inch square of towel, in a Cuban hotel, he has richly earned it by browbeating the landlord and scolding and feeing the servants.

## CHAPTER IX.

SHOPPING.—STREET SIGHTS.—LA FUERZA.

THE delights of shopping, " on the American plan," are unknown in Cuba. In cases of rare importance and urgency, the ladies drive to the shop-doors, and such goods as they wish to examine are brought out to them. A clerk standing by a volante, displaying piece upon piece of delicate linen lawn and sheer *piña* to the fair inmates, or trying pair after pair of kid and satin shoes upon their dainty feet, is no unusual sight.

In general, however, when a *Cubana* wants anything, from a spool of thread to a silk robe, she calls, in a voice more clear and penetrating than soft,—for bells are also among things unknown,—" Atanasia!" (or Juana, or Maria, one of which names will be sure to fit), and some unadulterated, unmitigated Africaness comes forth from her lurking place, turbaned and barefoot, and drops her slovenly courtesy. To her, "*la señora*" delivers a writing, setting forth the nature, quality, and quantity, of the article which she needs; and the messenger goes forth, and presently returns with a considerable assortment of the goods required, on her head or in her hands; to be examined and selected from in the lady's own room, assisted by a small crowd of children, servants, and other disengaged members of the household. Time is of no account in the transaction. Frequently, the servant trots back and forth four or five times between mistress and shops, cheapening, questioning, and exchanging, ere the bargain is concluded; and nearly the whole day is consumed in the business,—i. e., the servant's day. Another phase of the affair is also noteworthy—the number and value of the goods thus entrusted to an ignorant, stupid servant. On one occasion when a set of jewelry was the thing desired, Atanasia shuffled home with twenty or thirty sets, varying in price from ten to fifty dollars! The science of thieving cannot have reached the perfection here which it displays in the United States:—in our modern Sodom, she would have been obligingly relieved of her burden on the first corner!

I was well aware, therefore, that it was a daring breach of universal custom to sally forth, on foot, for a morning's shopping, after the American fashion; but I trusted to my foreignness to excuse the innovation; and I knew that I could depend upon Juan's broad shoulders, and grave, well-known Spanish face to shield me from all unpleasantness. To confess the truth, I was in that state which is common to the American female mind, in view of shopping—perfectly sure that I wanted something, but by no means certain what! Or, to state the case more fairly, I wished to find some small trinkets or *bijouterie*—whatever might turn up—of unquestionable Cuban manufacture, and as full of pleasant suggestions of Cuban climate and manners as a rose is of perfume, to serve for mementos of Havana, and gifts to friends at home. If further justification of the step be required, it must be found in the fact that I was dying (in a figure) for want of exercise. Up to this time I had made use of "Cuban feet," i. e., the volante. I now desired to satisfy myself, by a brisk walk, that my own were still fit for service, and not Cubanized into merely ornamental appendages, good for nothing under the sun but to adorn with fanciful French boots and slippers, and repose upon a footstool for the admiration of all and sundry. I had tried to keep them somewhat in training by pacing up and down the galleries and roofs of the hotel, followed by the wondering gaze of its Cuban inmates, till I was indescribably sick of the tame performance. All the more, that it invariably recalled the forlorn image of a royal lion which I once saw marching restlessly up and down his narrow cage, with a disdainful indifference to all spectators, and an eye of sorrowful longing for the freedom of his native jungle.

Juan and I were soon deep in the intricacies of the narrow streets of the old city—so narrow that a stranger is apt to pass the first hours of his explorations in wondering when he will get out of the lanes and into the streets; but he will find only a few worthy of the name, and those outside the walls. In the older streets, I was often obliged to flatten myself against the walls of the houses, to avoid being swept off the narrow pavement by the furious passage of a *volante;* a vehicle which dashes so recklessly through the streets and round the corners, that, if the wide, high windows were less strongly iron-grated, it would be certain to plunge headlong into a drawing-room now and then, in some of its rash turnings and erratic progressions. Many of the streets were quite roofed with awnings, stretched from side to side; and it was easy to imagine one's self walking under the vast tent of Peri-Benon, of Arabian Nights' fame, if there were only a few turbans and caftans about to help out the illusion. In truth, there is an almost ridiculous incongruity between the quaint, Oriental aspect of Cuban architecture and manners, and the modern French fashions—stove-pipe hats and close-fitting pants. In one sense, certainly, Paris *is* "the world."

The walls of the houses are often two or three feet in thickness, built of an irregular mixture of stones and mortar, and then stuccoed and painted. Although they are seldom of more than one story, the front wall is not less than twenty feet high, the top being ornamented with urns or carvings, and the roof sloping back to an interior court, upon which most of the rooms open. If the house boasts of two stories, the lower part is occupied as a store, or devoted to the kitchens, offices, and stables; and the upper floor is reached by a wide staircase from the court, leading to a corridor above. The entrance is wide and lofty; the doors are double, of exceeding thickness, and further strengthened by bands and knobs of brass or iron till they look fit to resist a battering-ram; and the windows are without glass and iron-grated like a prison. The floors are of marble, tiles, or stucco; the walls whitewashed or frescoed; the ceilings high, and often open to the roof, the beams of which are made presentable by painting, staining, or carving.

But, before the stranger has time to notice all these peculiarities of Cuban dwellings, his eyes are dazzled by their brilliancy and variety of color, where all the hues of the rainbow meet and mingle in odd and bewildering contrasts. One house has walls of a light green, with pink cornices and mouldings; its neighbor is a delicate blue, with salmon trimmings; the next is gray and orange, with some admixture of white,—or lilac and yellow, or pink and blue,—all shimmering and quivering in the hot, glowing air, until it seems like a vast, radiating, dissolving view. Nevertheless, after the first surprise is over, and your eyes are a little wonted to the dazzle, you discover that these vivid tints are in exquisite keeping with their surroundings. The tropics suggest color and demand it. It cannot easily be too profuse nor too gorgeous, albeit a better taste might preside over its use.

You are next made sensible of the peculiar compound odor of the streets of Havana, very perceptible to newly-arrived noses, but not so easily resolvable by them into its components. The scientific formula would probably read something like this:—" smoke of tobacco, four parts; steam of garlic, three parts; aroma of negro, two parts; miscellaneous garbage, one part." Nevertheless, Havana is not an unclean city in some senses of the word; it has none of that griminess and stickiness of filth which makes New York an abomination to the eyes and a stench in the nostrils, at certain seasons of the year. The dryness of the atmosphere and the arid sunshine, transform most impurities into a fine, cloudy dust; which is kept down in the city by means of sprinkling, but becomes a sufficient nuisance on country roads,—for during my month's stay in Cuba, there has been no rain.

Strangest thing of all, perhaps, to a foreigner, is the fact that as soon as he appears on the streets of Havana, he is taken into the very heart of its domestic life. The broad doorways are wide open, and the window-gratings do not, in the least, obstruct his observation of what occurs within. As he passes along, so close to the windows that he could easily thrust his arm between the iron bars to its full length, he sees ladies chatting and sewing—rocking, meanwhile, as if their lives depended on the regularity and continuity of the vibratory motion; he sees children playing, and servants dusting and scrubbing, and meals being served and eaten; he even gets glimpses of cooking, washing, and other domestic processes, going on in the courts and kitchens in the rear; and he may possibly find himself involuntarily witnessing the finishing touches of a fair *señorita's* toilet. If a lady plays or sings, it is for the benefit of the entire neighborhood, stationary and transient; if there is a conjugal quarrel, every passer-by gets a taste of its bitterness; and there is a continual cheery interchange of greetings between the inmates of the dwellings busied about their ordinary occupations, and their neighbors and acquaintances passing by in **volantes** or on foot—the salutation always being "*Adios!*" which answers to our "Good by," instead of the hurried "How d'ye do?" which serves us for chance meetings.

The "Calle de Mercaderes" is the Broadway of Havana, though the streets of Obispo and Riela are scarcely less busy and attractive. Jewelry stores are many and handsome; dry-goods and fancy-goods are everywhere; book-stores are good, though not plentiful. A certain corner store makes a specialty of wax-tapers for the devout, displaying them of every size and color, from an immense waxen pole that might serve as a sign for a barber's shop, to tiny pink, blue, and white tapers, fit for illuminating fairy halls. A certain other is devoted to *abanicos*, otherwise fans, ranging in price from fifty cents to a hundred and fifty dollars; the first of which the shopman tells you is "dumb," that is, incapable of the fan-language wherein the *Cubanas* are so well versed, and consequently not worth a groat for purposes of flirtation; while the latter, he assures you, will lay the whole male population low at your feet. "See what a fine snap it has!" he proceeds, opening and shutting it with a report that nearly makes you jump out of your skin. And having exhausted both language and gesture upon its perfections, he ends with that kiss on the finger-tips which signifies things unutterable. Linens and laces are temptingly cheap; so are palm-leaf hats; so are Spanish books; but having satisfied all reasonable wants in these lines of trade, better shut your ears and your purse. Unless you like to go to *La Dominica*, and lay in a stock of guava jelly and marmalade for the home-table. It is good, it is cheap, it will keep (with proper care) till the end of time. Buy a hundred dollars worth, by all means—if you can afford it!

The merchants do not put their names over their doors, but each shop has its own pretty or fanciful title which figures alluringly on its sign; and when your bills are sent home you find that you are indebted to " The Pearl," " The Sunbeam," " The Casket of Jewels," " The Garland of Flowers," " The beautiful Marina," or " The Ladies' Delight," instead of plain John Jones, or Seth Brown: and you pay them with unwonted pleasure, the sweet suggestions of the poetic names having shed a golden sheen over the otherwise prosaic transaction.

But, oh! the fabulous prices that those dark, handsome, villainous shopkeepers, with their courtly bows and complimentary phrases, had the face to ask me for their wares! and the smooth falsehoods that they poured into my amazed ears, swearing, by every saint in the Spanish calendar, that articles which had the marks of French and German manufacturers legibly stamped upon them, were wholly and immitigably Cuban—Cuban from their earliest inception to their latest finish! It was very amusing, too, to see how evidently Juan was regarded in the light of an inconvenient and provoking obstacle in the way of trade; and how one salesman sought to engage his attention, and get his back turned, while another attempted slyly to impose upon me some worthless, tinselled article, with a magnificent price.

After patient investigation, I came to the conclusion that the only articles of indubitable Cuban workmanship, were cigarette holders, palm-leaf hats, canes of *manati* skin, a coarse kind of shoes of undressed leather, for plantation wear, and a few articles of kitchen and bedroom furniture. If I had insisted upon anything further, I must have taken samples of sugar, molasses, and cigars.

As a last resource, I sought for stereoscopes, hoping to get some faint shadows of the beauties, the quaintnesses, or the antiquities of the city, to help me to bring them more vividly before the vision of home friends. Many of the merchants were persuaded that such things had been taken sometime, and were for sale somewhere,—others thought not,—and after hunting the "somewhere" through fifteen or twenty shops, I concluded that the last were right, and gave up the search in disgust. For it was verging toward noon, and I was heated and weary with my long walk through the close streets and burning summer air.

I went out of my way a little, however, on my return route, to take a look at "De Soto's fort," the oldest fortification on the Island. It was erected under the auspices of the discoverer of the Mississippi, to protect the little town from the depredations of French and English buccaneers, when it was only a stopping-place for Spanish vessels plying between Spain and Mexico. It is a gray, weather-beaten, antiquated structure, so much of it as belongs to the original fort; but it has been roofed over, and topped by an additional story, to make it serve for barracks; which modern climax destroyed whatever interest and inspiration I might otherwise have gotten out of it. I could have shaken myself for the irreverence and irrelevance, but instead of thinking of De Soto's romantic voyage and adventures or picturing the long, heart-wasting watch of his wife, Isabel de Bobadilla, for the return of the husband who had already found a grave beneath the Mississippi's yellow waters, I was perversely reminded of certain patched-up photographs that I have somewhere seen; in which the smart *coiffure* and sprightly features of a modern belle were fitted on to the stout, comfortable figure, and old-fashioned garments of her grandmother; or a boy's rosy, chubby face was joined to the shrunken limbs and "lean and slippered pantaloon" of an octogenarian. Neither did there seem to be any sufficient reason for this absurd resemblance, since the additions to the fort do not appear to be of very recent date.

And now, friends mine, go back with me to the hotel, and from an airy, shaded balcony, look out over the city and suburbs, gilded with noontide glory. See how the sunshine gathers all things in its passionate embrace, — spires, houses, palms, and gardens, — and breathes over them a soft, delicious languor. The air is full of the soothing murmurousness of gauzy-winged insects, swarming and floating and shining; and somewhere afar is a faint, faint sound that must come from the ocean. The atmosphere is of a mellow, creamy tint, quite different from its clear whiteness at the North; you think it must have been filtered through gold or fused in a crucible with amber, ere it was shed over this enchanted isle; or you wonder how many ripe, gorgeous, glowing sunsets it has dissolved and holds in solution, to give it such wonderful softness of tone, and rare luminousness of tint. Seen through this warm, palpitating medium, objects do not stand out sharp and clear, as in our colder atmosphere; their outlines soften and waver and grow vague and dreamy, and their colors are smoothed and blended, until you cease to think about details, and know only that you are living in a picture, and breathing sunshine—sunshine which is sweetness to your lungs, and repose to your heart. Your cares are soothed; your pains and ills fall from you like ill-fitting garments; all the dark realities of your life have a rainbow border, like objects seen through a prism. Your intellect is enervated, but your imagination is enriched; you no longer aspire to be a philosopher, but you are inly persuaded that you were born a poet, and have mysterious kinships with palm-groves and flowers. Sweet snatches of rare old songs come fitfully to your lips—gorgeous bits of Arabian Nights, imagery float hazily through your memory—air-castles rise, rose-hued and radiant, on the sapphire foundations of the cloudless sky—existence is become a luxury, and life a dream!

## CHAPTER X.

### FROM HAVANA TO MATANZAS.

I HAVE taken my last look (for the present) at the tomb of Columbus, and my last drive on the *Paseo de Tacon*—I have enjoyed a final view from *El Cerro*—I have said *adois* to our friends, Mrs. and Miss R.,—I have packed my trunks, I am going to Matanzas! Under a certain hospitable Spanish roof, in that second city of Cuba, I am invited to spend some months. For this I came over the sea, and all my sojourning and sightseeing in Havana have been but an idle loitering by the way, a pleasant prologue before the drama begins. Now, I am to plunge into the central flow of Cuban domestic life, leaving every waif and suggestion of the United States behind. Hereafter, I am to talk Spanish, eat Spanish, live Spanish,—do everything but dress Spanish, that is beyond my power of conformity!

Juan rouses me from an after-breakfast day-dream, to say that the cars will start in half an hour. "The cars!" I repeat, half unconsciously, "we go by rail, then?"

"Of course," says Juan, looking at me attentively, "how did you expect to go?"

"On the Emir's carpet," say I, still dreaming of the

Arabian Nights, and Haroun al Raschid. "Or, at least," —suddenly awaking to present quaint realities,—"in a huge *volante*, with twelve horses, and six postilions, and no end of silver plate and jingle!"

Juan's swarthy face darkens visibly. Pure-blooded Spaniard that he is, with the true peninsular contempt for Cuba—which is regarded merely as a mighty sugar-cane, out of which the Home Government annually squeezes sixteen or seventeen millions of revenue—he is not yet prepared to hear, with entire equanimity, the delectable and profitable province satirized, as he thinks, by an alien and a Yankee. "You will travel," he replies, slowly, and with dignity, "by as good a railway as ever you saw in your life, smooth and level as a ballroom floor; and at as rapid a rate as ever you did in the United States."

Nevertheless, oh! irate descendant of an hundred *hidalgos*, permit me to think that a railway seems an incongruity in Cuba: the harsh shriek of the locomotive, echoing over the palm-fringed valleys, steeped in sunshine and silence, sounds shriller and more dissonant than elsewhere. Ruskin opines that the world would be better off without railways, and desires that the capital thus employed might be diverted to the establishment and maintenance of schools; and in Cuba, it is easy to become a convert to his opinion. One is even ready to go farther, and dispense with the schools also! I suspect the "Cubaneras" do it, in effect. Their conversation is a storehouse of vivid imagery, an inexhaustible fount of graphic and animated narrative of home

4*

incident and daily routine,—but woe to him who seeks to convert it into a mine of information! Now and then, my New England temperament escapes for a moment from the languid, soothing spell of the delicious climate, and, "after its kind," asks questions.

"Can you tell me when the Morro was erected?" I asked, one day, of a stout, placid *Habanera*.

"*Dios mio!*" exclaimed she, with a low rippling laugh, "I am asked the age of the Morro, and I cannot even tell my own!"

No doubt thine ignorance was the true wisdom, soft daughter of the tropical noon! *Cui bono* to reckon how many years the Morro has looked out on the shimmering sea, or how few it has taken to mellow thy beauty into its somewhat over ripeness? Albeit, not in the tropics alone is the female memory unreliable with respect to age. In lands nearer the Arctic Circle than the Equator, I have met with the same mistiness of recollection.

On another occasion, I startled a dreamy *señora*, lazily rocking herself to and fro, and deep in the luscious, golden round of her third orange, with the question:—

"What is the population of Cuba?"

Looking upon me, with eyes wherein amazement and contempt were at a drawn battle, and with the grand, imposing gesture of a tragic queen, she responded:

"What do I know about population? Ask me how many shirts my husband has, and I can tell you!"

Possibly thou wert right also, languid child of the sunbeams! What need it matter to thee, or me, whether a few thousands more or less of stately Spaniards and lithe Cubans drive, or fierce Coolies and brutish Africans toil, in thine isle of perpetual summer? Can we not lounge and dream our lives away in Boston rockers? or thrust our arms, shoulder-deep, into the cool, odorous green of orange boughs, and pluck and eat the Hesperidean fruit? But wherefore said'st thou "*shirts*," oh! olive-cheeked and night-eyed daughter of the tropics? For "shirts" is humdrum and prosaic, suggestive of close and wasting toil, of breaking back and straining eyes, weary with eternal stitching of "band, and gusset, and seam." If thou had'st said, "how many gold and silken embroidered slippers," or sheeny and beaded watch-cases, my discomfiture had been complete!

Juan and I rattle and swing to the depot in a *volante*. Then I am left in the waiting-room for some moments, while he attends to tickets, permits and checks. Here, I find myself, for once, the "observed of all observers,"—not so desirable a position, by any means, as it sounds! However, after returning as many of the glances levelled at me as I can, conveniently, I decide that my neighbors are justified in staring, if my travelling costume is as much of a queerity to them as theirs is to me! The ladies are all attired in silk or muslin, as if for an afternoon at home, without bonnets, gloves, or wraps; two only wear the Spanish mantilla of black lace which I have seen at church. Their long trains—which they never hold up—sweep the pavement. Their flitting, glistening, coquettish fans—always in motion, and now and then opened and shut with a sharp, sudden snap, only attainable by long practice—make the room as brilliant as if it were swarming with butterflies. They have no parasols; I have not seen such a thing in use since I came to this Land of the Sun, where it would seem to be almost a necessity. But Cuban ladies never go out in the middle of the day, while the sun is hottest, if it can be avoided. When they do, the overhanging volante top is a sufficient protection, or if they choose to ride with that thrown back, they face shine and wind "like a man." No, I do not mean *that*, either—for the men all wear hats! Such exposure has its legitimate effect on the complexion, and the "fair sex," in Cuba, is uncommonly dark.

On the floor of the room are squatted some half dozen negresses, in the capacity of ladies' maids. Their heads are gorgeously turbaned, of course; but their dress, in other particulars, seems designed for a broad caricature of that of their mistresses. Others, in a lower order of servitude, are clad in a single garment, a coarse sort of "baby-frock," slipping off the shoulders, and frequently gaping in the back enough to reveal the shining ebony skin and firm, strong muscle beneath. If, by any chance, one of these is so fortunate as to own an under-garment, it is sure to be "Isabella" color; and lest any of my friends should inquire forthwith for that new tint on Broadway, or Main street, I will just mention, *en passant*, that it gets its name from a certain Spanish Queen, who vowed to the Virgin that in consideration of some favor which she desired, she would not change her linen for a year. And she kept her vow! Isabella color is very common in Cuba.

There are two railway routes from Havana to Matanzas. One, known as the "Regla route," is very direct, and measures about sixty miles; the other winds through the interior of the island, to bring out the sugar crop, and lengthens the journey to nearly one hundred miles. Being offered my choice, I designated the latter, as it would give me a better opportunity of studying the country.

The cars are quite homelike in appearance, bearing the name of a well-known Massachusetts firm; but so dingy, from long use, as to suggest the need of a fresh importation. They differ from ours only in having cane backs and bottoms to the seats; upholstery being almost unknown in Cuba, as it is thought ill suited to the climate. They who know how long my existence vibrated between cushion and pillow, before I came hither, will wonder that I live to make the statement; and the recollection of our luxuriously stuffed furniture is infinitely aggravating to an invalid. Moreover, the Cuban race lounges so naturally and persistently, I marvel that it does not provide itself with the means to do it thoroughly. The comfort of a cane-seated sofa is not patent, to me!

My journey is a bewildering dream of beauty,— albeit, with a touch of the fable of Tantalus about it, inasmuch as I am borne swiftly past pleasant villas— trees laden with tropical fruits—flowering vines, climbing and rioting everywhere—lime and aloe hedges—dense, dark thickets and jungles—bright, glancing waters—and mazes of brilliant blossoms, belonging to an unknown flora,—yet cannot pause to touch, nor taste, nor even look, long enough to imprint anything more than the merest outline sketches on my memory. The stations, as with us, are always located in the most uninteresting spots;—I find nothing there to repay attention, save a few loungers and hucksters, in attendance to discharge their respective duties; i. e., stare at the train and dispose of their wares.

I am somewhat surprised to discover that Cuba is not so flat a country as its cane-growing reputation would seem to indicate. To be sure, the valleys are quite level, and admirably adapted to that kind of culture; but they lie between rocky and wooded ridges, and one is never out of sight of the graceful, pleasing undulations of a chain of hills; or a blue, hazy mountain peak is seen across a sea of cane fields, and satisfies the soul with that sentiment of aspiration, that suggestion of the infinite, without which the loveliest landscape soon becomes monotonous.

The trees are a continual surprise to me. The acacia is homelike enough, certainly, and I have become familiar with the mimosa in our own Southern States,— but the *mango*, with its dark, broad leaves, and wide-spreading branches—the drooping, rustling *coco*, laden with green, melon-like looking fruit—the *bamboo*, with its slender, reedy stems, and graceful, pendant foliage— the *banana*, looking as if a sugar cane had suddenly made up its mind to become a tree, and was in a fair way to realize its ambition—the *ceiba*, giant of the forest, lifting its magnificent, regal canopy high above everything near it—the *jaguey marcho*, worst of parasites, stifling the largest and strongest trees in its cruel, wily embraces—the *bomba*, bearing aloft a fruit of the size of a watermelon, strikingly suggestive of broken heads to whomsoever may venture underneath,—these soon exhaust my small store of interjections and exclamation points, and leave me with nothing to say for the palm, which follows us all the way in graceful groups and groves, and is preëminently *the* tree of the tropics— Beauty's last and most perfect Apocalypse!

Now and then, across the dark, green billows of the cane-fields, at the end of a long, straight avenue of palms or orange-trees, we behold a large, stuccoed mansion, with ample provision of broad, shady piazzas; near by are a long, flat roof, and a tall chimney spouting forth dense columns of black smoke; several smaller buildings are grouped together in the vicinity; and the whole looks like a miniature village, but is really an "*ingenio*," or sugar plantation. Anon, we pass a degenerate "*cafetal*," or coffee estate, which branch of agriculture is slowly dying out in the Island. It looks like a pleasant bit of landscape gardening, untimely arrested, and given over to decay. But, as I shall have opportunity, by and by, to examine and describe these things in detail, I will not dwell upon them now.

Farther along, we discover a different kind of habitation, a rude, and somewhat dilapidated, wooden structure, with rafters of bamboo covered with dried palm-leaves, and surrounded by an acre or two of cultivated ground. In the doorway, sits a slender, lithe, indolent figure, lazily puffing at a cigar, with a hound stretched at his feet. This is a Cuban *montero*, a man that in character and social *status*, much resembles the "poor whites" of our South. It is difficult to say how he lives,—for he has a lordly detestation of labor,—but his wants are few, the soil beneath his feet is of incredible fertility, the sky above him does not so much as frown for many months in the year, and the climate is one of marvellous friendliness and amenity. Bananas and *malangas*, growing almost spontaneously at his door, serve him in lieu of bread; the streams supply him with fish; and in order to breed game-cocks for his amusement, he must, of necessity, keep a few hens. He is seldom, or never, too poor to keep a horse, nor to load it with queer, cumbrous, silver-mounted trappings. Astride of this animal, which is at once beast of burden and bosom friend, he roams about the country in most idle, nonchalant, and independent fashion; smoking, gambling, and cock-fighting; and investing any chance gains in lottery-tickets. For the rest, he is quick-witted enough, but utterly uneducated; warm-hearted and generous, but quite capable of repaying provocation or insult with several inches of the heavy, silver-handled *machete*, or cutlass, that hangs by his side; and he is entirely without ambition, for the despotic Spanish laws rob him of every incentive to improvement, and close every path to distinction.

At Melena, there is a longer detention than usual, until, the patience of the passengers being all "unwound from the reel," some one goes forward to investigate. Then, we learn that we have been the subjects of one of those gracious interpositions of Providence, which awe the boldest heart, and make the most scornful lips tremble for a moment with something like a prayer and a thanksgiving. Some portion of the engine suddenly gave way, just as the train stopped; and certain repairs, thereby made necessary, are the cause of our delay. If the accident had occurred when the train was in rapid motion, it is impossible to say what damage and loss of life might have followed! The intelligence stops, for a brief space, even the incessant motion of Cuban tongues, there is a silence and a shudder, and many cross themselves devoutly, and say aloud, "Gracias á Dios!" (Thanks be to God!)

When we are again in motion, night is closing in; behind us is the Western rosiness, before us, the Eastern purple gloom. Symbolic, it seems to me, of the wondrous change which has been wrought in the world, since Columbus came over the sea;—for the West is no longer the synonyme of ignorance, idolatry, and barbarism. Thither not only the "star of empire takes its way," but the brighter luminaries of science, art, literature; while over the once radiant Orient settle the dark shades of superstition, the dim night of despotism, the sombre gloom of decay.

We reach Matanzas at half past six, and I look out curiously for a first sight of the spot which is now to be my home; but nothing can be seen distinctly through the dark veil of nightfall. On the platform, Don Cecilio, Juan's younger brother, greets me in courteous

Spanish phrase, telling me that he throws himself at my feet (though he does no such thing!), and conducts me to the family carriage,—a large French barouche. On the box is a coachman in such magnificence of crimson and gold livery, and so pompous of mien, withal, that I am quite awed by the sight, although he lifts his hat on my appearance, and punctiliously holds it three inches above his cranium, until I have taken my seat. But he has the air of doing it as a specimen of finished deportment, and for artistic effect, rather than out of deference to anybody whomsoever. Then a rapid drive through the gas-lighted city shows me that Matanzas has many of the characteristics of Havana; but the streets are wider and the general effect lighter and more airy. Ere long, the carriage stops before the door of the Sámanos, the stately Don Enrique himself hands me out, I am ushered into a large, brilliantly lighted *sala*, I undergo a confusing number of ceremonious introductions, and receive a corresponding amount of ceremonious Spanish welcome. The house and its contents are unreservedly placed at my disposal, and every member of the family (figuratively) kisses my hand, or is laid at my feet. I come out of it all with but one distinct impression,—that my hostess, Doña Coloma, is by far the prettiest, most graceful, most *spirituelle Cubana* that I have yet seen.

Now that some weeks of the quick, silent weaving of the threads of habit have wonted me to the place and people, it is difficult to recall the strangeness, the bewilderment, the almost forlornness, of that first evening among them, after Juan had gone forth in order to make sure that neither counting-house nor fixtures had run away during his absence, and I was left to my own slender resources for the further prosecution of the acquaintance. The Sámanos knew no word of English, and my Spanish, having chiefly been used for book intercourse hitherto, was not sufficiently at my tongue's end to carry me very smoothly through a sustained conversation with a roomful of strange people. So, after the most easy and obvious topics had been exhausted, I looked at them, and they looked at me! and if Doña Coloma had not had a marvellous store of animated and expressive gestures at command, and an ease and grace of manner altogether perfect, the situation must have been awkward. But she smiled and nodded, and asked questions and helped me to answer them, and improvised small pantomimes, and called upon the children to show me their accomplishments; and one of them played, and another sang, and a third danced; and thus the evening wore on, not unsmoothly, until eleven o'clock; at which very early hour, according to Cuban standards, I was allowed, in consideration of my travel-worn condition, to withdraw to my own room. If some shade of home-sickness met me there with the insidious question whether, after all, it was worth while to have come over the sea for three or four months of this sort of thing, it shall not darken these pages. For the morning light dispelled it with other shadows; and in *that* shape, it visited me no more.

## CHAPTER XI.

### EVERY MORNING.

SCARCE a fortnight had elapsed, ere I felt myself thoroughly at home under the Sámano roof, and life had settled to a regular and familiar flow. Possibly there are those who would like to look closely into its quiet current, to know what the home-life of Cuba really is, what its occupations, its anxieties, its pleasures, its vexations, its courtesies. For such, I give, in this and the two following chapters, the history of a day—of any and every day; for, with few exceptions, the faces of all are so much alike that it is hard to discover any distinguishing trait.

Scene opens about eight o'clock, A.M., in my room. As the occupant thereof is buried in a profound slumber, or steeped in the delightful languor of the very last morning nap, you will have time to examine the apartment and its furnishings, before the *dramatis personæ* appear upon the stage. It is long and narrow in shape, and not less than twenty feet in height; the open roof showing plainly all the beams and rafters used in its construction. The floor is of quaint red and brown tiles, and there is a Turkey rug before the bed, put there since my advent, with some kindly intention, doubtless, of an approximation to my former habits of life; but I daily wish it were back where it came from, the reason of which ungracious and ungrateful sentiment will appear hereafter. The furniture looks meagre to an American eye, and lacks many things deemed essential to comfort in homes now distant (geographically—but very present to my inner vision!); yet it is fully up to the Cuban standard, and comprises all that is necessary to tropical life; where nature does so much for one's comfort and pleasure that the shortcomings of art are easily forgiven. By way of compensation, there is a superabundance of mere adornment,—the hangings, counterpane, sheets, pillow-covers, valance, and even the towels! being all elaborately trimmed with broad edgings and insertions of lace, of Catalonian manufacture, and often of fine quality. In this department, also, may be noticed a dingy figure of the Virgin, of such extremely unlovely and forbidding an aspect that the label underneath— "Madonna de la *Misericordia*"—seems absurdly misplaced.

At the east end of the room, facing the street, is a large window, of the usual quaint and clumsy construction of all Cuban wood-work. It opens on a sort of balcony, full fifteen feet wide, running across the front of the house, and overlooking market-place and bay. One end of this balcony is occupied by an aviary, densely populated with South American birds of brilliant plumage, whose wild, piercing notes are among the first sounds that greet me in the morning.

But the door opens. Enter Francisca, a young girl

recently imported from the Canary Islands, and the only white servant in the house—white, by courtesy, mark you, for there are really only degrees of dark in Cuba. This child of nature has a queenly figure, a majestic carriage, a bright face, and a voice as sweet as the birds of her native isle. Her morning greeting, considered as speech, is slovenly enough, being exceeding provincial; but regarded as sound, it is fresh and clear as a song. She brings me a cup of fragrant coffee, with milk and sugar, imparts such items of domestic news as are already current, and vanishes. The coffee having been sipped slowly, as becomes its quality, I rise and betake myself to the *chase*—a regular morning pastime. Armed with a pin and a piece of thin muslin lightly wrung out in water, I proceed to turn over and examine carefully, one by one, all the garments which I removed the night previous; hidden in the folds of which, hosts of blood-thirsty cannibals—known to the scientific world as *Pulex irritans*, and vulgarly denominated fleas—are waiting, with exemplary patience, to be put on again this morning, and renew their banquet on human flesh. At the faintest glimpse of a black speck, down goes the cloth with a vengeful slap; which, being wet, embarrasses the motions of the insect, and, being thin, permits me to see its form distinctly enough to run it through with the pin, which I do, "with a will." But I have learned not to rely too confidently on its decease, even after this operation; having had the mortification, on several occasions, to see my captive, on the removal of cloth and pin, hop off as gayly as if nothing had happened to it. In this event, I pursue it through garments and across tiles; and here appears the great inconvenience of the aforementioned rug, which is as discomfiting as a morass or a furze-field to a sportsman. If the flea strikes that, the chase is up, and the course of justice thwarted. I have grown learned in flea-lore, through this "sharp practice;" I think I could write a biography of one of the race, with great minuteness of detail and accuracy of facts.

The operations of the toilet are sometimes still further retarded by the necessity of rubbing the starch out of any articles needed from the last week's wash. I have not yet succeeded in convincing Paula, the laundress, that when I say, "No starch," I mean precisely that, and am prepared for no compromise whatsoever. The Cuban practice is to starch all garments, without exception, to the utmost degree of stiffness. How they manage to wear them, I cannot imagine. The sensations of a foreigner are best described by a certain Herr Wagner that I met in Havana. "The first time that I sat down in a clean shirt from a Cuban laundry," said he, "I thought I must have landed on a pile of broken crockery. And when it became necessary to put on a Cubanized night-shirt, I sat up till two o'clock in the morning trying to rub the scratch and the crackle out of it. As for pocket-handkerchiefs, you might as well use sand-paper!"

Being dressed, I step out on the balcony, where I pray you to join me, for much may be seen from thence which is novel and interesting to unwonted eyes. Leaning over the parapet,—which is thick enough to stand a siege, and dates back to the last century,—you will see that the house fronts on a large open space, in the angle formed by the Bay of Matanzas, and the River San Juan. Over the way is a row of volantes, waiting to be hired; in the middle is a string of packed mules, pausing to rest; nearer, a half dozen drays, piled with jerked beef from Buenos Ayres, or tobacco from the famous "Vuelta Abajo," or wine and oil from Spain, are waiting to discharge their loads in the warehouses of "G. and Co." Farther along are an ox-cart and team; the yoke is a clumsy wooden bar, laid on the animal's head, and tied to his horns by stout ropes; the draft comes, therefore, on the creature's horns and head, rather than on his shoulders; and he is guided by means of a long leathern thong, fastened into his nostrils. Soldiers, sailors, *paisanos*, coolies, and negroes, are continually passing, furnishing a gay and animated panorama for all eyes that gaze. Street-venders are plenty and picturesque. Yonder is a Chinese crockery peddler. His stock in trade is contained in two large round baskets, suspended from a kind of bamboo yoke on his shoulders. He calls attention to his wares, not by a cry, but by tossing in the air a half-dozen plates or saucers, and, by the sleight of hand peculiar to his race, causing them to fall one upon another as he catches them, with a sharp clash and clatter that is heard above everything else. Next comes a seller of *dulces*,—a neat-looking mulatto girl or negress, with a basket on her head and a tray in her hand, both filled with divers kinds of sweetmeats, suited to the popular taste; by the preparation and sale of which many decayed families support themselves, sending their only remaining servant into the street to dispose of them. After her comes a *panadero*, with a huge, flat, covered basket on his head, and two or three palm-leaf bags hanging on each arm. These are all filled with bread, in the form of rolls, of excellent quality; which he is distributing to his regular customers. There is no such thing as home-made bread in Cuba: the bakers furnish an unobjectionable article, and deliver it fresh at the door every day. On the plantations, it is obtained from the nearest towns or railway stations. Next, you see an odd figure of a poultry dealer, from the country. He wears a hat like a small umbrella; his shirt is of striped linen, and very likely, hangs *outside* of his pants; he is perched on top of a large saddle and a small donkey, and flanked by two great panniers, out of which stick the heads of three or four dozen of live chickens. Yonder is a negress crying "*Naranjas! naranjas, dulces!*" (sweet oranges); and another has a basket of fresh cocoa-nuts on her head. This latter fruit is always eaten here while the rind is yet green, and the pulp soft enough to allow of its being stirred up with the milk, and eaten with a spoon. It is said to be more wholesome thus, than in the shrunken and dried form in which it comes to us.

One of the saddest of the street-sights is the chain-gang, on its way to the government works on the quays,—a long line of vicious or stolid faces, marching to the clank of the fetters which link them together in forced and fearful companionship: one of the funniest is a patient little donkey, so thoroughly packed with green corn, fresh cut for feed, that you see nothing but a moving mass of verdure, reminding you of the "marching wood of Dunsinane;" unless the animal is coming directly toward you, when you see his poor nose in the midst of a circle of dainty green, just out of his reach; and he might fitly parody the lament of the "Ancient mariner" something in this wise:—

> "*Fodder—fodder* everywhere
> And not a *bit to eat.*"

If you go to the farther end of the balcony, and look into the "Calle O'Reilly," you may see a small herd of cows standing at the side-entrance, and chewing the cud, while the driver milks one of their number. The first time I witnessed this, I inquired of my host if he kept cows. "No," he replied, "it is only the milkman." I stared, and he explained that it is the custom, in Cuba, for venders of milk to drive their cows to the doors of their customers, and milk the quantity required, on the spot. I commend the practice to my own countrymen, nauseated with a deluge of stale or adulterated milk.

At first, I found an infinite deal of amusement in this motley show, but already the charm of novelty is worn away, the quaint, graceful, or picturesque lines smoothed to the tameness and soberness of every-day life. But beyond it lies a view, of which one tires not so easily—the beautiful bay, with waters now blue, now green—now heaving softly as the bosom of a sleeping maiden, now lashed by the north-wind into white, dashing crests of foam—now turned to molten gold by the sunshine, now lined with a silvery moonlight path that seems ready to take one to far-off, fabled *islas encantadas*—always full of ships lying at anchor,—with flags and streamers of every nation and hue, and gayly painted sail-boats and lighters, and steamers plying in and out;—a scene of brilliant and changeful hues, ever new and ever beautiful. Nor is this all. The bay is almost landlocked, and on either side stretch away green hills, crowned with white villas and gardens; and into the dreamy distance drift groups of palms, and stand clear drawn against the morning's blue or the evening's pink and gold. Farthest of all—now veiled in mist, now clearly lit by the daybeams, now crimsoned and purpled with sunset lights and shadows—is the San Juan mountain, where my eyes rest last and longest as the most eligible point in the landscape whereon Thought can stand a-tiptoe, and strain her eyes over the blue ocean for just a faint glimpse of the dear New England hills, which are fairer now than ever before, as seen through the golden medium of a "light that was never on sea nor land!" It is good to sojourn, for a time, in a foreign country,—not only on account of the fresh sensations, the enlarged experience, the new veins of thought, which it opens to one, but to learn how much of life's sweetness is compressed into that little word "home." Cares and trials, it is true, enter its charmed circle; so the rose has many thorns, yet is accounted fairest of all the flowers!

At ten o'clock, the gentlemen come in. They rose early; they partook of a cup of coffee and a thin cake or cracker, and went forth to the quays, the custom-house, the ware-rooms, the banks; for all out-door business is done, if possible, before breakfast, ere the day has reached its melting-mood.

Breakfast is now served. It is decidedly *à la fourchette.* It might answer for dinner as well, by reason of the variety and substantial nature of its dishes, except that it lacks soup and dessert. The first course is always fried eggs and boiled rice. This seems to be *de rigueur;* after that, you may eat what you please and in your own order. Doubtless, there is a beefsteak pie, mysteriously flavored; and there is certain to be a *tortilla con seso,* or brain-omelette. Chops are plastered with a mixture of eggs, herbs and olives, wrapped in paper, fried, and served with the wrappers still on. The stranger is often deceived by dishes which keep the look of old acquaintance to the eye, but break it to the taste. I was served, one morning, with what I took for codfish cakes, but which turned out to be a wonderful compound of chopped meat, raisins, tomatoes, eggs, onions, mashed potatoes, and I know not what beside! I was unable to tell, after I had partaken of it, whether I liked it or no, and my mind is not more clear about it at this moment! Fish are abundant and various. One kind enchants our eyes with all the colors of the rainbow, the process of cooking not having in the least impaired the brilliancy of its prismatic adornments; another is so minute that you wonder that people take the trouble to catch and cook it, nor is the problem solved after you have eaten four or five at a mouthful.

There is a decanter of wine and another of water, and a mixture of both is used. The glasses are a cross between tumblers and goblets, and are always placed on the table in finger-bowls, and remain there throughout the meal. Coffee is served at the end.

The dining-room must needs be airy, for it is entirely open, on one side, to the sky and the court. There are *jalousies*, to be sure, but I never saw them closed. In one corner is a piece of mahogany furniture, in appearance half-safe and half-sideboard. Lifting the lid, a large hemispherical stone basin filled with water is disclosed, the bottom of which is pierced with a single minute hole. Opened in front, it reveals a stout stone jar, into which the water from the basin above trickles slowly, drop by drop; also two or three fancy jars, with handles, for drinking purposes. Water thus filtered, is pure and palatable, and tolerably cool. The filterer is called an *estelladora*, and a duplicate thereof may be found in nearly every house on the island.

For the rest, the breakfast is merry and social, and bright with the faces of children. The Sámanos all belong to the order of "born teases," and long practice has given them wonderful skill in the art of provocation, so that *la señora* leads rather a thorny life of it among them. They are Spaniards, and she a Cuban; therefore, she is kept under a continual fire of jests and sarcasms, touching the language, customs, and character of her beloved compatriots. It is amusing to watch the little lady under this treatment; at first she assumes an indifferent and supercilious style of demeanor, determined not to be teased; then she shrugs her shoulders, and gives an expressive little gesture, as if she were shaking off a shower of paper pellets; next her face begins to darken, and her eyes to expand, and finally, the bucket of her forbearance being overflowed by some particularly tantalizing "last drop," a flash of forked lightning darts from her black eyes, the words burst forth in a torrent, and indignant remonstrance, energetic retort, and expressive pantomime, are all marshalled into array to confront and confound her foes. I think she would have the best of it, if they were not so many; but three against one, each with a characteristic and skilful mode of handling his weapons, is rather unequal odds. So the warfare goes on, until one after another of the assailants falls into paroxysms of uncontrollable laughter,—the Señora stops in the middle of a sentence, and laughs too, and the skirmish is ended.

## CHAPTER XII.

#### DURING THE DAY.

BREAKFAST over, the working day begins. The Cuban ladies, having far less pretension to the name of "lilies" than their northern sisters, do likewise toil and spin,—using these words to describe all sorts of plain and fancy sewing, and especially, for an interminable process of pulling half the threads out of a piece of linen, and working over the remainder with an elaborate pattern of leaves and flowers; which seems to be the very *ne plus ultra* of needle accomplishments,—being taught in all the schools. So, unless I have letters to write, I join my hostess in her own or the adjoining room; and we sew and chat together, the stream of our conversation being subject to many interruptions from children and servants. Exactly how many of the latter there are I have not yet learned, as new faces are continually meeting me in out-of-the-way corners; but they are ugly, ignorant, good-natured, noisy, chattering creatures, with not even a "gloamin' sight" (as Andrew Fairservice would say) of the fact that there is a time to keep silence as well as a time to speak. They are continually dawdling about, in grotesque attitudes and absurd attire, producing many quaint pictorial effects;

and affording much amusement to visitors, and a corresponding amount of vexation and care to their employers. One of them, Juana by name, and belonging to the African tribe of the Lucumís, is a continual study to me; I am so sorely puzzled to decide exactly what nice degree of upward or downward gradation would place her on a level with the baboon. When not at work, she is usually found crouched in a corner making mouths at the wall, or grinning at her own huge, ill-shapen shoulder, which she has an apish way of slowly lifting out of her loose-fitting frock, following it closely with her eyes until it is on a level with her ear, and then letting it fall with a grunt, which performance often occupies her pleasantly for a quarter of an hour at a time. If called, she answers in the harshest, most guttural, most unintelligible jargon conceivable, resembling more the cry of a bird of prey than the human voice.

The cook is a Chinese, formerly one of the class known as *Coolies;* whose sombre, discontented, mutinous faces meet one at every turn in the island, and stir the heart with indefinable pain and pity. Ricardo, however, seems happy enough when he is in a good humor; he served out his term of bondage years ago, and is now his own master, or, at least, may choose the whereabout and mode of his service. He fills other and more important posts than his nominal one; in reality he is steward, butler, and housekeeper. The kitchen communicates with the dining-room by a long staircase from the court, up and down which he travels fifty times a day, in the regular discharge of his duties, but goes into a tearing passion if, by any chance or mischance, the number is increased to fifty-one. And the rage of a Chinaman, be it understood, is unmatched for fire and intensity. The other servants, who quarrel among themselves all day long by way of pleasant pastime, fly before him, or huddle together like a flock of frightened sheep; while he hurls among them threats and anathemas, like a shower of bombs, and apparently doing as good execution. If the uproar penetrates to the *sala*, or there seems to be danger that he may resort to other and more dangerous missiles, Ricardo is summoned before his mistress. In the attitude of a stage-hero, he listens to an eloquent compound of reprimand, remonstrance, entreaty, and gesticulation; and departs humbled. If all else fails, a threat of dismissal immediately reduces him to order. It would break his heart to leave the family,—especially the children, all of whom have been born during his administration. Two or three years ago he was suddenly taken with a fit of discontent and would-be independence, and conducted himself in such a manner that, one morning, his wages were quietly paid him and he was told to go in peace. There was a mournful leave-taking of the little ones, a silent packing-up, and a moody departure. The day wore slowly away. At dusk, Doña Coloma was desired to look into the court. She beheld an affecting picture—in water colors. The central figure was Ricardo, on his knees and dissolved in tears. Around him hung the children, also dissolved in tears. The negro servants filled up the background, likewise dissolved in tears. To avert another deluge, she bade him return to his old quarters, duties, and behavior; which he did forthwith, greatly to the satisfaction of all parties. Doubtless, he is a fixture for life.

One of my chief amusements is to lean over the gallery looking into the court, and watch Ricardo's preparations for dinner. His method is certainly original. Just outside the kitchen is a long table for his convenience, over which hangs a double row of hats, of every shape, size, and hue,—straw hats, felt hats, silk hats, sailors' hats, farmers' hats, gentlemen's hats, ragged hats, brimless hats, crownless hats, black, white, and gray hats,—gotten, heaven only knows where, but enough! in number and variety, to stock a second-hand hat shop. Out from the little recess of a kitchen, red with the glow of a large furnace, rushes the Chinaman, hair flying and frying-pan in hand—slaps hat the first on his head with so furious a blow that it is a miracle he does not knock himself flat—dashes frying-pan on the table, and sprinkles the contents with salt—flies back to the fire, and gives a kettle a stir and a shake—darts out, seizes frying-pan with a flourish, and flings hat to the farthest corner of the court—dashes frying-pan on the fire, and stirs energetically for a moment—makes a dart at another hat, and puts it on—snatches a plate from a cupboard, and hurls it on the table *carefully!*—reproduces frying-pan, and inverts it over plate—raises the dish to a level with his eyes, and surveys it critically—shakes his head disapprovingly, and sends hat the second spinning in the air—returns the meat to the frying-pan and the pan to the fire, crowns himself majestically with hat the third, folds his arms and falls into a fit of abstraction—rouses himself, produces a bake-pan, marches gravely into the middle of the court with it, examines the contents minutely, cuts a pigeon-wing of rapturous delight, and hurls his third piece of head-gear straight upward, which lodges on the roof—covers bake-pan, and dons hat the fourth—dives into depths of kitchen and reappears with a stew-pan containing vegetables—drains off the water on the pavement, hurls hat the fourth into the slop-barrel, and crowns himself with the next in order of succession—transfers vegetables to a dish—suddenly becomes conscious that he has transgressed a strict rule that no slops shall be emptied in the court, and makes a frantic rush at a towel—rapidly wipes up the steaming liquid, puts towel into his pocket, and springs up three feet with a yell—hastily pulls it out, and throws it, in company with hat the fifth, at the furnace, in a vein of severe irony,—brings out a soup-kettle, sets it down in the court, stirs it, tastes it, walks around it, shakes his head at it—flings hat the sixth at his head with extraordinary accuracy of aim—adds divers condiments to the soup and bears it to the fire—takes off his hat, looks into it solemnly for some minutes—appears to find what he seeks, for he puts it on again, and immediately pours the soup into the tureen—dishes up some vegetables—takes tureen in both hands and commences mounting staircase to dining-room—becomes suddenly aware that he is still covered with hat the sixth, and, with a shake and a toss of the head, sends it rolling down the steps—places tureen on the table, and goes back for the other dishes—shouts for Francisca to come and help him, and shies hat the seventh at her as she descends the stairs; which performance goes on, with slight variations, until his whole assortment of head gear is strewn about court and gallery in curious confusion. Juan asserts that if he were deprived of his hats he could never serve the dinner creditably, and I am inclined to receive the statement in perfect faith.

At one o'clock, P.M., a certain dusky incarnation of probity, Atanasia by name (who may not only be trusted with untold gold, but will stand the severer test of being left in charge of unnoticed and nearly valueless trifles), gives a smarter set to her turban, shuffles out, and presently returns with a basket on her head, filled with fresh, yellow oranges, or ruddy bananas, and topped by *panales*. These last are a confection of eggs and sugar, made into white, frothy-looking bars, six or seven inches long, and designed to be dissolved in water, with a few drops of oil of annis, or the half of a lemon, which mixture makes an agreeable and nutritious beverage. Francisca peels the oranges as we do apples, sticks a bar of the *panal* in a goblet of water, and brings all to me, where I sit. This is our usual lunch, with only some slight variation in the article of fruit. The cashew, mamey, paw-paw, melado, citron-melon, guava, etc., offer us, now and then, a choice between acidity and insipidity; but none of them can institute any successful rivalry with the sweetness and richness of the orange and banana. The guava, though so great a favorite when made into jellies and marmalades, has, in its natural state, an intense flavor of rottenness, which nothing short of a long course of persevering and determined effort, can bring a stranger to regard with aught but the extremity of disgust.

The afternoon is so like the morning that you would be puzzled to distinguish one from the other, except for a slight increase of temperature, and a dimmer dreaminess in the mood of the air. The servants dawdle over their avocations more sleepily than ever, rousing themselves occasionally with a little quarrel; and it is amusing to see how stately and courteous they become at such time, hurling "*Señor*" and "*Señora*" at each other, as if these titles were a new and efficient sort of missile. Doña Coloma has finished one piece of work, and taken another in hand, which she executes over a long heavy cushion, held across her knees; bending over it with an industry and pertinacity wearisome to witness. What prevents her and her sister Cubans from stiffening into the shape of the letter Z, and growing to their chairs! By way of killing time, I inquire what she is making. "A towel, for a birthday gift to a friend." Said towel being a strip of fine linen, about two yards long, across each end of which she is embroidering, by the pulling-out-of-threads process, a border six inches wide; and which is further to be adorned with rows of lace. When finished, it will be hung, scarf-wise, across an ornamental knob, with which every Cuban bedroom is furnished. Regarded as an ornament, it is an extremely pretty thing; but I recommend all persons given to much bathing, to provide themselves with a dozen thick, durable towels, before they accept of the hospitality of a Cuban roof; for nothing will there be furnished them for their abstersions, beside the above-described dainty, elaborate, altogether admirable, but highly unserviceable "*toalla*."

Doña Mariquilla (a guest like myself) is busy with a sort of scarf, composed of alternate strips of muslin and embroidery, and edged with a frilling of rich lace. Pursuing my investigations in her direction, I am told that it is a "*sudario*, for (as I understand it) *un señor;*" i. e., a gentleman. Whereupon I commune with myself, for a season, after this fashion. "*Sudario*—I wonder what that means! Obviously, from the Latin *sudarium*, which signifies, primarily, a cloth for removing perspiration, and secondarily, any napkin or handkerchief. But this fanciful creation cannot be intended, even in the most remote and exceptional way, for any such service; neither can I conceive what possible use 'a gentleman' can make of it." Completely puzzled, but not quite ready to confess my ignorance, I consult my Spanish dictionary, and learn that "*sudario*" implies "winding-sheet." Now, I have seen so many queerities in the way of costume, and such abundant evidence of the semi-barbarous taste of the Cubans for decoration and bedizenment, that it would not surprise me to behold a corpse decked out with marabout feathers and gold lace; so I accept this definition in perfect faith. Composing my countenance, therefore, to a becoming degree of solemnity, I next inquire of Doña Mariquilla "if she has lost a near friend?" She looks at me in great amazement, and I am forced to explain myself.

"I understood you to say," I stammer, "that you were making that—*sudario* for a gentleman, and I presumed it must needs be for some friend."

"Oh!" returns she, smiling, "I said it was for *el Señor.*"

Now "*el Señor*" signifies "the Lord." A winding sheet for the Lord! I seem to be innocently verging toward blasphemy. "Doña Mariquilla," I exclaim, in desperation, "*will* you tell me precisely what a *sudario* is, and what it is for!"

Thereupon, the fat, good-natured, motherly lady, in wide-eyed wonder at the heathen darkness wherein I am groping, pours forth a voluble explanation that this term is applied, in Roman Catholic parlance, to the scarf which is usually wrapped around the loins of the figure of Christ, in the crucifixes, common to every house, and nearly every room, in Cuba. "She has one at home," she goes on enthusiastically, "a splendid one! a very large one!" (extending her arms wide to give me an idea of its size), "and as a labor of love, she is making a fine new *sudario* for it; wherewith she shall adorn it with great ceremony, when she gets home, and invite her friends in to see how grand it is!"

Now, I am getting used to small images of this sort: there is one affixed to the wall of the room where we are sewing, at this moment—a bit of lead run in a mould, and then gilded—which excites no greater emotion in my mind than what is, I fear, a very unchristian contempt for people who need such "helps to devotion." But when it comes to an ugly Horror of nearly life size, with thorns and nails delineated with pre-Raphaelite minuteness, great, red drops of blood, and a face of ghastly suffering, I am apt to turn sick at the sight, and make a rush for the nearest point of egress. Not that I do not realize, to the full, how good it is for us all to have our blessed Redeemer's sufferings in continual remembrance, but not in that grossly material shape,—which seems to make of the cross merely a horrible instrument of human torture, and robs it of all spiritual significance, all infinite power, all ghostly comfort. Wherefore, Doña Mariquilla, if your house is shadowed by the presence of such a nightmare of a crucifix, I retract, on the spot, my promise to visit it. I do not think I could sleep well under the same roof with so uncomfortable an inmate; and to grow familiar with, and careless of, its dolorous aspect, would, it seems to me, be the worst calamity of all.

My attention is next fastened on a ring, worn by Doña Mariquilla, the stone of which is so peculiar, in color and shape, that I beg to be allowed a closer inspection. According to Spanish custom, it is immediately placed "at my disposal" and its owner tells me, unsolicited, that it is made of the tooth of her father, which was extracted, to that end, after his death; in order that she might have a *part of himself* as a remembrancer! I restore the ring hurriedly, undecided whether I am most horrified at the cool hardihood of the proceeding, as it first appears, or touched by a certain curious, dreary pathos and tenderness, which I discover to be latent therein.

The entrance of the two little ones, Christinita and Rafaél, creates a diversion. Both are stark naked—the day being very warm—except for a tolerably thick coating of the dirt from the court, where they have been playing. Have you any notion how excessively filthy a sullied *naked* child is? Not the grimiest nastiness of rags and tatters is at all comparable to it. Nevertheless, Christinita (who has a fancy for me) stretches up her chubby arms and insists on being taken, with such absolute confidence in my reciprocity, such entire faith that she is going to be fondled and made much of, that no human heart not wholly incrusted with stone, can balk her expectation. So I swallow my disgust, and take her on my lap, to rehearse the one English word which I have taught her—"Pretty." Odila, *ætat* five, knows several, only she has a curious knack at misplacing them—invariably saluting me with "Good by, sir;" by way of morning greeting and emphatically pronouncing things "all r-right" (with a preternatural roll of the *r*) which she knows to be decidedly all wrong. She can sing "Yankee Doodle," too, which she has caught from Juan's habitual whistle, and which she accompanies with a queer, comic, impromptu dance; for Odila is a cross between fairy and imp, gifted with a marvellous spontaneity of prank and caper, and can dance in perfect time and character with whatever music is played before her. She is also a child of many moods, and of curiously extravagant expressions. In her happy moments, she accords me a high place in her affections, covering my hands, the hem of my robe—my feet even, if she can get at them—with rapturous kisses, treating my shawl, books, and other belongings, to enthusiastic hugs, and calling me her "*angel*," her "*amada*," her "*linda lindisima*"—when "presto, change!"—something goes wrong, and my devoted little admirer becomes a furious little demon, who stands, Samson-like, clasping the stone pillars of the corridor, and wishing she could pull the roof down on my head and her own!

With her comes her shadow—an exceeding black one! It is round, grave, staring, and good-natured; it is aged five; it is called Ramona; it is the child of Atanasia. It follows its little mistress everywhere, shares her playthings, her candies, her scrapes, and her punishments; accepts her caresses and her blows with the same placid satisfaction; and never makes moan nor murmur till bedtime brings the one thing unendurable,—namely, separation,—whereupon, it sets up a howl that almost raises the roof.

The children are soon engaged in a game of romps, and the foreign observer is confounded by their frequent use of the Sacred Name,—"*Dios mio!*" being the common expletive of small creatures who can scarcely utter it plainly. Before I well know what I am about, I am telling their mother how careful Christian people are, in my own country, to instruct their children to avoid such profanity, and how Society has taken the matter in hand, for those who are not Christians, and made it a rudeness to swear in her courts.

She looks at me wonderingly, and says, "They are *good* words, are they not? Why shouldn't we say them!"

A way of looking at the subject which would never have occurred to me!

It is now time for the two oldest daughters of the house to return from school. But not alone,—public opinion would condemn that, though the school were on the next block. Atanasia is sent to act as their *duenna;* also, to bring back on her head, even as she carried it forth this morning, a clumsy little chest containing their slates, books, school aprons, and needle-work, the key of which hangs by a ribbon from Dolorita's neck. Putting a question or two with regard to the school's *curriculum*, I find it rather limited. Reading, writing, a little arithmetic, and less geography, are counted all-sufficient for *girls!* If more is insisted upon, a skimming of grammar can be had. "What possible use can they make of anything farther, unless they are to teach?" asks Doña Coloma. "Of course, we give them all needful accomplishments."

Apropos to which, Dolorita's music-master bows himself in. That stately young lady of ten summers has been diligently practising her piano-lesson (hitherto untouched) for the last fifteen minutes, in expectation of his arrival. With outward patience, he endures a half-hour of blunders and discords that must give him an inward lockjaw. Thus far, the music-lesson might do as well for Boston as Matanzas; but now comes a variation. He seats himself at the piano, and strikes the chords of the piece that Dolorita has just played, be it finger-exercise, waltz, study, *pastorale*, or what not; and she sings it, in a high, thin voice, but in passable time and tune, making use of the syllables,—fa, sol, la, fa, sol, la, mi, fa;—in which performance the remaining half-hour is consumed. And this curious repetition of the piano-lesson with the voice is a regular thing; no matter how ill-adapted for singing the exercises may be, nor how far they transcend the compass of the child's voice,—though the latter difficulty is partially overcome by singing the notes an octave or two lower. I am unable to divine what is the object of this very peculiar musical training.

## CHAPTER XIII.

### EVERY EVENING.

AT four p.m., Ricardo appears before his mistress, strikes an attitude, and announces dinner. As the roof which shelters me is in the constant exercise of the largest, most generous hospitality, and no amount of unexpected company could cause any embarrassment where the daily bill of fare is as varied and as bountiful as ours; I may venture on the liberty of inviting you all to dine with me—after I have whispered in your ear a timely warning. "Look not long into the soup, though it be golden with saffron, neither linger with the *pilau* of chicken, neither disport thyself greatly among the vegetables dearest to thy heart; for more things are to come after than were ever dreamt of in any other philosophy of dinner than the Cuban, and the guests are expected to taste, at least, of all: therefore it behooves them not to partake to their special delectation, of any; but to walk daintily and discreetly among the good things provided, lest they be filled to repletion, ere they are aware, and be compelled to choose, finally, between the Scylla and Charybdis of bursting themselves or offending their host."

Fortunately, the dishes are all placed on the table at

the outset, so one has the advantage of seeing what is expected of him. Soup, colored and flavored with saffron, comes first, of course; then the meat and vegetables boiled in the soup,—among which you will notice bananas, or plantains, with the skins on; then salad. Next come stews, in endless variety; then eggs, in omelets; then vegetables; then infinitesimal roasts. Yonder seems to be a meat-pie; try it, by all means, and see what you can make of the contents. "Chicken—pork—tomatoes—onions—peppers—hard-boiled eggs—almonds—raisins"—you stop confounded, "*clams!*" (certainly, why not?)—"olives!"—and here you get bewildered, and give up the investigation, wondering what is *not* in a Cuban pie! Taste the green peas, stewed with tomatoes and eggs; the string beans, dressed like salad; the baked beans, mixed with shrimps or sausages. These things are to be eaten in course, and your plate is shifted for every one. For drink, you will have Catalonian wine, of undoubted purity; and the Spaniards always mix it with water. Now comes the fish, which has a different place in the Spanish meal, you see, from that which it occupies in ours. There are several varieties; among them you will notice our rainbow-hued friend of the morning, which, in its border of green leaves, is a study fit for the pencil of Claude Lorraine. Our host inquires if you will take "*bacalao*," which somebody explains is *codfish;* and feeling quite certain of your ground, you acquiesce, and receive upon your plate a thick, dark, greasy mass, wherein the codfish is so masked by oil, tomatoes, and the eternal saffron (which is one ingredient of all Cuban soups and stews) that you will fail to recognize it as an old acquaintance.

Having steered warily through all these (and many more, of which I spare you the full catalogue), you feel yourself at peace with the world, and ready for the dessert. First, we have preserves, all new to us, but all most delicious; then confectionery; lastly, fruits. Then the table is cleared, and coffee is brought; so also is a silver dish of lighted coals, called a *candela*, and a bundle of cigars. The master of the house lights one for himself, and passes the bundle to his next neighbor. Smoking is the one thing, which, in Cuba, momentarily reduces all classes to a level. The coachman may ask his master for "a light," the slave his driver, the soldier his general-in-chief, and it is never refused; and a mere wave of the hand is sufficient, by way of thanks. Now, if you dislike smoking as much as I do, you will make your escape, returning thanks, generally, for what you have eaten, and particularly, that you have been asked to eat no more, for the extremest limit of human capacity has been reached.

The next act of our day-drama is to come off out of doors, to my great gratification. The almost constant confinement within doors, to which the softer sex is condemned in Cuba, is extremely trying to foreigners, accustomed to more freedom, and who have not, moreover, the powerful and absorbing attraction of domestic cares and duties to keep them steady within so contracted an orbit. Now and then I get mutinous, and threaten to go out and explore the city and suburbs by myself, on foot; but Juan shakes his head gravely, and asserts that I shall repent of it, in dust and ashes, if I do; and his sister looks profoundly disgusted at the mere mention of such a thing. So, by way of a *pis-aller*, I pace furiously back and forth, from the front balcony, through sala, dining-room, gallery, open passage, and laundry, making divers circuits to avoid prostrate children and babies, white and black, and encouraged by the plaudits of half the household, gathered to witness the performance; for a Cuban is unable to conceive of motion for the mere sake of motion, and is disposed to regard as a fool any one who prefers to walk when he can sit, and as very far gone in idiocy if he chooses to sit when he can lounge or lie down.

But the carriage waits. Doña Coloma in delicate *piña*, Doña Mariquilla in black grenadine, Odila in white muslin and scarlet ribbons, the three-year-old Rafaél in the gorgeous uniform of a colonel in the Spanish army, and myself, descend to the piazza; and are handed into the vehicle by Don Enrique, or Don Cecilio, or Juan, one of whom leaves the counting-house to render us that polite attention, and returns thither as soon as it is paid.

The *señora* directs her coachman in clear, bird-like tones, which pierce through the rattle and clangor of the vehicle. "*Dobla al derecho, Amavedo!*" she cries, and we go to the right; "*Al izquierda, Amavedo! dobla al izquierda!*" and we turn to the left with a lurch that unseats us all, and makes it doubtful, for a moment, whether we are in the carriage or out. But this is only a cross-street, with a pavement that seems to have recently sustained the shock of an earthquake; by and by, we shall have smoother going.

First, we drive to the "Paséo de Versailles," which is even finer than that of "Tacon" at Havana, inasmuch as it lies along the margin of the bay, commanding a view of the shining water, the ships at anchor, and the encircling hills. On the left is the Campo de Marte, where a battalion of soldiers, in gay uniforms, are going through with their evolutions; and at the end are the castle and fort of San Severino.

Here, all Matanzas is to be seen at this hour, driving up and down and around, exchanging nods and greetings with acquaintances, and closely observing whatever foreign element presents itself. It is a brilliant and striking scene; yet it grows tiresome, taken as a regular dose,— the same scenery, the same soldiers drilling, the same people, day after day, with no variation except in the toilets. So, now and then, I petition my companion to leave the *paseo*, after a few turns, and go a little way up the bank of the Yumurí or the San Juan; both of which rivers run through the city, and give to certain quarters of it a Venice-like character. Or we drive out to the *playa*, a delightful strip of sand-beach on the south side of the bay, where the children and I gather shells while *la señora* waits and dozes in the carriage. But it is plain that she finds it dull pastime, and I care not to take her too often out of the groove wherein her life has run so long, that it runs not satisfactorily elsewhere. Most frequently we remain in the *paseo* until it is nearly dark, when we follow the soldiers out on their march to quar-

6

ters, see them defile in, while the band plays its last piece, and then go home to prepare for the *retreta.*

This takes place in the "Plaza de Armas," a very handsome square, laid out with walks, palms, and fragrant shrubs and flowers. In the centre is the inevitable statue of some one of that succession of Ferdinands (I believe it is the seventh), under whose auspices Spain went so steadily down hill for four centuries, that she finds it difficult to turn about and ascend, even now. On the east side is the residence of the *Comandante,* or governor of the department; on the north is the *Licéo,* a mixture of lyceum and club-house, and the remaining sides are filled with handsome dwellings and shops.

Eighteen years ago, in this square—so calm, so fair, in its silver moonlight dress—fell *Gabriel Concepcion de la Valdez,* a mulatto, a patriot, and one of the very few popular poets of Cuba. He was accused of taking an active share in that wide-spread movement of the slaves to gain their freedom, which sent such a thrill of terror throughout the island in 1844. He was tried, condemned, and sentenced to be shot. It is related that the first volley failed to touch any mortal part, and the brave victim, bleeding from several wounds, but erect and undismayed, pointed to his head: "*Aim here,*" said he, with as steady a voice as if commanding a battalion. The order was obeyed, and the second volley sent the strong, heroic, yet tender soul, to a land where, we may trust, it found gentler judgment for its errors, and wider scope for its talents, than in that which gave it birth.

However, no shadow of that tragedy lingers here tonight. All around the enclosure is a broad pavement, lined on either side with gas-lights and seats for spectators. Outside of these are the volantes and *quitrins*, closely wedged together, and filled with the beautiful *Matanzeras*. The band is stationed at the foot of the white statue, sprinkling the air with sweet sounds, even as the flowers sprinkle it with sweet odors. Overhead are the palms and the stars. It would be hard to find a fairer, gayer scene.

The etiquette of Matanzas, less rigid in this particular than that of Havana, allows ladies to alight from their volantes, if they like, and take a turn or two around the square, if duly escorted by father, or brother, or husband. You see scores of them, therefore, walking round and round, with that graceful, undulating motion peculiar to Cuban women, and pausing, now and then, to rest upon the seats. They are dressed as for an evening party,—long trains of sheer muslin, or sheeny silk, sweep the pavement—bright sashes wave—jewels glisten—polished shoulders gleam white by gas-light, and rows of gentlemen stare and comment as they list. It seems to us a very public exhibition, and a little inconsistent with the strictness of Cuban customs in other matters.

At nine o'clock the music closes with the celebrated Cuban dance,—a strange, monotonous, half wild and half sad melody, which makes you doubtful whether it was intended to set you dancing madly, or to lull you to a dreamy sleep. The Cubans, however, seem not to be troubled by any such question; you can see that their feet involuntarily keep time to the music, and I am told that, at their balls, the sound of this favorite dance rouses the most languid of them into a sudden enthusiasm and intoxication of dancing. This over, the band marches away to the sound of its own music, the *volantes* rattle off, and the show is ended. Some of the promenaders linger a while, if the evening is fine; others go to the "*Louvre*," to eat an ice with *barquillos*, or take a cup of coffee, and then the *Plaza* is left to the moonlight, and the sentinels guarding the palace.

Very often, we go from the *retreta*, to pass an hour at the house of another branch of the Sámano family, residing in the city. This abode shall be briefly described, not as anything exceptional, but as a fair specimen of an average Cuban city dwelling.

The marble floor of the hall is on a level with the stone pavement of the street, and would join it but for a somewhat elevated door-sill. Stepping over this, the first object that confronts your astounded gaze is the *quitrin*,—elegantly trimmed and glistening with silver-plate, it is true; but still, giving you the impression that, by mistake, you are entering the house through the stable! Between this hall and the *sala* is an arched opening, closed by a light iron-grating,—the *quitrin*, therefore, is always in sight; indeed, in some cases there is no division whatever, and the vehicle occupies one end of the apartment in stately grandeur, but the room is so vast that it is not in the way. Back of the parlor is the dining-room, through which the horses are taken to the stables in the rear of the court; their hoofs striking sharply on the stone floor, and convincing the foreign observer that there are many good reasons for the lack of carpets in Cuba! I have had the pleasure of witnessing this performance many times, with much inward amusement, as you may imagine, and congratulating myself, meanwhile, that my countenance is not always the mirror of my thoughts.

Back of the dining-room is the court, over which an awning is drawn during the heat of the day; and in which a few roses, lemon-trees, and vines, are growing, giving it a cheerful touch of greenery and blossom. Upon it the doors of the sleeping rooms open. All are on one level. It is not unusual to see one end of the court roofed over, to serve as a dining-room.

The large windows of the *sala* are raised one step from the floor, strongly iron-grated, and project about a foot into the street, affording an unobstructed look out, and an equally unobstructed look *in*. If you are passing outside, you often see the *señoras* and *señoritas* standing in these, and gazing at the outer world through the iron bars; with so much of the aspect of prisoners, that, at first, it makes you melancholy to look at them. You fancy that they suffer from the tyrannous restraints of their social customs, and are longing to escape. Your compassion is utterly wasted. I do not believe the desire to "get out," except in a volante to the *paseo* or the *retreta*, ever enters the Cuban feminine mind.

Entering the *sala* you will find its furniture separated by magnificent distances. There is a fine Erard piano, a cane-seated sofa, two or three tables, and a few good pictures. There is also in the middle of the room a double row of chairs (chiefly rockers) facing each other, and with just space enough to pass between them; and you will suspect that the children were enjoying a game of cross-questions when you entered, and there was no time to set things to rights. But it is the universal arrangement, and you will find it in every *sala* on the island. The gentlemen are expected to take one row, and the ladies the opposite one, unless there is a disproportionate number of either sex, which makes it necessary to encroach upon the space allotted to the other. Never take a seat elsewhere—you will commit an almost unpardonable breach of decorum,—but if the row is too short to accommodate a sudden influx of visitors, a servant will straightway piece it out to the required length.

A cellar-like dampness pervades most of the apartments, and I am glad that the lines have fallen to me in a dwelling of a different sort; for Don Enrique, like many Cuban merchants, lives over his counting-room and warehouses, nor thinks his social standing at all lowered by his so doing. Indeed, the Captain-General himself must needs live over the government offices when he is in town; and of all curious Cuban combinations, perhaps not the least curious are the very common ones of elegant mansions with busy warehouses.

At the Sámano *réunions*, we all sit in the inevitable double row of chairs, in the middle of the *sala*, in full view of the street, and rock and talk at each other at about an equal rate of velocity. Sometimes, I am fain to pass off my knowledge of Spanish for something even less than it is, in order to escape from the weariness of being civil and sociable in a foreign tongue, and to be free to use my eyes and ears to the best advantage.

In one thing, the Cubans are less formal than we: the use of the Christian name among friends and acquaintances is universal, and also of the diminutives "*ito*" and "*ita*." "*Don*," and "*Doña*" are prefixed where a little more formality is desired. "*Señor*" and "*señora*" are used, alone, precisely as we use "sir" and "ma'am": they are allied to the surname when it becomes necessary to distinguish *which* "Don Juan" or "Doña Maria" is meant, or on occasions of extreme formality. For formal introductions, and superscriptions to letters, both titles are used, thus;—Señor Don Juan Sámano," "Señora Doña Maria Sámano." Very likely, the latter would sign herself "Maria *Legran, de* Sámano,—Legran being her maiden name,—and you would be quite safe in addressing her accordingly. To an unmarried lady *señora* takes the place of *señorita*, but *Doña* applies to both married and single.

In the circle whereof I write, my own Christian name is already current, but so disguised by the prefix "Doña," and the suffix "ita," and the Spanish pronunciation of the initial letter, that I find some difficulty in recognizing it as one of my belongings.

Listening to the talk around me, I am struck by a peculiar, rising inflection at the end of every sentence, and clause of a sentence; tantamount to a note of interrogation. Señora Arcila, moreover, introduces a questioning "eh?" between every particular of the remarks she is addressing to me, which seems to say, "Do you understand it? can you believe it?" the whole running something as follows:

"You see her uncle wanted to marry her, eh? and the Bishop of Havana forbade it, eh? and so they sailed yesterday for the United States, eh? and they will doubtless get it done there, if they pay handsomely, eh?"

I venture to express my surprise that there should be any question of marriage where there is such consanguinity. Unto which she replies: "Why, *I* married my own uncle, eh? did you not know it, eh? We had a dispensation from the Pope, eh?—paid three thousand dollars for it, eh?"—and so on, until I am ready to cry out, "Yes, yes, I believe it all and ten times more, if you like; only do talk like a Christian, and not keep me nodding, after the manner of a Chinese mandarin, with that eternal 'eh!'"

An odd, wizened, Don-Quixotic figure now enters, leaning on a gold-headed cane, and bowing to the ground. He is presented to the foreign lady with *empressement*, as Señor Don Miguel Santamaria. She has heard of him before. He is remarkable, dietetically, for having drunken nothing but cocoa-nut water (or milk, as some call it) for twenty years; and intellectually, as having written and published a book in praise of that beverage,—also several poems. Somebody suggests that he shall recite one of the latter for her delectation. He does so, with a passion of emphasis and an energy of gesticulation that are—to say the least of them—

supererogatory. Some one then mischievously hints to him that *she* has been known to string rhymes together. Whereupon he lays his hand upon his mellow old heart, and looking more Don-Quixotic than ever, protests that, though he has often desired to know English, never did he desire it so ardently as now, that he might have the inexpressible pleasure of hearing her recite some of her " versos," in return for his. Soon after, he casts himself at her adorable little feet, kisses the hands of the mistress of the mansion, and elaborately bows himself out of the room.

Immediately, the roguish young Don Ruperto gravely gives a perfect imitation of the old gentleman's voice and manner, even to the recitation of some of his verses, and a wonderful fac-simile of his ceremonious departure. Everybody laughs, but the mimic's mother,—she scolds. Such treatment of their late visitor "is *vergonzoso ;*—it is *escandoloso ;*—it is everything that is disgraceful and discourteous!" So it is; but it is also very amusing.

We are also entertained with music. Mercedes—the eldest daughter of the house—plays exquisitely. Her audience is not confined to the *sala ;* an appreciative group gathers outside the window, and listens attentively to the end. Every hat is then lifted, a low, but emphatic " *Gracias* " is heard, possibly a compliment, or two, to the young lady's talent and beauty follows; then the group scatters. Perhaps she acknowledges this tribute by a slight bow; perhaps not; it doesn't matter either way.

On one occasion, the lady of the house is excused

from seeing us on the plea that she is "suffering from the quarrel between the Bishop and the Captain-General." I don't quite see how that can be a personal calamity, and Doña Coloma explains to my puzzled face that it is a Cuban custom to name epidemic colds after some recent national or local misfortune. The last wreck, or powder-mill explosion, or a possible invasion of *filibusteros*, or the resignation of a government official, is assigned as the reason why your friend denies himself to you; which is to be understood as a pleasant way of saying that he has an influenza.

If we spend our evenings at home, there is sometimes a rustle on the staircase at a late hour, and in flutters a bevy of bright dresses and glistening fans; the toilets and their wearers being fresh from the *retreta*. Children accompany their mammas, decked out in flounces and white satin boots, and manage their fans and eyes with nearly as much skill. There are no introductions; but those who meet in a friend's house enter into conversation without that formality, and need not recognize each other when they meet again, unless they choose. Introductions are seldom given, without first having asked the consent of both parties.

At ten, there is an informal supper of *pacienzas* (a kind of hard biscuits) and wine, for those who like it, and the day is over. Step out on the balcony with me, and take a last look at the phantom ships on a silver sea before us, and the "Southern Cross," gleaming on the horizon's utmost rim, and spiritualized by its legend of "*In hoc signo, vinces*,"—and so, good night!

## CHAPTER XIV.

### THE VALLEY OF YUMURÍ.

OCCASIONALLY, the foregoing programme is varied by excursions to points of interest in the vicinity. Among them, that to the valley of Yumurí stands preëminent. It is said to be the loveliest spot in all Cuba. It has been likened to the "Happy Valley" of Rasselas, and the "Valley of Delight" of Rafi-Eddin. It is declared that he who is not quite ready to yield up his mortal breath at sight of the bay of Naples, at once succumbs to the valley of Yumurí. All of which it is as well to believe. The tourist should have large faith.

The valley takes its name from the river flowing through it. The latter, tradition affirms, was called Yumurí—which signifies "I die"—in commemoration of the last words of a certain Indian, who was drowned in its waters by the upsetting of his canoe. This also the tourist will believe, though the river's current is neither rapid nor deep. For the name is soft and musical, and even this bit of a legend gives a kind of historic interest to the stream; inasmuch as the said Indian must have been one of that gentle and simple race which welcomed Columbus to these shores as a god, and which the Spaniard thereafter enslaved and exterminated.

Besides you and me, dear reader, the party will consist of my hostess, and other members of the family, Mrs. and Miss R. (recently arrived from Havana for the purpose), and several invited guests. The gentlemen and Miss R. are to go on horseback, the rest in *volantes;* for we are told that no carriage could stand the roughness of the road by which we are to travel. You and I are a little surprised at this, not yet seeing what advantage those cumbrous, noisy, swaying vehicles, whereat we have laughed so much, can possess over a good carriage; but we shall be wiser ere our expedition is finished.

We were to have started at three o'clock, but delay seems always to be the first thing on the programme where a large party is to be gotten off; and it is nearly four when we descend, to find the saddle-horses standing on the stone floor of the piazza, each held by a swarthy, bright-eyed, half-clad boy, and the *volantes* drawn up outside. Here, an unforeseen difficulty occurs. The saddle intended for Miss R. is discovered to have the horn and stirrup on the *right* side, according to universal Cuban custom; and she very naturally doubts her ability to ride in such unwonted fashion. However, she is persuaded to mount and give it a trial. Mrs. R. and I are handed into a *volante*, the gentlemen spring to the saddle, the servants, porters, grooms, etc., assembled to watch " *las Americanos,*" wave courteous *adieux*, and we are off.

Don Enrique leads the way, on a handsome black horse, which he rides like the accomplished gentleman that he is; a certain powerfully framed, black-bearded, and black-browed *Capitan* Garcia, of Castilian birth, takes a position on the right of our own *volante*, by way of escort to the foreign ladies; and Miss R., Juan, and Cecilio, fall into the rear, choosing to take a slow pace until the lady gets accustomed to her saddle. We lose sight of her at the first corner—rattle briskly through the city—cross the bridge—pass the barracks, the hospital, and two or three handsome suburban villas,—and then, commence the slow, rough, toilsome ascent of the "Cumbre." Ere long, we are high enough to overlook the rear road for some distance, but our horsewoman and her escort do not appear; and Mrs. R. begs me (for she speaks no Spanish) to inquire the probable cause of the delay. Questions and surmises follow, and a halt is ordered till the loiterers shall arrive. Meantime, we enjoy the view, which is already very beautiful—the square blocks of the horse-shoe shaped city, with its pair of shining rivers—the bay and shipping glowing in the rays of the westering sun—the neighboring hills and distant mountains—and afar, the blue waves and white sails of the boundless ocean.

We take ample time to study all these details; still our friends do not appear. I inquire if they may not have taken some other road, and am told that there is no other road,—a piece of information which I do not deem it necessary to impart to my trembling companion, who is clinging to that last hope. Neither do I think it expedient to utter my involuntary inward comment, that "one such is enough": a road like this in the immediate vicinity of a city of forty thousand inhabitants, speaks more pointedly of the indolence and sloth of the Cubans, in matters not directly related to the making of money, than anything I could say. At length Don Enrique grows impatient and uneasy, and sets off, at a hand-gallop, to solve the mystery; reappearing again in a short time, to say that Miss R., finding herself unable to ride in such reverse fashion, has wisely returned to the house, and will follow us as soon as another *volante* can be found. Satisfied with this explanation, the cavalcade again moves on.

Our way is still upward, and the road grows rough in tolerably exact proportion to the rate of ascent. Gullies yawn beside us; rolling stones give very insecure footing for the horses; rocks heave up like billows and lift us on their brown shoulders; and my respect for the *volantes* grows with every revolution of the enormous wheels. Being so large, they pass easily over the irregularities of the road; being so strong, they are not readily broken; while the distance of the horse from the vehicle gives one a pleasant assurance of security from his heels, in case he goes down—a danger which seems imminent, at times. My sympathy for the hard-worked animal, however, increases in the ratio of my respect for the *volante ;* he toils, pants, and stumbles on, dripping with perspiration, while his companion, whose share of the labor is limited to carrying the postilion, steps easily and jauntily, making one to see that, even to horses, the good things of this life are unevenly distributed. I bethink myself that Bishop Butler half admits that his masterly argument for the immortality of man applies as well to animals; and am soon lost in a wild maze of speculation as to how much the admission may be good for, and whether the Indian is so far wrong in believing that his horse and hound will share his Paradise,—when Mrs. R. recalls my wandering thoughts, and points to a cactus-crowned wall which we are passing.

The variety of these prickly plants growing thereon is really wonderful; and they seem to form quite as effectual a barrier against intrusion as the broken glass and iron spikes often used for the same purpose. The grounds thus enclosed are radiant with oleanders, pomegranites, and other brilliant flowering shrubs; while oranges, bananas and cocoa nuts tempt one, by their luscious profusion, to wish that laws respecting "*Meum and Tuum*" had never been framed. So we trot on, up hill and down vale, passing several small "*haciendas*," or plantations,—past sugar-cane fields, pine-apple gardens, palm avenues, and mahogany trees, until the last hill is surmounted, and the first glimpse of the valley of Yumurí, breaks upon us. Looking down a steep hillside, worn into deep gullies by heavy rains (of such regularity, that they look like a row of gigantic columns) we see a gently undulating vale, feathery with palms—billowy with cane—golden with an ever-present flowering shrub, peculiar to the country—a thread of silver winding through it, to show what a small beginning in life, as a brook, the river Yumurí has,—and all around, green hills, with sun-gilded crests, and sides mantled with shadow. But this is only the beginning of enchantments. Riding along the brow of the hills, our eyes are delighted with a succession of lovely and changeful pictures, until we reach a point on one side, where we all alight, and scramble a little way down a steep, rocky path, bordered by a thicket of shrubs, till we stand on the summit of a hill that thrusts a rough, scarred shoulder out into the valley, and a complete view of its whole length and breadth is before us! It is of such an exquisite, ethereal, and pathetic beauty, that all voices are hushed, all hearts touched, and we gaze in absolute, breathless silence! The valley is vast, in extent, and deep down below us, in position; yet its minute, microscopic features seem very near in the transparent air, very distinct in the flood of sunset light which both reveals and transfigures them; and those same slanting sunbeams, give it a tremulous, palpitating grace, which makes it appear unreal and unearthly—a thing to dissolve and vanish even while we gaze and wonder. There is no habitation to be seen in it, no form of man; it is a tract of enchanted ground—a lovely opening into fairy-land—a vast piece of weird mosaic—a picture of Eden before man had breathed upon and dimmed it;—yet none of these images fully expresses its peculiar, exceeding charm. Like the master-pieces of art or of poetry, it has a nameless and intangible beauty, a consummate deliciousness, that baffles comprehension, and seems to belong almost more to the domain of faith than that of sight.

Right opposite to us, two lofty mountain-peaks lift their rugged brows to look upon it admiringly, throwing long shadows across its gilded floor,—for behind them the sun is going down, round, red, in cloudless glory— and *he* too seems to be gazing, wondering, lingering, loth to pass on and leave it behind! I know not what feelings stir in the hearts around me, but my own, after a little, swells with an indescribable sense of pain that this entrancing vision will have so soon passed out of my life, never again to be present to actual vision, however it may haunt my memory; for its subtle fascination and appealing beauty wind themselves into my soul, and cling there, with a pleading, persistent tenderness,— whispering, in siren tones, " Abide with me and be my love!"

But the sun has dropped behind the mountains, and the valley begins to fill with shadow, as with a sea! The clouds darken, the outlines tremble and blend, the tufted palm-trees sink out of sight,—swiftly, too swiftly, the purple billows climb the hill-sides, until all is submerged; and, looking across the deluge which has swept over that fairy world, we see the dark forms of the mountain mourners sharply outlined on the pink and gold background of the sky. What subtle link of association brings before me that lovely picture of the " Christian Martyr," which used to hang in Goupil's window?—a fair female figure, drifting in transparent, rippled waters. Do I expect to see some sweet incarnation of the drowned Valley floating on the surface of that purple sea?

Sighing as we go, we turn our backs on the darkened picture, and climb back to the road. Life is full of strange contrasts, and we next find ourselves in a sugar-house close at hand, belonging to the "*ingenio*" of "*La Victoria*,"—and feel much as if we had been suddenly transported from Paradise to Pandemonium. The establishment is not a large one; and the mill is of the primitive sort, somewhat resembling an old-fashioned cider-mill. It is turned by five or six pairs of oxen going round and round in a dusky gallery above; the negro drivers of which keep up a continuous yelling and screeching that may truly be called infernal,—it makes us put our hands to our ears. They are hideous, vicious-looking creatures, too (the dusk and the noise may be partially responsible for that), so that the pistols in the belt, and the sword by the side, of the overseer, seem not a needless precaution. This latter personage, by the way (here known as the *mayoral*), is politely cutting up sugar-cane for us to chew, while we are making these observations,—a refection not to be despised when once the taste for it is acquired. We are glad to escape from this noisy Erebus to the vats below, though it is even hotter down there, and the half-naked attendants, seen through clouds of vapor, might be taken for Macbeth's witches over their cauldron. The process of sugar-boiling and drying is shown and explained to us, but as I shall witness this operation by and by, on one of the largest and completest "*ingenios*" of the island, worked by steam, I pass over it now. Finally—a last attention always paid to guests—teacups are filled from the boilers, with a cocoa-nut dipper, and commended to our lips. The draught, however, is not much to the taste of anybody except Don Cecilio and myself; but we linger, sipping the hot, sweet beverage, and chatting with the *mayoral*, for a considerable time; and are compared by Miss R. to two old maids, drinking tea!

Emerging from this den of sweets, unrefined and unadulterated, we are confronted by a row of negresses, each with a bouquet to present to the ladies. We accept the flowers with thanks, and they receive a donation from Señor G—— with courtseyings and ejaculations grotesque and indescribable!

Then follows a pleasant ride home in the moonlight, and a charming, silvered view of city and bay, as we surmount and descend the last hill. We enjoy it all keenly, but we do not talk much about it;—in truth, when the recollection of that wondrous valley, transfigured in the sunset and drowned in the shadow, comes before us, we feel as if we should never talk any more; for a fair, cherished friend is buried out of our sight, and the earth cannot ever seem so bright again. What words will embody to others the lost grace, the evanescent loveliness, or the exquisite pleasure and tender pain that we have experienced!

## CHAPTER XV.

### LAS CUEVAS DE BELLAMAR.

"YOU don't really mean to say that you are going to spend the rest of the winter in Matanzas?" said a certain John Bull to me, in a gently amazed and supercilious way, as I was quitting Havana. "Why, there is nothing worth seeing there but the Caves, and you can do *them* in a day."

If we dwelt in the Palace of Truth, I might have responded that we can "do" some persons in less time than that; it takes scarcely more than a glance to arrive at their sum total of national arrogance and personal conceit; but Talleyrand affirms that words were given us to enable us to conceal our thoughts, and in my answer doubtless they fulfilled their mission.

I did not then know how unfounded was the gentleman's assertion. Nothing worth seeing at Matanzas? Had he never seen (or only failed to appreciate) the beautiful, far-reaching views from the Cumbre? Had he forgotten the Valley of Yumurí, loveliest and tenderest landscape that ever charmed mortal vision? Did he never hear of the soft beauty of "Los Molinos?" Had he never felt his soul rise and flutter around the grand, blue dome of the "Pan," in a vain attempt to climb to the full moral height of its airy sublimity? Let me record it here, that in the matter of pure air and lovely scenery, Matanzas has greatly the advantage of Havana; and for all persons who can content themselves outside of "May Fair," it is much the more desirable residence. Invalids, especially, should never pitch their tents in Havana; almost any other spot in Cuba, where a reasonable amount of life's comforts can be secured, is a better and a kindlier abiding-place for them.

But to the Caves! Even His High Superciliousness, from across the Atlantic, endorsed *them* as worth seeing; and inasmuch as we do not intend to pass by on the other side of any opportunity of doing good—to ourselves,—nor of letting it be done to us through the revealings of that spirit of beauty which is so nearly akin to the spirit of love, we will go and see them!

In accordance with the hints of my hostess, I donned for the expedition certain short and loose garments which would neither embarrass motion nor suffer quickly from moisture, and which had already established some small claim upon the washtub; so I found myself a veritable grub among butterflies when I joined the other ladies of the party, whose toilets had not been made under so wise a supervision. The sun was sending long, slanting beams across the valley when our *volantes* were set in motion; and some fear was expressed lest night should be upon us, ere our inspection of the caves was concluded. To which Don Enrique responded, with a grave face, but a twinkling eye, that "as caves were seen to better advantage by torchlight than daylight, it didn't much matter!" Don Gustavo, a travelled Cuban, who has seen something of most countries under the sun, and picked up a smattering of divers tongues, rode on the right of my *volante*, and entertained me with a cheerful miscellany of four languages, which had but one drawback—it was frequently unintelligible. The quickest wits will now and then lose the track of sentences that begin in English, slide into French at the first stumble, relieve their embarrassment by a German expletive or two, and end comfortably in the speaker's native Spanish.

Our route first lay along the margin of the bay, where the waves, linking hands, came rushing up almost to the horses' feet, like troops of sportive children, and then broke and retreated, amid shouts of laughter and showers of spray. Just here, making the most of the broad outlook over the water, and the advantages for sea-bathing, boating, etc., three gentlemen have built summer villas, which, being the fairest examples of their kind in the vicinity, deserve a passing notice. The walls are stuccoed, and painted in bright colors, with facings at their base, three or four feet high, of blue and white Dutch tiles, figured in quaint patterns, and highly polished. In front is a broad piazza, with a heavy pediment, supported by white Doric columns; and through the wide-open windows we catch a glimpse of various large and lofty apartments, all *en suite*, with cool marble floors and white muslin draperies, and elegantly, but simply, furnished. In the midst is a court, with a sparkling fountain in its centre, encircled with broad-leaved plants. All around are blooming gardens; and lemon and orange trees, blossomy and fruity, lean over the iron railings. A group of dark-eyed *señoras* upon the piazza completes the picture, and inclines one to think that suburban life in Cuba is as enjoyable as anything ought to be, in a world which one must some time quit.

Just beyond is a group of wooden houses, which the natives point out as a curiosity—having undergone a sea voyage from the United States, together with a number of carpenters, who put them up in their present position. They belong to the common, ugly class of tenement houses; and neither their bare, clap-boarded sides, nor their loop-holes of windows, are calculated to impress the Cuban mind with the superiority of foreign over native architecture.

A short distance beyond these, our road turns to the south and begins to climb the hills, which cluster everywhere around Matanzas; and we are jolted over stones and jerked through gullies, at a rate that sets our words and ideas to knocking their heads together in a most uncomfortable and bewildering fashion. I wonder if there is a tolerable country road in all Cuba! Certainly, such a one as we are now toiling over, within two miles of the second city in the island, and on the route to Cardenas, a flourishing seaport town, does not promise much to reward further investigation. We jog on for a mile or two, with frequent pauses to breathe the jaded horses, until we reach a wide extent of table land, and trot briskly up to the door of a low, wooden building in the centre; when our postilions drop from their saddles, and we read on a conspicuous sign, "Las Cuevas de Bellamar" (The Caves of the Beautiful Sea.) *Here!* There is a general exclamation of surprise. I own myself an ignoramus in the matter of caves, and possibly my anticipations were as absurd as they are proved to be unfounded; but I certainly expected to find the entrance to our subterranean destination in the side of a cliff, or at the bottom of a ravine, or in some other place giving evidence of former convulsions of nature. To come upon it, therefore, under a prosaic shanty, in the midst of a broad plain, smiling and peaceful as if it had never known change or disturbance since Eden blossomed under the footsteps of Eve, was utterly subversive of all pre-arranged ideas; and I alighted in a state of extreme humility, minded to take whatever came thereafter, and be thankful.

While Cecilio registered the party in the visitors' book, I strolled around the room, and noticed its attractions. Divers views of the caves adorned its walls, to give visitors a foretaste of the wonders awaiting them, and several cases of stalactites stood around, by way of further whetting of the appetite; while a stand of refreshments, with a goodly array of bottles, performed the same office, in a more literal sense. In the centre was a covered staircase leading—to the bottomless pit, I conclude, after looking down! for I see the steps fade away through various gradations of dimness into darkness and nothingness;—and *this* is the entrance to the Caves!

The guides are now ready with flaming torches, and we commence our descent. In due time we touch bottom, and find ourselves standing in the midst of the "Gothic Temple,"—the largest of the caves, though scarcely the most attractive, at present. For the stalactites being so near the entrance, have been somewhat soiled by the admission of outer air and dust, and have lost much of that luminous whiteness which is one of their chief beauties. Still, the forms of pillars and arches are very perfect and majestic, and we gaze silently, with a mixture of wonder and awe. Pulpit and altar there is none. Nature is the priestess, and she offers the living sacrifice of hearts that are hushed beneath the vast dome into mute praise and fervent love. The guide tells us that, two or three years ago, the Bishop of Matanzas held a service here, with crowds of people to witness it,—an esthetic performance of which I should never have suspected that stout, round-faced, yet most dignified and reverend prelate. What a spectacle it must have been! The gorgeous vestments of the priests, the wreathing lights, the clouds of incense, the solemn roll of chant and anthem among these grand pillars and arches, covered from broad base to airy summit with the minutest and delicatest tracery of frostwork!

At one extremity, pendent over a deep chasm, is a mighty stalactite, which looks like a stately human form wrapped in the Roman toga. I thought of Curtius;— it needed but the horse to make the old Latin tradition visible to modern eyes, in strange, ghostly characters,

7

that may be older than itself. The fissure is of unknown depth; I threw in a stone, and heard it tossed back and forth adown the rocky sides, till the sounds died away into silence.

Leaving the "Temple," we are led by a rough, rocky path to the "Gallery of Icicles;" the roof being adorned with clustering, pointed pendants of translucent stalactites, and the floor with tapering masses of correspondent stalagmites, except where a path has been cleared.

Farther on, the empire of Fantasy begins, and her lovely or grotesque creations confront us at every step and beckon from every corner. Each stalactite takes the shape of leaf or blossom, insect or animal, in such bewildering profusion of beauty or oddity that it is impossible to take note of all; the whole being a rich kaleidoscopic mystery that changes with every change of the position of the spectator. Here, an arch Cupid peeps out from a mass of tangled vines; there, a spray of leaves and blossoms charms us with its delicate finish; here is an owl, and there is a cat; and yonder a stalagmite which, when the guide's torch is held behind it, becomes "A Lady's Skirt,"—soft, sheer folds of snowy muslin, with a dainty, fluted flounce at bottom! Farther along, the exquisite purity and loveliness of a "Vase of Flowers," seemingly carved out of dazzling pearl, leaves us no room for incredulity at the guide's statement that a certain rich American offered two thousand dollars for it, and was refused—as he ought to have been; otherwise the cave would have lost one of its chiefest adornments.

The traditionary step between the sublime and the ridiculous is much shortened here; often there is only a handbreadth between loveliness and deformity, and frequently the two run together in queer combinations of a lily growing out of an ugly, horny head, or a bird's wing attached to a rough, shapeless excrescence. Methought I had hit upon visible types of a moral fact. The continual, unnoted accretions of daily life shape characters into forms as imperfect and incongruous as these; the sweetest flowers of devotion and loyalty sometimes blossom out of the foulest relations, vices branch off into virtues, good and evil are inextricably blended, and only God can tell which shall ultimately predominate. But may He not, out of the fulness of His power and patience, bring all these unfinished material forms to final perfection and beauty? And is He not also, by the light touches of circumstance, and the silent influences of His Spirit, rounding into symmetry characters that now seem odd and ineffective jumbles of inharmonious elements?

A pair of stalactites which have succeeded in joining their stalagmites below, and grown into a remote resemblance to human limbs, are introduced to us as "Maximilian's Legs,"—christened, doubtless, in days when the name of the unfortunate Austrian prince was more easily associated with mirthful ideas than now. Hereabouts, I am the Columbia who first discovers to the world a fair, white, crystalline—pig! alike ignorant of swill and mud puddles; and it will probably be pointed out to succeeding visitors as the "American

Lady's Pig." For we are now in the vicinity of the "English Lady's Bath;" and all who wish to behold it, are invited, singly, to go down on all fours, and follow the guide into a small, dark aperture at the right. Crawling through mud and water for a yard or two, and knocking my head against divers projecting points, I am rewarded by the sight of a small, circular apartment, with three or four feet of clear water at its bottom; wherein, I am assured, a certain "Inglesa" once insisted on bathing, whence its name. As there is no standing-room within the apartment, and the irregular, dirty path outside offers small accommodation for toilet purposes, one doubts if the lady's comfort were much increased by the indulgence of the whim! Albeit, we are dripping with perspiration, because of the extreme heat, and our temples throbbing, by reason of the confined air; so we accept an invitation to drink from the spring, and find the water quite palatable, though its temperature does not suggest an Arctic origin.

We next enter "Benediction Hall," which shows no fitness for its name, that I can discover, but where the white stalactites cluster in even greater opulence of loveliness, and wilder fantasy, than elsewhere; and we pant with an oppressive sense that a flood of undetected beauty is surging over us, of which we can grasp and keep only the minutest fraction. If we turn back a moment, fresh graces blossom out under our eyes, airy creations have sprung up magically since we looked there last, and as many more are waiting to surprise us if we look again. There are exquisite and marvellous specimens of flowers, foliage, and vines, twined by the fairies, doubtless; with things ineffably absurd thrown in, here and there, by some mischievous gnome or elf. The infinite fulness of beauty, and the variety and fertility of grotesque extravagance, are altogether confusing and indescribable; to examine them thoroughly would take a lifetime. At the farther end, a stately row of alabaster organ-pipes, in a case of daintiest frostwork and pearl, causes us to wonder why it was not placed in the "Gothic Temple" yonder,—an inquiry to which the oracles of the cave return no answer. Its beauty takes on a more transparent, ethereal grace, as the guides' torches are held behind it; and that beautiful term, "frozen music," is no longer a purely poetic conception, but lives in my memory henceforth, a divinely white, airy, exquisite actuality.

By this time we have learned that our guides are not only dispensers of light—material and metaphorical,—but careful guardians of the caves' treasures also, keeping strict watch over us, and interposing quickly between the stalactites and any despoiling hand. There is reason in the precaution, for if each visitor were allowed to break and carry away at will, there would soon be nothing left but the mangled remains of these lovely creations, wrought by the light, magical touches of centuries of falling drops. Many of them are unspeakably delicate and fragile, crumbling under the softest touch, obliterated by any accidental pressure; the floor of the cave is covered with their white fragments. Nevertheless, to a born curiosity-lover, like myself, the idea of quitting this realm of enchantment without a single memento of its wonders is intolerable; but linger and watch as I may, I am sure to find a pair of dark, bright eyes fixed upon me. The most persistent pair belongs to a young negro, who brings up the rear of the procession; evidently, he has orders to leave no one behind him. Determined not to be baffled, however, I adopt another set of tactics. Turning suddenly upon my ebony follower, in the midst of a narrow, tortuous, ascending path, I hold up to his view a bright silver piece, point to the stalactites, and motion him to pass on. The dark imp is neither obtuse nor incorruptible. He grins, marches forward, holding his torch at a convenient angle over his shoulder, and looking straight forward; while I hastily secure two tolerable specimens, and go on my way rejoicing. So does he, and I suspect that he had still further cause for self-gratulation; for on reporting my stratagem and its success to one of my companions, she assumed my position in the rear, and I went forward to cross-question the head guide about the caves; thinking that it might be well to keep his attention occupied at this juncture. Virtue is ever its own reward! I gathered a quantity of information which I should otherwise have missed.

The entrance to the caves was once the site of a lime-kiln, the bottom of which suddenly "fell out" one day, to the consternation of the owner, and his lime vanished from sight. He and his assistant, when they had sufficiently recovered from their fright, set their wits to work on the subject, and reached the wise conclusion that they had happened upon a mine of precious metal, or a receptacle of hidden treasure. Swearing each other to secresy, and agreeing to share the profits, the one remained upon guard, while the other set forth to buy up the land in the immediate vicinity; which, not being deemed very valuable, he secured at a moderate price. Exploration was the next thing to be thought of; and after much deliberation and hesitation, the more courageous of the twain consented to be let down through the opening by a strong rope, with a light in one hand, and a signal cord in the other. He went down—down—down! to what seemed to him a frightful depth, when his courage gave out, he pulled the cord, and was drawn up without having touched bottom; reporting that he had seen an immense vaulted roof, flashing with *diamonds*—and nothing more! This was, of course, the "Gothic Temple," in its pristine whiteness and brilliancy. What an awfully grand sight it must have been to the terrified observer, suspended in mid air under its arched ceiling, and between its stately columns, whose bases were lost in the depth and darkness of the unknown Below! Farther experiment revealed the real nature of his possession to the disappointed purchaser; yet his treasure was not proven altogether "magician's coin;" for the caves attract large numbers of visitors, who are made to pay well for the sight, and have turned out a veritable mine of wealth to the owner, albeit not just of the sort he anticipated.

It takes time and labor to prepare the galleries for

the reception of visitors; the stalagmites must be cleared from the path, irregularities smoothed down, and chasms bridged. This has been done for three miles from the entrance, by two different routes, so that the visitor needs not to pass twice over the same ground. And the guide stated that other galleries, not yet made ready for visitors, had been explored, to a much greater distance than those now open; and that in one of these was a lake that must be crossed by means of boats. So the Mammoth Cave of Kentucky may yet find a formidable rival in her Cuban sister, when the full extent and attractions of the latter are made known.

It was aggravating to hear of these added wonders, and not be allowed to behold them; still, our first enthusiasm was beginning to flag, we were dripping, panting, and weary, and when we reflected that there were still two or three miles of fresh enchantments between us and egress, resignation was not unattainable. Our return-path led through new variations of white splendor,—dainty carvings, and quaint distortions, and dim ghost-peopled vistas,—infinite in detail, but similar, in general effect, to the galleries already visited. Four stalactites of great beauty and perfection deserve special notice. The "Virgin's Mantle,"—rich, graceful folds, of a delicate rose-tint and satiny texture, all glistening and glittering with brilliants. The "Lake of Dahlias,"—a frozen pool, studded with curious involuted projections, of a tawny yellow. The "Three Angels,"—a triad of white figures, sitting side by side, in an attitude of grief, with drooping wings and veiled faces, any one of which might serve for a representation of Bailey's Earth-Angel, who was "ever weeping." Last, and I think, most beautiful—though it is hard to choose where all are so lovely, and each has its own peculiar and exceeding charm—a seemingly frozen waterfall,—sheet and foam arrested and mute, yet clear and bubbly still, and absolutely flashing and flaming and dancing with light, from every point, as the guides wave their torches before it. This has received the expressive name of the "Cascade of Diamonds."

So we bade adieu to this realm of the gnomes and wizards, and climbed that detestable staircase, pausing to rest now and then, and wondering not that the first explorer refused to be dropped all at once into those dim depths and mysterious vastnesses; and finally emerged into upper air and daylight, to laugh (when we had gotten breath enough) at the queer figures we made. Boots had sunken all distinctions but that of size under one thick, democratic coat of mud; skirts were wofully splashed and stained; sleeves and collar limp and shapeless; hair totally unconscious of crimp and innocent of curl. The grub came best out of this ordeal; the butterflies looked as if drenched and blighted by a sudden shower, and utterly deprived of their moral expression.

The guide advised us to pace the room awhile, until we were somewhat accustomed to the comparative coolness of the upper air, if we desired to escape colds; so I obediently dragged my weary frame up and down, while my friends rebelliously sank on the nearest settee, and amused themselves—and me—with witty commentary on my performance. The "best, last laugh" was mine next day, when one was reported in bed with rheumatism, and another speechless from hoarseness.

Our ride home by moonlight was charming enough to merit a separate paragraph; but having already said enough in praise of the Cuban Luna to be set down as hopelessly moonstruck, I forbear, on the present occasion, at much cost of inclination.

## CHAPTER XVI.

A PROCESSION.

TIME was when the Roman Catholic Church was a power in Cuba; but a military despotism cannot safely tolerate any rival authority, and she was long ago forced into a subordinate and almost slavish position. The government owns all the church edifices and other property; appoints and removes the clergy, when it chooses; fixes their salaries; and in short, exercises whatever authority, in ecclesiastical matters, it is its pleasure to assume. The results are a sad lack of religious control and discipline—very observable in the almost universal disregard of the Lord's Day, and in certain dissolute practices of both clergy and laity,— and a want of moral power in the Church, which is one great cause, doubtless, of the extreme prevalence of practical infidelity among the male population. A bishop cannot remove a presbyter, except by resort to a tribunal where the government has a voice, and is certain to have its way, in the end; which way is extremely likely to be influenced by other than spiritual motives, and to tend toward other than spiritual ends. The civil law allows slaves their time on Sundays, outside of a certain limit, in order to enable them to purchase their freedom, if they wish; and many persons choose to employ them on that day, from lack of principle, or out of charitable considerations; so that it is quite common to see housecleaning, whitewashing, painting, etc., purposely postponed to the Lord's Day. Whites and quadroons, or mulattoes, live together in open concubinage, for the civil law prohibits the intermarriage of the races; and they avoid the Church, because she, since she is not allowed to marry them, must needs put an end to such relations, ere she receives them into her bosom. These things are no small obstacles to the Church's work and influence, even where there are earnest desire and effort to do the one faithfully, and exert the other beneficially.

This much is patent to the most casual observer of the religious life of the Island, and I do not claim to be much more than that. I early discovered that it was the merest waste of time, and most useless torture of feeling, for me to attend the services of the Romish Church with any purpose of devotion, or hope of benefit; although I did my best to go in the spirit of sympathy, and not of opposition, with a genuine desire to find points of agreement rather than of difference, and holding fast to the theory that an earnest and spiritually minded Christian may pray anywhere, beside anybody, and be nothing the worse for it. Unfortunately for the theory, I found it impossible, in practice, to shut my ears to prayers addressed to the Virgin and saints, or my eyes to observances which I inwardly stigmatized as "profane mummery;" and which stirred my soul to indignant protest, or cool disdain, or set me to rehearsing all the long controversy between Rome and the Church Catholic, until I was in no frame of mind to be benefited by whatever shreds of purity of doctrine, or beauty of ritual, the former might have to offer me. Nor could I settle it comfortably with my conscience to make these services, Sunday after Sunday, a spectacle or a study; knowing well that the study was not in the cause of truth, but for the gratification of curiosity. I was driven, therefore, to the conclusion that a quiet reading of our own helpful and satisfying Liturgy, in my own room, was the best, as it was the most convenient, method of fulfilling the letter and spirit of the fourth commandment, and sharing the " Communion of Saints," which was open to me.

Nevertheless, I have witnessed various services and ceremonies, at odd times, and certain domestic observances have come under my observation, which may furnish matter for thought and interest.

On my first coming to Matanzas, I went to see a "*paso*," or procession,—a religious ceremonial with which Protestants, and even Romanists, in the United States, have no acquaintance; except in an extremely limited and modified form. Certain crowded, squalid quarters of Matanzas, chiefly inhabited by blacks and coolies, have been severely visited with small-pox during the winter; and this *paso* was designed as a propitiatory act, to procure an abatement of the epidemic. At dusk, our carriage took a position at the corner of the " Plaza de Armas," directly on the route of the procession; where, for an hour, we awaited its appearance, while the crowd grew dense and denser around us, until the Plaza surged with a sea of human heads, and the street behind us was packed with vehicles and spectators. The orderliness of the vast multitude was one of its pleasantest characteristics,—no ill humor, no shouldering, no fighting, no incivility, though the great mass of those on foot were of the lower orders of society. "*Señor*" and "*señora*" resounded on all sides, as courteously exchanged between housemaid and hod-carrier as between countess and general; and the crowd swayed to and fro with as much unanimity as the waves, yielding to the regular motion of the tides. Less agreeable, though not less noticeable, was its evil odor. The daily pint of water, allowed to people of the better sort, probably shrinks to some quantity not worth mentioning, among the lower classes.

By and by, the universal patience was rewarded by the vision of a long line of thick, clustering lights descending the Cumbre, far away to the right, and apparently sailing by its own volition on a sea of darkness, or obedient to the waving of an unseen magician's wand; which curious and beautiful illusion was the prettiest sight of the evening. Very slowly the lights approached, heralded by the notes of a band of music, and preceded by two or three companies of cavalry to clear the way. Then appeared a considerable company of negro-women, all dressed in white, and each bearing a flaming torch,—said to be, without exception, mourners for friends who had fallen victims to the pestilence.

They were succeeded by a heterogeneous mass of women and children, black and mulatto, all carrying torches, and dressed in every sort of gaud and gew-gaw wherein the African heart delighteth; grand with long, sweeping trains, and marching on with that stately, erect, easy carriage which is theirs by right of their universal practice of carrying heavy burdens on their heads. Next came a gigantic negro, a true Anak of his race, ringing a large dinner bell ("only that and nothing more!") with all his might and main, and with evident relish of his performance;—he being the *avant courier* of a certain St. Sebastien, a life-sized figure, borne, on a platform, on the shoulders of four stout men. Now, hats began to come off in the crowd, in token that an element of solemnity had been introduced into the scene,—a thing sadly lacking hitherto. I looked very scrutinizingly at the image, but, knowing nothing whatever of the character and achievements of the said Saint, to add any ideal or derived lustre to his image, I was unable to discover anything in its bare literalness, but an ugly, brown, semi-nude, and altogether inartistic representation of the human figure; the complexion of which forced me to conclude that, like Murillo, Placido, and other persons of genius, the saint had African blood in his veins. Following him was a large body of torch-bearing men, corresponding in color to their patron and leader.

A second bell-ringer now smoothed the way for the passage of the Virgin, in the shape of a doll, two or three feet high, in great magnificence of golden and jewelled array. Her platform was decorated with flowers and tinsel, guarded at the corners by small gilded cherubim, and escorted by three or four priests in their robes. More hats were now lowered, and I saw some lips moving in prayer, which served to check the somewhat irreverent course, of comment in which we were indulging, lest we might be giving offence to some of these "little ones," children in faith, if not in fact. Then came another long file of torch-bearers, but the Virgin had wrought a change of color—miraculously, or otherwise,—and whites now filled the ranks of the procession; yet it was plainly to be seen that the representation was chiefly drawn from the lower classes.

Next, appeared a large crucifix, with a life-sized figure of the Saviour, fashioned with the usual minute and revolting attention to details. I could have compounded, thankfully, for a dozen Virgins, and any computable number of saints, in the place of this one crucifix;—seeing it, I became sensible that, somewhere in my veins, there must run one great drop of blood, directly inherited from some uncompromising iconoclast, of Cromwellian times. It was borne by black-robed priests, and followed by a small company of ecclesiastical, civil, and military dignitaries; each with his torch, and all in excellent humor, apparently, for the sound of their half-suppressed chat and laughter broke somewhat harshly upon the surrounding silence. All hats were lifted, as the crucifix passed; the crowd crossed itself reverently, and the hush was general and prolonged.

A band of music playing a dirge-like march, and a regiment of infantry, closed the procession. The line of lights defiled slowly down the street, and disappeared under the black arch of the Cathedral as instantaneously and completely as if it had been the Gate of Oblivion. I could have wished it were—for certain adjuncts of the ceremony!

As a sanitary measure, the procession failed lamentably. Nothing short of a miracle could have prevented its legitimate effect,—to spread contagion, and increase the pestilence. A few days later, the government, taking a more sensible view of the situation, issued an order prohibiting all crowds, for any purpose whatever, and enforcing certain precautions and restrictions; which, after some weeks, was followed by a marked abatement of the disease. Still later, the city was officially declared free from epidemic; and thereupon, a *Te Deum* was appointed to be sung in the cathedral, at which the reader is invited to "assist" in the next chapter. As the *Comandante*, with his staff and escort, is to be present, it will be necessary to go early.

## CHAPTER XVII.

A TE DEUM.

MATANZAS has but three churches for the accommodation of its forty thousand souls; and of these, the Cathedral only will repay the stranger's visit. It is a structure of dark stone, with nothing impressive about it, but its size and its aspect of hoar antiquity. The Cuban climate has a knack of dealing with buildings of comparatively modern date in a way to make them look as if they had witnessed the lapse of centuries; therefore this gray old edifice, upon which it has been at work for nearly two hundred slow-paced years, must needs have acquired a look of extreme venerableness. In truth, its severe plainness, approaching to shabbiness, seems but the natural condition of its time of life. It has outlasted all taste for adornment, all Grecian and Gothic vanities, all care for keeping up appearances, and comfortably slidden into the white-headed, broad-brimmed, loose-coated, and slip-shod period of architecture, corresponding to the same epoch in the life of man. It is flanked by two rough towers, the taller of which is not without architectural pleasantness to the eye, and moreover, contains a fine chime of bells.

Within, it is vast, dim, and bare. There is an acre or two of stone flags, by way of floor, but in a state of chronic insurrection and upheaval, in the nave, and, in front of the altar and shrines, worn away by the reverential footsteps of many successive generations of penitents, now slowly crumbling into dust. There are also divers large, lofty, sombre-browed columns, sturdily setting themselves to their age-long task of supporting the ponderous, cavernous, gloomy arch of the roof; also a high altar of white marble; and furthermore, nothing but a musty odor of vanished years, a harsh-toned, severe-tempered organ, and the shrines, pictures, relics, etc., which are common to all Romish churches.

Our hour of waiting serves to record these particulars, and to watch the arrival of Matanzas's female aristocracy. They gather in great strength; the vast amplitude of the nave is soon filled with prayer-carpets, kneeling figures in black dresses and mantillas, fluttering fans, missals, and rosaries. From pillar to pillar, a single row of benches forms a kind of barricade around them, outside of which gentlemen crowd, in such numbers that there is danger of this slight defence being carried by inadvertency.

At nine o'clock, the chimes break upon the ear, with a somewhat unsatisfactory tone, it must be confessed; attributable, doubtless, to the fact that they are not rung, but beaten with iron bars, by a dozen stout negroes; which indignity the grand, old bells resent, as they have a right to do, by keeping their wealth of sonorous music pent up within them, and giving out only a dead, muffled sound, which savors more of protest than jubilation. The *Comandante* immediately presents himself, steps warily along the out*skirts* of the sea of crinoline which has overflowed the nave, and seats himself upon one of the benches, near the altar,—a pleasant-faced, portly gentleman, with two or three stars and orders glistening on his breast. He is attended by several officers, nobles, and gentlemen, his staff, and an escort of soldiers,—which latter forms in the vestibule and near the door. He and his companions are accommodated with tall, lighted tapers, by an attendant priest; they rise, and the *Te Deum* commences.

To say truth, it is chiefly remarkable for clangor. There is none of that clear, piercing melody of boys' voices, for which I had looked; the singers are all men, chosen (it is impossible to avoid the conclusion) for the strength of their lungs, and with small reference to any other quality whatsoever. The organ lends all the grumble and bellow of its hoarse pipes, a dozen or two of violins and violincellos screech and groan in concert, and the brass instruments of the military band throw in clash and crash *ad libitum*. Moreover, several small tea bells, or something similar, are rung furiously by the altar boys; the negroes above are belaboring the poor chimes with their best will; and cannon and volleys of musketry are fired, at intervals, just outside the door. I have a suspicion, too, that there is a popping of fireworks somewhere; but whether on the roof, or under the floor, or close at my back, it is impossible to say; nor does it make any manner of difference. The din is fearful; it sounds like two or three Fourth of July celebrations rolled into one; but after its separate parts have lost something of their grotesqueness and prominency by repetition, one becomes sensible of an odd kind of grandeur dominating the uproar, the product of such an immense volume of sustained and jubilant sound. Between the roll of the cannon, we are able to make out a few words of the *Te Deum*, enough to show that it is the same grand, ancient Latin hymn, whereof the English version is so dear to our hearts; but toward the close, we discover that certain ascriptions to the Virgin and Saints have somehow been ingrafted upon the mighty, majestic branches, and its beauty is tarnished henceforth for us.

The celebration of the Mass follows, with even more than the usual splendor of robes and pomp of ceremonial. We send some scrutinizing glances around us, with the design of learning to how many of those present it is really an act of worship; and their number, judging by appearances (the deceitfulness of which I would in nowise underrate), is mournfully small. Even the doctrine of the Real Presence does not keep dark eyes from wandering, and fans from operating a system of covert telegraphy; while the negroes look on with a stolid receptivity, which seems less indicative of faith than superstition. Yet be it recorded that I have seen devotion in these Romish churches—devotion as real, absorbed, and fervent, as is possible to the human heart. Women that crept quietly into shadowy corners, and wrestled, as did Jacob of old, with a Presence dread, Divine, for a blessing to be granted, or an affliction to be withheld or withdrawn. Faces more earnestly and pathetically appealing than ever I saw in the home churches; for this Cuban race lives out its inner self far more frankly than we do, and is neither so apprehensive of observation, nor so sensitive to it, as our hardier, more self-contained and self-controlled race. Hands clasped convulsively over a forgotten rosary, while lips trembled with the passionate pleading of prayers that were not reckoned among the prescribed number of *Pater Nosters* and *Ave Marias*. But this was at quiet matins or vespers, when the few who came, came to pray, and the old Cathedral looked vaster and dimmer and lonelier than ever, for its scattered, isolated worshippers;—not on days of High Festival, like the present, when all the world goes to church, in its worldliest mood, to enjoy the spectacle.

I know not precisely at what point in the service our attention is drawn and held by one rapt, innocent, adoring face in the *Comandante's* train, which might well serve as a model for a picture of that young Catholic saint, beheaded by certain Jews of old time, whereof the legend runs that the lovely, severed head went on singing hymns and saying *Ave Marias*, for a day and a night afterward, to the extreme amazement and terror of the executioners. It is the son of the Count ——, not yet old enough to have outgrown his childhood faith, and slid into the common Spanish infidelity;—not the keen, hard, witty infidelity of the Frenchman, skilful at finding out the joints of the Church's armor, and making clever thrusts therein; nor the phlegmatic, dispassionate, thoughtful infidelity of the German, offspring of a mind lost and gone astray amid its own intellections, and blinded by dust of its own raising; but an infidelity of disdain, last resort of men who have flung aside their allegiance to the Church of Rome in the extremity of disgust at its deceptions, its assumptions, and the scandalous lives of many of its priests; and who have not sought, nor care to seek, for anything better to fill the empty place. I think I could count on the fingers of one hand, all the males that I have seen, during my whole stay in Cuba, engaged in any voluntary act of devotion; if I except that rapid crossing of brow, lips, and breast, which runs like a ripple through the crowd gathered in the Cathedral, at the elevation of the Host; and seems more a matter of habit, or of courtesy, than an expression of devotional feeling, so little of solemnity, or even of attentiveness, is there in it.

After the elevation of the Host, the *Comandante* and his friends are relieved of their tapers, which they surrender with great alacrity; their attention having been chiefly engaged, hitherto, by the onerous necessity of keeping them upright. This has been signally wearisome to a spruce young aid-de-camp, who has several times been on the point of putting out his neighbor's eyes with his taper, while his own are busy with the bright challenges thrown to him from the nave. Now, the party seat themselves comfortably on their benches, and look around them with the manifest intention of making up for lost time.

At last, the priests bring their droning, nasal, monotonous intoning of the prayers to an end, and the strange rite is over. The congregation waits, standing, until the *Comandante* has bowed himself out, and then disperses slowly, with a birdlike twittering of talk among the women. Then, the long shadows of the columns again stretch unbroken across the stone floor, the dim, duskiness steals back to its wonted corners; and the old, white-haired sacristan, hopeful of a chance of turning an honest penny, offers to show us the little chapel and sacristy. We decline; we have seen them all before, and know there is nothing in them worth visiting, or recording.

## CHAPTER XVIII.

#### SUNDAY SEEINGS AND DOINGS.

"EL DOMINGO" is a trying day, in Cuba, to whomsoever has in his veins the faintest coloring of that blue blood which is responsible for the sour asceticism and rigid formalism of the "Blue Laws" of Connecticut,—one of the most notable examples in history of the axiom, that "extremes meet." No matter how substantially the blueness has been toned down by some few generations of a healthier growth of religious life, and a more genial apprehension of the character of the worship due to a God whose highest name is "Love," he cannot get through the day without more shocks to his principles and prejudices than are wholesome or agreeable. The domestic business goes on, with the accumulated impetus of a fresh relay of hands; the counting-houses are suggestively half-open; the shops are brilliant and busy; the chain-gang labors on the Government works; and the tide of human life sends its fullest and gayest flow through the streets and squares of the city. In the morning, people go to Mass, or to business, according as they are devout, or no; but the evening is unscrupulously sacrificed, by all classes, on the altar of Pleasure. The theatre then gathers its most brilliant audience, the *retreta* its densest crowd, the shops and restaurants their best customers.

In vain I shut myself in my room; sounds most unsabbatical invade and destroy my quiet. The children are all at home,—for Sunday preserves enough of its *holy*-day character to shut the schools and public buildings,—and there is a fivefold gush of antic and merriment through the house. Dolorita seizes the opportunity for practice, and strums waltzes and marches on the piano with an energy and diligence worthy a better work. Moreover, the opera company at the "Teatro Estéban," on the upper side of the Square, is rehearsing for the evening, with wide-open windows; the street-criers are vociferous and hopeful; and just up the street, a nomadic menagerie allures the public with the would-be lively notes of a wheezy and dismembered brass band. In the course of the forenoon, Atanasia appears, tub on head, to give my room its weekly drenching;—I use the word advisedly, for she commences by emptying three or four pails of water on the tiles, with the object of drowning out the fleas, as well as of washing away the dirt. Driven forth by this flood, I find the *sala* and dining-room in the hands of housemaids, and possibly of whitewashers; the laundry is in active operation; Ricardo bakes, boils, stews, and scatters his hats, in an ambitious attempt to concoct a dinner that shall surpass all former achievements; and the only refuge is in Doña Coloma's own room, where she pursues her elaborate stitching or intricate embroidery precisely as on other days. There are a few high festivals and saints' days, marked with a double cross in the Spanish calendar, on which she would think it well to intermit her work; but this is not one of them,—indeed, I think they fall oftenest on a week-day.

Later, the house takes on a festive aspect; its mistress makes a grand toilet; little Rafaél is put into his scarlet uniform; Christinita is made ill-at-ease, bashful, and enchanting, in white lace and muslin; and the servants deck themselves out with whatever gala-day finery they may possess. There is more than the usual number of guests at dinner; and among them are sure to be two or three bronzed sea-captains, whose ships, gay with a holiday dress of bright bunting, ride at anchor in the harbor, while they spin yarns of every material and hue, and recount hair-breadth 'scapes and hair-brained adventures on every sea and every coast; which if they be truth, shame all the marvels of invention. To one of these, who has a rare natural eloquence, and a wonderful faculty of so arranging his material as to throw forward all the picturesque points without injuring the perspective, it is a treat to listen. The only drawback is in thinking it over,—the very excellence of the work breeds suspicion;—seldom do life's actual events group themselves so artistically as in the captain's narrative.

The interim between the dessert and the announcement of the carriage is seized by Doña Coloma, for a little catechetical instruction of the children; to which I listen with an attention that would assuredly bring her proselyting instincts into active exercise, if she had any. I learn the nature and design of penance, the routine of confession, the catalogue of the principal saints, etc. I find that the commandment forbidding the worship of graven images is expunged from the Roman Decalogue, as it needs to be (to make all consistent, the third and fourth ought to follow it); and I conclude that the coveting of one's neighbor's wife is an offence of great frequency and universality, since it is counted deserving of a separate statute,—which splitting of the tenth commandment in two makes up the required number. I am also taught how to cross one's self after the elaborate Cuban fashion, *via* the children standing before their mother; who proceeds as follows, suiting the action to the word:

"Therefore, we have to sign and sanctify ourselves, by making three crosses; the first on the brow, in order that God may deliver us from evil thoughts; the second on the mouth, that He may deliver us from evil words; the third on the breast, that He may deliver us from evil works; saying, 'By the sign of the Holy Cross, deliver us from our enemies, O Lord our God; In the name of the Father, and of the Son, and of the Holy Ghost, Amen, Jesus:'"—and at the word "Jesus," the ends of the fingers and thumb are brought together, and kissed devoutly.

In which observance it is hard to find anything objectionable, if it be piously practised. The teaching of it to the children, however, is apt to degenerate into a frolic. Dolorita, to be sure, goes through the performance with a lofty, pharisaical superciliousness; but Felipa's words and ideas are always tripping each other up; Odila's agile and irrepressible fingers indulge in various supererogatory crosses upon the oddest and most out-of-the-way members of her small body; and Rafaél is not quite clear about the distinctiveness of his nose and mouth, gets bewildered, embarrassed, and sulky, and refuses to cross himself at all.

It is now time for the usual drive. I go,—not that I should think of doing such a thing at home,—but no opportunity for fresh air and exercise is to be lightly thrown away, in this land of oriental seclusion; and furthermore, it is simply a question between tweedle-dum and tweedle-dee, whether my Sunday's sanctity shall be ruthlessly slain to me in or out of doors. There is even a chance that the murder will be something less barbarous in the open air, since my hostess, in consideration of my prejudices—as she deems them—often foregoes the crowded *paseo*, and gives me a quiet drive along the beach, cool and resonant with the dash of foamy waves, or orders Amavedo to climb a little way up the Cumbre, for one of its lovely views of the fair city seated between the mountains and the bay.

Returning from one of these drives, I notice lights in the cathedral, and beg her to stop long enough to let me see something of the vesper-service. The rosy glow of the sunset tips the pinnacles of the gray tower, as we enter the low-browed portal, but a twilight duskiness is already brooding in the quiet interior. There are no lights save the candles burning on the altar, where a single priest is intoning Latin prayers in a low, monotonous voice. A few worshippers, with faces indistinct and spirit-like in the dimness, are kneeling here and there, solitary or in little groups; telling their beads with evident singleness of purpose and sincerity of devotion, for they do not look up as we pass. There is no music; only the ghost of an organ looks grimly down from the choir, and suggests harmonies of whose divine pain it might have died. The gravity, the hush, the shadow, are all very good after the clatter and gayety and glare of the streets; I sit down on the end of a bench, and taste some rare moments of quiet, sweet enjoyment.

By and by, a second priest suddenly appears in the pulpit, with a sort of stage-effect, since the entrance thereto is concealed within the masonry of a column; and his dark-robed figure is seen in outline on the lighter background of the pillar. His sermon is full of rant and acrimony, and delivered with a superabundance of extravagant gesticulation, utterly inharmonious with the hour and the scene; so I soon tire of listening, and go on a pilgrimage to the shrines, and try to make out their images and pictures in the obscurity. I stand, for some moments, tracing the faint outlines of an old brown canvas, in the firm belief that they tell the story of the transformation of biscuits into roses, in St. Elizabeth's apron; and am considerably nonplussed when Cecilio interrupts my comments and conjectures with the statement that I am looking at a picture of Salome, bearing the head of John the Baptist on a charger! Finishing my studies abruptly, I signify that I am ready to go.

On another evening, we enter the cathedral in the

same unpremeditated fashion, and find that we have come unawares upon a most solemn and touching service,—solemn and touching even to those who have no faith in its efficacy,—a mass for the souls of the dead. If the building was dusky at our previous visit, it is absolutely dark now: the night which is fast gathering strength outside, is already dominant here,—it may have fallen from the gloomy arch of the roof, or arisen from the dank floor in vapory and sombre exhalations. A single taper burns upon the altar, by which the officiating priest intones his solemn prayers; but its rays penetrate only a little way into the obscurity of the nave; the tall pillars have a grim and spectral aspect; and the roof, corners, and organ-loft are mere masses of heavy shadow. The floor is strewn with dark, formless objects; they might be automatic figures, or strange, nocturnal animals, or a hundred other things, for aught that our eyes tell us; but some fine, spiritual vision makes it clear to us that we are in the presence of sorrowing human souls, that the air is thick with tears and heart-break, and heavy with impassioned supplication. Each one is so isolated in the silence and sombreness as to be free from every distraction and constraint, yet feels the soothing presence of many other stricken, mourning hearts, and knows that its prayers; on their upward way, are blended with many consonant petitions, the unutterably tender and pathetic harmony of which cannot fail to touch the ear of the All-Father.

But vainly I seek to give you an adequate conception of the impressive solemnity and weird suggestiveness of the scene—the vast, ancient edifice, venerable with the consecration of the prayers of many vanished and ghostly generations—the one taper, shining like a star in the midnight of the chancel—the low, subdued chant of the priest—the intervals of awe-struck silence —the shadowy, motionless forms of the scattered penitents, that seem but dim hints of other scarcely more substantial shapes that may be lurking in the remote corners, or peering down from the dim arch aloft. Its influence — spell — magnetism — what you will!—dominates prejudice, and vanquishes resistance, in every heart that has some time bled over a grave (and few there are who have not); it tyrannizes over me to such a degree that I am constrained to seek out a dim nook, and straightway drop on my knees. But my dead, thank God!—all of whom I have the dear right to say "mine"—have died "in the communion of the Catholic Church, in the confidence of a certain faith, in the comfort of a reasonable, religious, and holy hope;"—I need not pray for them, if I dared! But there are others, not gone down to the Silent Land, yet as dead to me as if the Spring grasses and violets had drawn their inexorable bars between our faces, for whom it is still permissible to say the prayer of faith. And may it add some touch of tender blessing to their far-away lives!

The voice of the priest at the altar dies away into silence, and there are some moments of a stillness so deep, so utter, that I involuntarily hold my breath; yet so subtly interfused with intense, powerful emotion, that the sound of a shriek would really be a relief, and

I momentarily expect to hear one from some overcharged and sensitive heart. Instead thereof, a rich, tender, thrilling voice seems to grow out of the hush—certainly it does not *break* it!—to whose wondrous music of tone and melody of modulation I listen entranced, for a time, without being at all cognizant of the sense of its words. Presently, I perceive that it is talking quietly of the Fatherhood of God, of His unresting care for the Universe, His tender taking of thought for those who never think of Him, the lavish fall of His sun and rain upon the just and the unjust, and the dew-droppings of His bounty on the improvident and unthankful. Then, in deep, sombre, penetrating tones, it draws a Rembrandt-like picture of the terrible orphanage of the world if, by any means, the reality and the conception of God the FATHER were utterly lost and forgotten, and its place filled by some cold abstraction of Law or Destiny—a picture that curdles one's very heart-blood, and causes one's bosom to heave and strain with an oppressive, insufferable weight of ideal woe. "Only a picture now, thank God!" it says, in ineffably solemn and pitying tones, "yet certain to become, in some sort, a dread reality to all those, who, having despised God's mercy here, are cast out of the sunshine of His favor, and into the fire of His wrath hereafter!" Then, suddenly changing to a tone of perfect, joyous faith, it sets forth the comfort of knowing that God is, in a special and most tender sense, the father of those who trust in Him, and how confidently all such may commit their dead to His gracious love; ending with a wonderfully thrilling and pathetic appeal to the irreligious, by the memory, and for the sake, of those waiting, longing, imploring dead to become, in this full and final sense, His children. And the voice ceases just as it came, and the dark spot in the pulpit, which has seemed merely a sort of nucleus of the nave's mighty breadth of shadow, vanishes silently!

I know not how I got out of the church, but I found myself in the carriage, drawing a long breath, like one who has just escaped from the oppressive influence of a fantastic dream;—yet with a tolerably clear comprehension, for the first time in my life, how it is possible for a being endowed with reason (provided a heart and an imagination are super-added to that good gift) to be a Roman Catholic. It is frequently said, and with truth, that the services of the Romish Church appeal to the senses; but they also address themselves to something better and deeper—the sweetest and strongest affections of the human heart; and herein, probably, is the secret of their powerful hold upon women. Convince a mother—nay, give her a glimmer of hope, even—that her prayers and alms can lift the erring, lost soul of her child out of purgatory, and Rome has, ready made to her hand, the most patient, submissive, and liberal of disciples.

I record this whole matter partly for the sake of the moral which I draw from it,—that it is scarcely worth while to try to beat Rome with her own weapons. She is an adept in stage-effects and sensuous influences, in the management of drapery, light and shadow, sound and silence; and her skill and unscrupulousness in using them, put all such attempts at a frightful disadvantage.

Doña Coloma sets me down at home, and then proceeds to opera, *retreta*, or family reunion, as her mood dictates. And now, at last, a measure of quiet is vouchsafed to me; for the children are out or asleep, the servants are mostly off a-pleasuring, and the sweet, plaintive music of "La Sonambula," or "Lucia," softened and spiritualized by the distance and the evening-hush, does not seem harshly out of keeping with the hour. Or, it may be that Francisca, heart-heavy with homesick longings for her island-home, lingers on the balcony, and croons to herself and the sea an old, quaint, pathetic Spanish hymn, whose simple melody and exquisite feeling bring tears to my eyes. The refrain slips into an English dress thus:

> Woe is me!
> 'Tis I that offended Thee!
> But the rod
> Thou did'st endure, oh, my God!—

albeit, the idiomatic simplicity and tenderness of the remainder laugh translation to scorn. The Spanish language is exceedingly amenable to verse, by reason of its wealth of idioms, its profusion of ready rhymes, its rich and stately rhythm, and the figurative character of its phraseology; but its poetry is very difficult of translation,—all the finer essence escapes in the process. The real truth being, perhaps, that its beauty is oftener due to music of sounds, and harmony of versification, than to high and sustained poetic thought.

Of such domestic religious observances as grace at meals, and family prayers, I have seen nothing; which is, by no means, to be admitted as indubitable evidence that such things do not exist. The observer in foreign countries is in continual danger of classifying individual traits as national characteristics, and cannot safely argue, except after a very long sojourn, that what he does not see is never to be seen, nor that what he sees once is commonly to be seen.

He will not go amiss, however, if he set it down in his note-book that an oratory, or chapel, or something similar, is to be found in every Cuban dwelling. My hostess has, in her own room, a large case of rosewood and glass, containing: First, a crucifix of extremely antique appearance, with angles and edges that have been rounded off by the teeth or tongue of Time, until it has greatly the aspect of a sugar-toy that has been subjected to the ordeal of an infantile mouth, being an heirloom of the House of Samano, handed down from eldest son to eldest son through many generations, and valued accordingly. The scarf—I should say "sudario!"—which enfolds the loins of the figure of Christ, is studded with family jewels, and its ends are drawn through a costly diamond ring, the wedding-ring of *la señora*. Secondly, a highly lugubrious-faced image, with a golden nimbus around its head, a veil of rare, time-yellowed lace, and a black velvet robe, garnished with jewels; which represents the Virgin as the "Mother of Sorrows." Thirdly, a silver censer for burning incense. Fourthly, a silver cup, and sprinkler, for "holy water,"

Fifthly, three vases of artificial flowers; and a number of smaller ornaments, which need not be catalogued. By the side of the case are two heavy silver candelabra, and a dainty porcelain lamp. The flame of the latter is never suffered to expire; all the day and night long, its small glow admonishes the bystanders to keep their spiritual lamps trimmed and burning. Its care is one of the religious duties of the mistress of the household, and I think I never saw a face of greater consternation than she exhibited one day, when a mischievous puff of wind (or might it have been the disembodied, but still militant spirit of some grim old Roundhead!) during a "norther," made a sly, swift dart at the flame and instantly extinguished it.

She calls this case a "chapel," and as she plainly considers it a sacred spot, wherein she sees typified the whole life, death, and teaching of Christ, and through which grace and benediction flow unto her and her household, I am half-ashamed that I can associate it with nothing but a show-case on Broadway, filled with dolls and trinkets for sale. This comes of difference in education. To her it is eloquent with signs and suggestions of holy things, and she says her prayers and tells her beads before it, doubtless, with faith and fervor. And if I smile to see, it is not in scorn, be it understood, neither with any assumption of superiority; but with an irresistibly amused recognition of the *naïve* and childlike nature that finds help in such devotional ladders, and with a thankful remembrance of that good grace which maketh us to differ. For no man can say, positively, that if the providence of God had placed him, at birth, within the vast, powerful machine of the Church of Rome, he would not have come forth moulded and chiselled to the pattern of the devoutest of her disciples. And one may hope that all fervent prayer finds out the Father at last, no matter how many forms of Virgin and Saint stand in the way. Happy, nevertheless, are all they who look straight up to the ineffable glory of the Godhead, when they pray; and behold the transfigured Humanity of the Son, unobscured by any image of the Mother—the woman,—who is, be it allowed, much better adapted to the genius and purposes of Rome, in the way of bedizenment, exhibition, and sentimental adoration.

But there is another aspect of this "chapel" which I should regret to miss, embodying a lesson good for me and all Protestants,—that spirit of loving sacrifice, that willing offering of one's most precious things to God, which does, in truth, dignify it with a sort of consecration. Manifestly, the Señora has not given of that which cost her nothing. Her own wedding-ring blazes on the crucifix, her cherished family jewels adorn the Virgin, and the solid silver candelabra were recently imported from Spain, expressly for this purpose. And these things are given, not lent,—never again to be appropriated to any secular use or adornment. Whatever you may think of the fitness of the gift, its preciousness must be allowed, and the grace of self-denial which prompted it. And every shrine, every altar of the Romish Church, tells the same story of self-sacrificing devotion. It were well for the whole Protestant world, if more of this spirit animated the hearts of its people, and were visible in its churches; if its gold and silver were oftener wrought into cross-tipped towers that should lift all humble and serious souls with Divine aspiration and joyful faith; if its labor were crystallized into walls that should be eloquent with silent ascription and vocal with spoken praise, for all coming generations; if the light and color of its gems were fused into the tender glory of stained windows, that should tell the stories of apostles and martyrs, or keep in remembrance solemn truths, through the lovely blazonry of emblem and symbol, for millions of eyes that are to open out of the future, and for whose education and destiny we are in some measure, responsible. The surplus jewels of our women, the costly upholstery and frippery of our houses—things that too frequently vulgarize rather than beautify them—would build a church in every village that should be a joy to the eyes, and a comfort and stay to the hearts, of all that looked upon it!

## CHAPTER XIX.

#### THE ENTRANCE AND EXIT OF LENT.

NO history of a Cuban winter would be complete, without some mention of the gayeties of the Carnival, and the solemnities of Holy Week. The former seldom get well under way until Quinquagesima Sunday. On the afternoon and evening of that day the whole city, apparently, gave itself up to fun, frolic, and folly. The streets and the *paseo* were flooded with maskers, mummers, and spectators, on foot or in carriages; while ladies in full dress, and children in every variety of youthful bedizenment, crowded the windows and balconies, to watch the ebb and flow of the fantastic tide.

The popular fancy seemed to run chiefly in the channels of noise and grotesqueness, overlooking the softer attractions of the picturesque and the humorous,—a tolerably certain indication that the lower classes had the masking and the active merry-making pretty much to themselves. Everywhere there were men disguised as women and women disguised as men, negroes simulating whites and whites simulating negroes, while impossible noses, chins, beards, and paunches, were the rule rather than the exception. Beasts and birds were numerous, and especially effective in point of vocalism; there were counterfeit donkeys that brayed, lions that roared, cocks that crowed, dogs that howled, and apes that chattered, in a way to shame the real article into silence forever. Instruments of music and of discord alike helped to swell the uproar; about every third mask twanged a guitar, or sawed a fiddle, or tooted a horn, or banged a tin pan, or rattled a gourd, or belabored a drum, with a zeal and zest wonderful to behold. Scores of these organized themselves into callithumpian bands, and paraded the streets, doing great execution upon sensitive tympanums. Scarcely less noisy were certain processions (of which I saw two or three), consisting of a grotesquely costumed leader, holding aloft an immense rat in a cage, and screaming "Catch this rat!" at the top of his voice; and followed by a double file of demoniacs, all frantically yelling in chorus, and in every variety of intonation from a squeal to a roar, "Catch that rat! Catch that rat!" These seemed to divide the popular favor with processions headed by a band of music, and made up of the most diverse and grotesque masks that could be coupled together. Conspicuous among these was an extremely tall man carefully arrayed as a fashionable belle, with gorgeous fan and preposterous train, arm in arm with a tiny woman in male attire, whose coat tails almost reached to her heels; the one playing the part of a coquettish maiden, and the other of a devoted and persistent swain, in apparent unconsciousness either of the spectators surging around them, or of the plaudits and peals of laughter that everywhere greeted their performance. Bringing up the rear of one of these processions was an enormous negro, in a gilded circle representing the sun, who amused himself with reflecting the rays of the real luminary into all the eyes in his neighborhood, by means of an ingenious arrangement of small mirrors, and grinned broadly whenever the victim manifested annoyance.

In the vicinity of the *plaza*, maskers, promenaders, volantes, and carriages, were so wedged together as to seem absolutely solid. However, by dint of patience, vigilance, and audacity, Amavedo slowly brought us to one corner of the crowded square, which we found to be flanked with movable kitchens for the preparation of dainties acceptable to the popular taste, and booths and tables for the selling and eating thereof. Fruit stands seemed also to be doing a thriving business; the owner of one of which vainly strove to tempt me with a string of small, withered, tough-looking, red apples, from my native shores. Vainly,—though I really cannot tell whether it was disgust at their uninviting aspect, or mortification at the sorry figure they made beside the fresh and luscious tropical fruits, or a rush of homesick memories, that forced me to turn my eyes away from them as quickly as possible. But I could not shut my ears to the following dialogue close to the carriage wheel.

"*Caramba*, José!" (*in the high shrill tones of a paisano*)—"what kind of things are those?"

JOSÉ (*hesitatingly*). "I—I—ah—ah—is it fruit?"

FRUIT-SELLER (*taking up the theme with animation*). "APPLES! *caballeros!* Fine, fresh apples! just in from the United States! Selling like smoke, too—these are all I have left! Try some? (*insinuatingly*) only ten cents each!"

Two apples are bought. The next remark is from José, mingled with sounds of spitting and spluttering,—

"*Caramba!* Tomás! what sort of people must they be who have no better fruit to eat than that!"

Tomás (*munching slowly and critically*). "I don't know (*munches*)—on the whole (*munches*)—I think I rather like it. You see (*munches*)—it isn't eaten in a hurry, and I always did like something to *chew at!*"

In this quarter, the masks were thicker and noisier than ever, yet I saw but one worthy of note—a Falstaff of such unwieldy proportions that it required three or four good natured friends to set him in motion, after every stoppage; but when once fairly under way, the crowd rolled back from his bluff sides like waves from a headland. At one corner of the *plaza*, a small space had been cleared, where somebody was continually going off into waltzes, jigs, or the favorite *danza criolla*, with a constant change of partners and musicians. And once or twice, a number of strange masks joined hands, and danced slowly round and round in a circle, accompanying themselves with a monotonous and even mournful chant, which had an almost funereal effect amid the prevailing fun and frenzy. It was a touch of the skeleton at the antique feasts—the inevitable suggestion of sorrow breaking up through all human mirth, yet investing it with a still stronger characteristic of mad, reckless jollity.

Occasionally, too, there was a strange pause in the

merriment, a contagious silence spread itself throughout the crowd, as if every individual therein had suddenly stopped to consider whether this furious revel was really worth his while,—whether it were possible to distil any drop of the true essence of enjoyment from this noisy ebullition of folly. And then the hubbub began again, forced and fitful at first, but gradually swelling louder and louder, till it seemed that every voice in the vast throng must lend its aid to the mighty aggregate of sound; while every face, young or old, white or black, beautiful or ugly, was lit up by a smile or broadened by a grin.

Yet, at best, it was plain to see that only the lower ranks of society gave themselves up heartily to the spirit of the hereditary festival. The higher classes might now and then dip briefly into the frolic, in the person of some youthful representative; but, for the most part, they contented themselves with looking on and laughing. It would seem that the motley show of the carnival, coming down to us from a ruder and simpler age, is best suited to rude and simple tastes. Flowing through the midst of the modern civilization, it still keeps its ancient hue and tone. For every mask, every absurdity, every fantasy, which is the sportive effluence of the present day, there are a hundred bearing the stamp of the broad, ancient humor; and whereat so many buried generations have laughed as to make them more melancholy than mirthful, in all thoughtful eyes.

Certain it is, that in the present instance, scarce any but negroes and children followed the sport with unflagging interest to the end. For myself, the limit to my enjoyment of grotesqueness and extravaganza being always quickly reached, I was glad when, on Tuesday at midnight, the last masker left the street, the last peal of laughter died away into the wholesome quietude of Lent.

During this season, the bells seem to ring almost constantly, and the services are numerous. Perhaps the church accommodation of Matanzas is not so inadequate as it first appears: it must be taken into consideration that its three houses of worship stand always open for the use of penitent or pilgrim, that it has a daily service, and that, on Sundays and all important feasts and fasts, one mass continually follows another, with a fresh priest and a new congregation, from early morn to dusky eve. Certainly, I never saw any of the churches overcrowded—or even well filled—except on occasions of unusual spectacular attraction. The ordinary Lenten services appeared to be but thinly attended, and the Lenten rule of life somewhat less strict than is usual in Roman Catholic countries. Nobody within the scope of my observation, abstained from the use of meat, except on the two last days of Holy Week. I had already noticed that no one seemed to think a fish diet obligatory on Fridays; and when I ventured to express my surprise thereat, I was told that Innocent VIII., in the fifteenth century, granted an unlimited dispensation from Friday fasting to the whole Spanish nation, in requital of their final expulsion of the Moors; which grace the Cubans inherit by right of lineal descent. I tell the tale as it was told me, not having taken the trouble to verify the statement.

Palm Sunday was observed by fastening the graceful leaves of the royal palm into doors and windows; and the devout wore bits of them on their bosoms or carried them in their hands. Often, they were braided into crosses, stars, rosettes, bracelets, and other pretty devices, by the skilful fingers of the ladies; who first have them blessed by a priest, and then bestow them upon their friends.

From the forenoon of Maunday Thursday until Easter morning, the city breathes an almost oppressive atmosphere of stillness and gloom. The bells are forbidden to ring,—the clocks, even, are prevented from striking the hours. Not a vehicle of any sort whatever is allowed in the streets; business is necessarily suspended; guards and sentinels march with arms reversed; flags are at half-mast; women attired all in black pass slowly through the streets on their way to church; it seems a city suddenly overtaken by some dire and widespread calamity.

On Good Friday, the churches are all hung with funereal drapery, pictures and images veiled, flowers, tinsel, and whatever is bright and cheerful of tone, covered or removed. The Cathedral is like a vast, dim tomb, filled with black-robed mourners. Such, at least, is its surface aspect, and it is hardly worth our while to look beneath. All day long, services are going on within its walls; and echoes of its solemn chants drift far down the silent streets. At dusk, a life-like representation of the dead Christ, on a large black-draped catafalque, is borne through the city, followed by a vast procession of priests, religious orders, charitable societies, civic and military bodies, and multifarious ranks of men, women, and children. On this occasion alone, of the whole year, the entire population may be seen in the streets and on foot, without exception of class, color, sex, or age. The millionaire elbows the slave; the silken robe of the countess touches, on one side, the unfragrant rags of poverty, and on the other, the pitiable garments of shame. There is a continuous, inarticulate murmur, like the roar of the sea, and there are occasional ripples of the elaborate crossing, before described,—but no loud talking nor laughter, no rudeness nor quarrelling, no tumultuous swaying to and fro of the dense human tide, no noticeable disorder of any sort. Nevertheless, decorous as the crowd appears, and devout as some few of its members undoubtedly are, there is a nameless something about it, in gross, betokening that it is come hither to enjoy a show, a spectacle, an objective display, rather than to take part in a heartfelt, religious rite. It is law and custom that have shut the shops and stopped the pulsations of trade and commerce, it is official obligation, on the one hand, and love of parade and excitement, on the other, which have filled the ranks of that immense procession; it is partly the prospect of scenic display, and partly the social instinct, which have packed together this vast concourse of spectators.

And in truth it is a sight worth seeing!—the long

river of wavering lights, shining on priestly robe and monastic gown, on civic pomp and insignia, on military uniforms and society banners; and flowing between dark banks of spectators, wherein young and old, rich and poor, dusky and fair, stand side by side under the clear-eyed stars and the tender, tropical sky! I wish I had bethought me to go through the crowd with a note-book, sketching a representative character here and there; the result must needs have been a gallery of portraits far better worth preserving than the caricatures of the carnival; but I did not, and in my memory the multifarious throng becomes a dusky, indistinguishable human mass. At least, the only figure which comes forth prominently to my mind's eye, is that of a massive negress, planted solidly upon a street corner, with a gigantic cigar in her mouth, and a broad, unctuous aspect of the serenest satisfaction. It would seem, to look at her, that the whole spectacle had been designed for her exclusive benefit.

The procession, having finished its course, disappeared from view, but the crowd seemed loth to leave the streets. At eleven, it was still surging to and fro, and I went to sleep by its murmur.

Early on Easter-Even, I was roused by a wild uproar without,—a mingling of shouts of anger and execration with sounds of blows and pistol-shots, that seemed serious. With visions of riot and revolution and slave insurrection chasing one another swiftly through my brain, I made a headlong toilet, and rushed to the balcony. There I beheld a wretched effigy dragged through the street, by a rope round its neck, and followed and set upon by a mob that spat upon it, that beat it with sticks and brooms, that cut it with knives and riddled it with pistol-balls,—that, in short, lavished upon it every cruelty and indignity which human ingenuity could devise.

"What does it mean?" I asked, wonderingly, of Doña Coloma, who soon joined me.

"It is Judas, the betrayer of our Lord," she answered, gravely.

The disgusting scene was closed by hanging the effigy from the highest attainable post; where it served as a target for mischievous boys and idle negroes, until fairly annihilated by persistent persecution. This was accomplished ere noon, when the Lenten quietude once more settled over the city.

But with the breaking of Easter morning, lo! what a change! In an instant, as it seems, the city passes from the extremity of gloom to the extremity of joy. Bells peal—trumpets sound—flags wave—drums beat—salutes are fired from the forts, and the ships in the harbor—*volantes*, drays, victorias, whatever goes on wheels, dash noisily through the streets—friends exchange glad greetings,—it is an universal chorus of rejoicing. The risen Christ is borne through the city in triumphal procession, and returns to the cathedral in season for a gorgeous scenic service. And let me not forget to note that, for the first time in this "Island of Flowers"—as it is poetically named—I saw the altars and shrines decorated with fresh, fragrant, natural blossoms, in place of the gaudy and scentless imitations usually found there. A *Cubana* would fain persuade me that the latter, representing more skill and money, are the worthier offering. I am slow to accept the conclusion. Even here, fresh flowers of the rarer varieties, offered daily, would cost more, in care and labor, than their waxen and muslin counterfeits, seldom renewed, and often faded by time and dingy with dust. And the gain in artistic beauty, in poetic sentiment and spiritual harmony, would be incalculable. Yet a second thought compels me to admit that I may here be talking nonsense. There is so little that is fresh and natural in the Romish ritual, that the use of artificial flowers may have grown out of a nicer, deeper sense of fitness than I possess.

It would be pleasant to close our account of Easter rejoicings here. But the faithful chronicle must needs state furthermore that, with its unwonted religious animation and cheerfulness, the city also assumed an unusual activity of secular business and pleasure. The shops were temptingly open, street-venders were noisy and busy, the *paseo* was crowded, the *retreta* exceptionally brilliant, in the afternoon there was a bull-fight at the *Plaza de Toros*, and in the evening an operatic performance at the *Teatro Estéban*. So I was told, at least,—for I verified none of these statements save by observations from my balcony. But thence I witnessed so many profane sights, and heard so many profane sounds, that further confirmation was unnecessary.

## CHAPTER XX.

### COSAS DE CUBA.

COUNTRIES, like individuals, have certain ways and habits peculiar to themselves, neither the origin nor the utility of which is always patent to others. Often, the fact that they exist is the best reason assignable for their existence. In Spain these things have been happily termed, *cosas de España*. I borrow the title, with an obvious variation, for a chapter devoted to such Cuban peculiarities as do not come easily under other heads.

And first, the climate. Anything more delicious can scarcely be conceived of. It does not smile at you one day and frown at you the next, *aujourd'hui votre serviteur et demain Judas*, after the changeable fashion of our northern summer; but day after day of genial warmth and unclouded splendor unfold before you, more intoxicatingly sweet and surpassingly fair as the season advances. The terms "winter" and "spring" seem almost to lose their significance in a land always green with verdure, fragrant with bloom, and luscious with fruit. A better division of the Cuban year is into two seasons, the wet and the dry. The former begins late in May, and lasts till October. During its continuance, there are daily showers, often accompanied by thunder and lightning; which serve to moderate in some degree the extreme heat. After them the sun shines out bright, the air is both fresh and soft, the verdure seems new-created, flowers open and scatter their perfume everywhere, and the afternoon drive is a delight. The dry season stretches from the first of October to the end of May, during which rain is of rare occurrence, the variations of temperature slight, the days all gold and sapphire, the nights all silver and amethyst,—indeed, says Frederika Bremer, "there could not be more beautiful nights in Paradise." To be sure, chill winds known as *los nortes* do now and then blow from the north, during the winter months, lasting, possibly, for forty-eight hours, whereat the Cubans shiver and grumble exceedingly; but the Northerner, accustomed to winds of much austerer temper, scarce minds them at all. Still, it is well to protect one's self by extra clothing, during their continuance, as colds for the careless are apt to come in their train. The mean temperature of the island, throughout the year, is declared to be eighty degrees; during the hottest months, eighty-three. In the middle of the day, it is generally quite warm enough to make rest, idleness, *refrescos*, and *siestas*, agreeable; though the heat is much mitigated by the sea-breeze, which regularly rises about ten o'clock, and subsides at four. Then, a delicious breeze from the land, fragrant with the breath of innumerable flowers, springs up; and the nights are rarely so warm as to interfere with sleep. It will be recollected, also, that the houses and habits of life are arranged to suit the climate: spacious rooms, lofty, wide-open doors and windows, marble and stone floors, cane-seated furniture, the cooling *refrescos* always at hand, the custom of doing all out-door business before breakfast,—all these things make the problem "How-to-keep-cool" much easier of solution than we are apt to find it during the hottest part of our northern summer.

Cuban courtesy is perfection itself, to outward appearance; but some of it turns out to be veneering and not true wood, on examination. When I call upon any of Doña Coloma's friends, I am told, with a sweeping, all-comprising gesture,—"This house is your home; it, and everything it contains, are at your disposal." Rendered into plain English, this means, simply, "I am glad to see you; pray call again." If it becomes necessary for me to ask, "Whose book is this? Whose *anything* is this?" the reply (if from the owner thereof) must needs be, "Mine, and yours also." If I express admiration of anything,—no matter what, horses, furniture, ornaments, the dress which my friend is wearing,—the invariable response is, "Take it, it is yours," or, "It is entirely at your disposal." This seems lavishly, and even embarrassingly, generous, until you learn that its English equivalent would be, "I am glad that you admire it." I remember an amusing little scene, in point. The elder Señora Sámano received a birthday gift of an embroidered handkerchief from her daughter, which she exhibited to Doña Mariquilla and myself, with a beaming face; and as we offered the expected meed of admiration, she repeated to each of us the usual formula, "It is yours," and then composedly folded it up and put it in her pocket, utterly oblivious of the fact that she had twice given it away!

Occasionally, some foreigner, more obtuse than the generality, accepts the gift thus offered, and the Cuban is forced to surrender it, or to explain that his phraseology will not bear too literal a construction! I must do him the justice to state that he chooses the former course, unless the article in question is of great value or indispensable necessity. Indeed, report says that a certain Havana nabob, being thus unexpectedly taken at his word, and too proud to retract, *did* actually send his fine carriage and horses, with his compliments, to the door of the simple-minded American who had accepted them!

One Cuban custom impresses me pleasantly—children always kiss the *hands* of their parents by way of salutation and leave-taking; the kiss on the mouth may follow if they choose. It is in strong contrast with the rude familiarity one too often sees in American children. Doña Coloma lifts the hand of her mother to her lips with a pretty air of reverent tenderness, and the stately old lady receives her homage with the dignified graciousness of a benignant sovereign; while I, looking on, am deeply touched by the beauty and fitness of the custom, its evident rendering of that honor to parents to which God has attached the promise of "long days in the land."

A young colored-girl, in gala-day attire, entered the

*sala* one evening, and with many courtesies and compliments, presented each member of the family a bit of gay ribbon, folded together, with a knot at one end, and a silver coin at the other. This was a pretty way of giving notice that a christening had taken place in the family of an acquaintance. On one side of the ribbon was printed the child's name, and the date of birth, and on the other the names of the *padrinos*, or sponsors. When the godfather, whose duty it is to provide these things, is very wealthy, the coin affixed is of gold.

Apropos to this: one of the house-servants had the honor to stand as godmother to the child of a friend recently, and after the ceremony was over, she brought her godchild to exhibit to us, in its christening finery. And very fine, indeed, I thought it, in its robe of white satin, and lace overdress, with a dainty frill around its small olive-colored face; but a closer inspection showed that this elegant toilet was a compound that would not bear resolving. The satin and lace robe was only a sort of apron, looking extremely well as long as the infant was held right side out in the nurse's arms; but on its being reversed, a quite unexpected background to so fair a picture was presented, of which the most noticeable feature was a dingy brown flannel petticoat!

Cuban children, white and black, are evidently considered to be yet in a state of paradisiacal innocence, and are clothed—or unclothed—accordingly. Rafaél, Christinita, and Ramona, are running about "sublimely in the nude," as *Aurora Leigh* hath it, for a good part of the time; ready to serve, at short notice, for *tableaux* of

Cupid or the Cherubim. One who has not had the advantage of being brought up to that sort of thing, cannot wholly enjoy their *poses* when the gentlemen are about: nevertheless, one of the very finest pictures in my Cuban gallery is the naked Christinita in the arms of her black nurse, and both fast asleep in a large chair; the fair, rounded outlines and delicate features of the Caucasian child being strongly contrasted with the black, brawny arm and coarse traits of the African woman. A better subject for painter's skill is rarely seen. Excellent types of two widely different, yet strangely associated, races; the ignorant, brute fidelity of the slave touchingly apparent in the close embrace wherewith, even in her slumber, she holds the child to her bosom; the fine lines of whose fair figure and prominent brow speak clearly of a more delicate organization, a higher intellect, a richer cultivation. I know not how long I stood musing before these eloquent figures—so long that even the rude perceptions of the negress felt the magnetism of my steady gaze, and she woke to stammer an excuse for being caught sleeping in the "sala."

Nor is nudity confined to the day only. Night after night I have seen the little ones laid, stark naked, on their hard beds, under a mosquito net, and left to go to sleep without other covering than the soft air. The dreamy journey being accomplished, a linen sheet may or may not be drawn over them, at the discretion of the nurse. It must be confessed that they thrive on this regimen. Healthier children, or more finely developed forms, are not to be found.

Next to no costume naturally comes thin costume. I have seen a boy of six years old, clad in pantaloons and blouse of sheer, white muslin,—nothing else—as I hope to be believed!

Moreover, if there be need of the services of a painter, whitewasher, or carpenter, in any Cuban dwelling, let not the foreign visitor be surprised nor disconcerted to see his shirt worn carelessly outside his pants! It is cooler thus, and less restraint upon motion. And time will teach her that, so far from having any cause to complain of his fashion of wearing the garment, she has reason to be thankful that he is not in his skin only, from his waist upwards.

One odd Cuban custom was made known to me through the medium of a tall, sullen-looking negress, named Rosa, once hired to assist in the laundry. Scarce a week of her occupancy had gone by, ere Ricardo, lynx-eyed in detecting offences and offenders, came to report that he suspected her of stealing. "Bring me proofs, not suspicions," responded his mistress, curtly. Two days after, the proofs were forthcoming, in the shape of an odd assortment of coals, candles, crackers, towels, stockings, thread, etc., etc., which the Chinaman had ferreted out of some secret corner and spread in order upon the dining-room table, like a collection of curiosities.

"Put them back where you found them, and send Rosa to me," said *la señora*, after a brief inspection.

The woman shortly appeared, glancing around her suspiciously.

"Where did you tell me that you worked last?" asked Doña Coloma, quietly.

"At Madruga, *señora*."

"Why did you leave there?"

"I could not get any more work."

"Take off your turban."

The negress started back with a cry of alarm and remonstrance.

The *señora* made a slight, significant gesture; and Atanasia, who was standing near, snatched off the turban ere the wearer comprehended what she was about. With it came an artistic padding of moss, doing duty for hair; and underneath was a bare-shaven poll!

"Enough," said Doña Coloma, "pay her her wages, and send her off."

And thus I learned that all blacks detected in thieving, even children, are immediately shaven; which brands them sufficiently, for a time, at least. It is not uncommon, in hiring strange negresses, to request them to take off their turbans,—a precaution which, in this instance, had been unwisely omitted.

Set it down as a creditable *cosa de Cuba* that intoxication is either very rare, or kept out of sight. I have not yet seen a case of it. The nearest approach thereunto was a negro, who went past the house singing noisily one night, and was, apparently, put under an extinguisher by the *sereno* at the corner.

Every resident of Cuba is required to give notice to the proper official of any change of domicil; of every increase or diminution of his household, whether by birth, death, arrival and departure of guests, lodgers, *et cætera*; and of all reunions, balls, parties, and other large entertainments, that he proposes to give;—in all which matters the government takes a lively interest. And if he is wise, he will put his name to no petitions, —certainly to none signed by more than two of his neighbors,—lest he furnish ground for an accusation of conspiracy and sedition, and consequent arrest and trial.

Moreover, if he wishes to engage in building, or repairs, he must first procure, and pay for, a license. But he must not construe this into an unlimited permission to blockade the street, and endanger the lives of unwary passers by. Wherever, at night, a pile of brick, stone, or plank, a mortar-bed, a gap in the pavement, or other nuisance occasioned by building, is found in a Cuban street; it will also be found to be surmounted by a pole and a lantern, making it visible afar off, and allowing its exact nature and extent to be seen and avoided. Any failure to set up this beacon is punishable by a heavy fine. The blockade will also be scrupulously limited to one third of the narrow street. What would New Yorkers, accustomed to obstruct their thoroughfares with building materials, and to tumble over them, at their own sweet will, say to restrictions such as these?

Of all *cosas de Cuba*, none is so irksome to ladies from the United States as the social edict which confines them so much within doors, forbidding them to drive or ride with other male friend than husband, father, or brother; and debarring them from walking, except to church, and then only under the protection of page, or *duenna*, or near male relative. Nor is this law to be violated with impunity, as I have reason to know. For one morning, Juan, having occasion to drive out in a buggy, invited me to accompany him, little thinking what a commotion so simple a proceeding was to excite. No sooner did we appear in the streets than everybody —men, women, and children,—stopped to gaze, as if spellbound;—people at the windows called to those within to come and look, and they who were called came, in every variety of dress and undress, and with every sort of implement, stopping not to don or drop anything. One man ran in his shirt only, women rushed to the windows with streaming hair, cooks came with frying-pans in hand, laundresses with flat irons, clerks with goods, and the merchant with his pen. They shouted—they laughed—they gesticulated—they gazed in open-mouthed wonder—they seemed to have gone stark, staring mad. We might have been tracked through the city by the dazed, wondering, excited faces that we left behind us. The thing was so ridiculous that it was impossible not to laugh; yet it was unpleasant, too, to be the subject of so much amazed and jeering comment, and I uttered an emphatic resolve to try the buggy no more. But Juan decreed otherwise. "We are neither of us Cubans," said he, "and in this matter, there is no good reason why we should be bound by their senseless customs. A morning drive, now and then, will do you good. And the people will soon get accustomed to the sight. A nine days' wonder never lasts ten." Which conclusion proved to be drawn from the fount of wisdom. Long ere its ninth appearance, the buggy, with its freight, was suffered to go and come through the city as unnoticed as any market wagon.

The Cuban way of attracting attention is by means of a sharp, sibillant sound, best represented by the letters, "P-s-t!" With this, servants are summoned, *volantes* stopped, street venders signaled, children called to order, and the notice of friend or stranger arrested. The Cuban mode of beckoning also differs from ours. The hand is held up with the palm outwards, and the fingers moved in a way that we should be certain to interpret as a sign to depart and be seen no more.

A noticeable *cosa de Matanzas* is the prevalence of images of the Virgin, one or more of which seems to be enshrined in every dwelling. It occurred to me to wonder whence these things came, and to ask if they constituted a regular branch of trade. To which Don Enrique replied, that they were much more common than formerly, owing to the fact that a neighboring commission and shipping house not long since received from Spain, to its great surprise and disgust, a large consignment of particularly ugly undressed dolls. Such, at least, they were at first supposed to be; but they proved to be invoiced as "*Virgenes santisimas*"—that is to say, representations of the Virgin. Scarcely better pleased with this view of the case, the firm nevertheless decided to put a good face on it, and duly advertised for sale, "*Virgenes santisimas*, direct from Spain." The rush that followed was beyond anything ever seen in Matanzas. The street leading to the warehouse was literally packed with *volantes,* wherein the fairest aristocracy of the city and suburbs patiently waited their turn to be served (to say nothing of humbler customers); and the whole lot of images was sold out at a handsome profit, long before the demand ceased;—each purchaser triumphantly bearing off her prize, to be fitted for use by being first decked in costly array, and then presented to a priest for consecration.

The dowry of a widow in Cuba consists of *one half the gain made during the years of wedlock.* For example, a neighbor recently died, leaving property valued at two hundred and fifty thousand dollars; he was worth thirty thousand at his marriage; the widow's share, therefore, was one hundred and ten thousand. This is giving direct and fitting testimony to the value of the wife's assistance to her husband; in advice, encouragement, economy, etc., and seemed to me more just than the "third" apportioned to her use by our laws. But if there be no increase? "Ay, there's the rub!"

Insect-life in Cuba is abundant and manifold, but when it develops in the shape of *arañas peludas* (hairy spiders) two inches long, and long-tailed scorpions vicious and spiteful enough to contain the combined venom of a whole generation of metemsychosed wasps, one prefers to examine it *post mortem.* To ants, however, I have become so accustomed that I do not always take the trouble to brush them off the articles which I am using; though I do object to have my washstand pitcher chosen by a whole colony bent on suicide, as a convenient means of quitting this sphere of existence. As for cockroaches, I have a suspicion that the floor of my room is alive with them o' nights; and scouts are frequently seen drawing a bee-line across the white marble slabs of the *sala*, on warm evenings, which no one seems to think it worth while to arrest. Mosquitoes appear to be but little troublesome to the natives, during the daytime; but they come in swarms to enjoy the flavor of what Doña Coloma calls the "thicker blood" of northern visitors,—a musical throng of them generally hovering around me when I am at work, while my companions are left unmolested.

But a really beautiful and interesting insect is the *cocullo*, or firefly of the West Indies, two of which I now have upon my table in an *impromptu* cage. Very docile are they in my hands,—to whose touch they seem to have become pleasantly accustomed;—taking kindly to a diet of moist sugar in lieu of the sugar-cane which is their natural food, and accepting a semi-daily bath in my wash-basin with much apparent enjoyment, floating about in the water for several minutes, and then spreading their legs and feelers as a sign that they are ready to come out. They are a sufficiently unattractive bug in their unillumined state, being of a dingy, earth-brown color, and about the shape and size of a large cockroach; but they become so glorified by the irradiation of those wondrous orbs of phosphorescent light which they carry about on their shoulders, that children scream with delight at the sight of them, and ladies make pets of them as I do, and even use them for ornaments on some occasions. I once saw a lady at the *retreta*, with a coronet, stomacher, and bracelets of them, and all the crown jewels of Spain could not have made her so resplendent. Their light is not a momentary flash, like that of our northern fire-fly; but it is emitted in a brilliant, steady ray, at will, and is of extreme beauty of tint, being of a slightly greenish yellow from one point of view, and of a pale red from another. It is a touching fact that the poorer classes are furnished with a most beautiful and inexpensive light for night-watchings, when sickness visits their dwellings, by confining a half-dozen *cocullos* in a cage, and suspending them from the ceiling.\*

Is it known to the medical world that the Chinese (in Cuba, at least) are wont to vaccinate in the tip of the nose? Doña Tomasita informs me that her coolie servant has recently undergone the operation at the hands of an expert of his own race, and is carrying about "a nose as big as a cocoa-nut." She further assures me that

---

\* It may interest some reader to know that the *cocullos* will bear transportation to the United States. The pair above-mentioned crossed the Gulf with me, and were my fellow-travellers for a month at the South. As it was necessary to carry them openly by hand, in order to attend to their wants and give them sufficient air, they attracted an almost annoying amount of attention in cars, steamboats, and hotels, as soon as nightfall brought out their splendor; bringing curious strangers in crowds, to inquire into their character and history. If I tried to partially conceal them with my shawl, it was only to be stopped at every turn with the good-natured warning, "You're a-fire there, somewhere!" In hotels where they remained long enough to become

this mode of vaccination is more effectual than ours, and never needs to be repeated;—but I vouch for nothing which comes not under my own observation.

A specimen of Cuban-English shall serve for *finale*. A certain youth, whom I meet occasionally, anxious to display his knowledge of my native language, often assails me with an idiom far more puzzling than any Spanish. He once informed me that, at a house across the way, they " swallowed boarders!"

" Swallow *what?* " said I, utterly at a loss.

"Boarders—*boar-ders*—how you call?—*huespedes?* "

"Oh," said I, enlightened by the Spanish word, "You mean that they take boarders."

" Si, señora; no is 'take' and 'swallow' the same? I take medicine, and I swallow it, too, no don't I?"

Furthermore, my young Cuban avowed that when he was in the United States he " did not *call on* the Episcopal Church, but on the Methodist!" It was with some difficulty that I repressed my inclination to

---

known, it grew to be a regular thing for them to hold a drawing-room reception every evening " by request,"—the guests seeming never to tire of watching their weird flight through the darkened room, with alternate thrills of terror and delight ; or of testing their recognition of me by observing how quickly they dimmed their light in strange hands, but immediately kindled it to its fullest brilliancy on being restored to mine. Both ended their career in Savannah ;—one apparently died a natural death, and the other, having escaped from its cage in the daytime, was mistaken by the chambermaid for a gigantic cockroach, and crushed accordingly ; so that I was disappointed in bringing either to my own home.

ask if the Methodist Church was inclined to be sociable and returned the call! And he added that he had told his American landlady that he would gladly take his old room, on his return, "if it was not *busy;*" and shortly afterward apologized for a "*mistake*" (that is to say, a stain) upon his otherwise immaculately white linen coat—white linen suits being the ordinary wear for gentlemen in Cuba.

Doubtless I commit equally absurd blunders in Spanish, but my friends are far too polite to make me aware of them. Long live the graceful Cuban courtesy, and may the years give to it a richer flavor of sincerity and truth!

## CHAPTER XXI.

### TO SANTA SOFÍA.

"CAPRICIOUS April" was sung by a northern poet. In the tropics, that graceful and freakish fairy is transformed into a lotus-crowned, olive-browed, slumbrous-eyed houri, full of soft, warm, languid life, whose breath intoxicates, and whose embrace soothes. Under her reign, Nature lapses dreamily into her "melting mood," and the earth steeps and simmers in the fiery glow of a sunshine that seems like a consummate extract of fine gold, poured red-hot over the palpitating landscape. Whosoever travels in Cuba, at this season, does so, as far as it is practicable, in the cool of the morning, while there is yet more gold than heat in the sunbeams. So Juan and I, vis-a-vis and alone, breakfasted sumptuously on fish, eggs, rice, and bananas, with due allowance of *vino catalan* and coffee; and then, as quickly as the thing could be effected, by means of a crazy *volante* and a covetous-eyed *calesero*, were transferred to a first-class car of the "Matanzas and Baró Railway," and were soon dashing southward.

The first object of interest was the *Monte del Pan*, now first seen close at hand, and discovering to us that it has many aspects wherewith to enchant the beholder.

Seen from Matanzas, it is a blue, aerial dome, fit to crown a dream-cathedral; from the Cumbres, it is a cone, sculptured sharply against the velvet sky; here, it stretches out in an irregular, serried chain, and is found to be not one, but many peaks, linking hands together for solemn conference, or sombre-browed companionship. Darting out from their shadow, we came upon a succession of soft, wavy swells and subsidences—fields of corn, cane, and *yuca*—vegetable gardens—orange groves—plantations of pine-apple, tobacco, banana, and cocoa-nut—colonnaded villas—and bamboo-framed, palm-thatched cottages. To these succeeded long reaches of level plain, thickly overgrown with wiry grass and savage shrubbery; and anon, came tangled thickets, bushy slopes, wooded and rocky hillsides, and wayward streams, whose deeply fertile banks gave life and luxuriance to a dense variety of succulent stems and gigantic leaves. Wild flowers of every hue and odor, and wild vines gifted with every peculiarity of creep and cling, covered the ground and the thickets. Among the latter, climbing and rioting everywhere, and too happy in its freedom to shut its eyes till late in the afternoon, the morning-glory mocked me with a strange familiarity in unfamiliarity,—so much more luxuriant was it, growing wild here, than in its cultivated state at home, and yet so little modified, in most of its characteristics, by difference of climate. Perhaps the loveliest "bit" that I saw that morning, was a crystal lakelet, whose banks were just a tangled mass of these cheery blossoms; and which looked like a large diamond flung carelessly into a radiant heap of sapphires, amethysts, and pearls. The flowers entirely hid the foliage,—the only hint of green about the picture being the placid reflection of the crests of two or three lofty palm-trees in the lakelet's smooth mirror.

The inhabitants have done so little to change this part of their country, or Nature has lent herself so kindly to their ways, that it is easy to think it is the very same landscape on which the eyes of the first explorers rested; whereof Columbus wrote so enthusiastically, deploring his inability to delineate the beauty of "the new heaven and new earth which had opened to his view," and making wondering mention of the fact that he had found "pines and palms growing together,"—those most characteristic types of arctic and equatorial vegetation dwelling here, side by side, in curious and picturesque harmony.

By and by, the wild and picturesque character of the landscape gives place to a more level and cultivated aspect; the hills recede to a soft, undulating line on the horizon; a green luxuriance of sugar-cane fills the valleys; lime and aloe hedges perfume the air; tall, white chimneys send up black columns of smoke; and compact villages, consisting of a small *plaza* and a street or two of contiguous houses, with the gray tower of a church rising among the red-tiled roofs, meet us here and there.

Through all these scenes we dart at the usual rate of railway travel, amid ever-growing heats, until the fixed fervor of noon is upon us, the tired sea-breeze swoons away in the distant hills, and the earth lies, sun-tranced and silent, under the glowing sky. We buy fruit, at the stations, from turbaned negro-girls, with soft, dusky eyes and illimitable lips; and we drink cool cocoa-nut water from the green shell. We stare lazily at our travelling companions,—mostly business men, in white linen suits; but a bundle of red shawls marks the whereabout of one woman, fast asleep, another is chatting merrily with her escort, and an old negress, crouched in a corner, with a pipe in her mouth, looks like a heap of ragged blankets, smouldering within, and sending out smoke from a chance opening. We buy the sixteenth share of a lottery-ticket,—not that we look for any favor at Dame Fortune's tricky hands, but because the vendor thereof is a one-armed soldier, pale and trembling from a recent amputation, with dark, melancholy eyes, and a face of hopeless misery. This is a pleasant way that the Government has of providing for her invalided servants; she gives them a small monopoly of routes and lottery-tickets.

Often, the stations consist of a single building, wherein the produce of the neighboring plantations is collected for transportation; one of them is in the midst of a canefield, and engineer and brakemen plunge into the green rows with drawn knives, and help themselves to a supply of this tropical refreshment sufficient to chew upon for the next hour. Here, idlers are few, and passengers fewer still.

About one o'clock, we change cars at Union, a town that seems a trifle more wide-awake than its neighbors;

and in the course of an hour, we are dropped at a little sun-burned and sleepy station in the heart of the sugar-country. Here, a tall, white-haired negro, with a sword at his side and a pistol in his belt, accosts Juan respectfully, conducts us to a *volante* in waiting, mounts the postilion-horse, cracks his whip, and we are *en route* for Santa Sofía,—an *ingenio* or sugar estate, owned by a branch of that House of Sámano, to whose overflowing kindness I am already so deeply indebted for Cuban sight-seeings and enjoyments. Our way lies through a lonely sea of sugar-cane, traversed by palm-bordered avenues, or lanes hedged with a dense and varied accumulation of tropical vegetation; through which we journey at a rattling pace, while Juan explains to me that our *calesero* goes armed, in order to be ready for the attacks of runaway slaves, coolies, and other desperadoes, who sometimes lurk in the cane and thickets, with intent to rob, and no insuperable objection to murder. And as our guide is a faithful servitor of his master, entrusted with all of the marketing and much of the expressage of the house, he is in special danger of molestation.

A drive of three or four miles brought us to the *casa de vivienda*,—a large, white, colonnaded structure, with interior court. On its broad piazza, a pleasant family party was gathered to welcome us, consisting of Don Gervasio, a grave and reverend Spanish *señor*,— Doña Carlota, a stately elderly dame,—their eldest son, Don Julio, Cuban born and bred,—his wife, Doña Angela, a highly accomplished and fascinating Barcelonian,

—a bevy of dark-eyed *señoritas*, and three lovely children. Here, I fell under the magic of a hospitality never excelled, within my experience, in the quality of putting a guest entirely at ease,—a hospitality so frank, so graceful, and so delicate, as to make my stay at Santa Sofía wholly delightful at the time, and surrounding it with a kind of halo, in the retrospect.

## CHAPTER XXII.

### THE INGENIO.

INGENIO—meaning literally, *engine*—is a word of elastic signification. Covering, in its broadest sense, the whole sugar plantation of thousands of acres, its meaning is first limited to apply to the large building devoted to sugar-making, and on entering that, it is found to be still further contracted to fit the powerful steam-engine which drives the works.

My first visit was to the *ingenio* building, or sugar-house,—a vast extent of red roof, one hundred and eighty feet long, and scarcely less than half as wide, supported on stout pillars, and pierced by a tall, smoke-vomiting chimney; under which roof the toilsome process of sugar-making goes on unintermittedly during the grinding season. The cane, fresh cut from the fields, is brought in carts to one end of the long building, where it is laid, by hand, lengthwise, on a flexible, revolving conductor made of wooden slats and links of chain, which conveys it between three huge, heavy, horizontal rollers, called *maquinas de moler*. From these it emerges, on the opposite side, crushed and dry; and a second conductor takes it outside the building, and dumps it into carts, when it is carried away to be first thoroughly dried in the sun, and then stored to serve as fuel for the furnaces. The expressed juice falls into a receiver beneath the rollers, whence it is pumped into a long trough overhead; through which it flows into a large reservoir where it is gently heated, and deposits whatever bits of cane and other impurities have accompanied it thus far. From this it is drawn into the first of a "train" of three immense caldrons, in which it undergoes a rapid boiling, the process of defecation being assisted by the admixture of a small quantity of lime; and is then successively ladled into the two remaining caldrons, and boiled, stirred, and skimmed, until it reaches the granulating point. Next, it is poured into large, open, shallow vats, and left to cool. When cold, it looks somewhat like the thick deposit sometimes found in the bottom of molasses hogsheads, and still more like particularly dingy and slimy mud. It is then shovelled into barrels with pierced heads, and, having now traversed the entire length of the *ingenio*, is removed to the *casa de purga*. The floor of this building is composed of narrow strips of plank, with openings between; and upon this the barrels are ranged, with their pierced heads downward, and left to drain. The drainage falls into an immense copper tank below, and constitutes molasses. The sugar left in the barrels is of the quality known as *mascabado* (frequently corrupted into *muscovado*), and forms the larger part of the imported sugar; the refining thereof being a separate business, mostly done in the United States.

However, in this *ingenio*, about midway of the building, and connected with the engine by a band, is a "centrifugal wheel," by means of which a better quality of sugar is made. The rim of the wheel is a kind of trough of perforated tin, into which a small quantity of the thick, dark mass from the vats is shoveled, the wheel is set in rapid motion, the centrifugal force throws off the molasses through the perforations, and the residuum is a dry and light-colored sugar, the best quality known to Cuban commerce. Furthermore, the planters make a small quantity of "clayed sugar," for home consumption; the unrefined mass being put into conical moulds of tin, with small apertures at their apices, which are then inverted, covered with a soft paste of clay and water, and left to drain. In time, the mass becomes dry and solid; and when removed from the mould, its base is quite white, a little higher it is of a pale yellow, and the tint deepens gradually to the apex, where it is almost brown.

But the mere mechanical process of sugar-making is by far the least interesting part of the scene which meets the eyes of a stranger, first ushered into an *ingenio*. There is a look of hard, steady, energetic industry about it, which he sees nowhere else in the island; and which seems wholly incongruous with the soft, languid reaches of tropical sky and landscape that smile upon him through the unenclosed sides of the building. Apart from this, however, there is a sombre, phantasmagoric character about the spectacle which will persuade him, for the moment, that he has somehow strayed into Pluto's own palace, wreathed in sulphurous vapor. There is an uncouth and demoniac appearance about the negro and coolie workmen—naked above the waist, and with no superfluous garments beneath it—as seen in the red glare of furnaces, or through misty clouds of steam from the hissing caldrons, that seems suited to no other locality. Add to this the hoarse, startling cries of the caldron tenders to the stokers,—"A-b'la! a-b'la!" "E-cha can-de-la! e-cha!" "Puer-ta!"—the mournful, minor chant of the workers at the carts and rollers, the *crunch* of the cane, the creak of chains, the whirling wheels and bands, and you will not wonder at the illusion.

I was directed to notice the engineer's apartment, hanging like a bird-cage from the roof, and reached by a ladder-like staircase. The engineer was a tall, powerful, sandy-haired, shrewd-faced native of New Hampshire, seated cross-legged on the frame-work of his engine, poring over a dilapidated copy of a home newspaper. He seemed glad to see a countrywoman, and did what he could for her entertainment. Seeing me look earnestly at a ponderous chain which was connected with the rollers, and had a grim look of unrelenting Fate about it, he began to tell me how an old slave-woman was once drawn into its cruel embrace, "kicking and yelling, and before I could stop the engine, her legs were torn clean off her body, and—" but here I broke in upon the horrible narrative with an energetic request that it might be left unfinished. The thing which sickened me most was the cool hardihood, verging upon jocularity, with which he treated the affair. But then, it was only a "*negra*," and too old to be of much value.

I asked some questions relative to the comparative efficiency of slave and coolie labor. "Wall!" said my compatriot, scratching his head reflectively, "the coolies *do* know a leetle the most,—but they are apt to be cross-grained, ugly chaps (to be sure, it's no wonder, considerin' how they're treated); and then they don't mind up and killing themselves, when they git mad, any more'n I do paring my nails. I'd rather have ten niggers to manage, than one Chinaman, by a long chalk!"

"Do you have much to do with the management of the hands?"

"Um!—no, not much,—that's the *mayoral's* business. But I call for what help I want about the engine, and I don't allow any meddling with my hands. And *they* know I don't stand no sass nor shirking."

"But you do not carry any weapons, nor whip."

"Wall! I guess not. But I generally carry my fists about me, and they do pooty well. I leave pistols and such like to the *mayoral.*"

Said *mayoral* being a short, dark, broad-chested Spaniard, with a face like a smouldering furnace, and an eye that had a perpetual threat in it. He was girded with a sword, and had a brace of pistols in his belt. Little mercy would any mutinous coolie get at his hands!

During my stay at Santa Sofía, the sugar-house exerted a curious fascination over me, and whenever other sources of amusement failed, I was sure to be drawn thither, and to be found hanging over the rollers, watching the cane slowly tending toward its hard fate, and listening to the wild chant of the Africans there at work; or inhaling the faint, sweet vapor from the caldrons, or seated silently by the centrifugal wheel, harvesting the abundant crop of analogies growing out of all. It was impossible not to notice, for example, how the cane became the agent of its own destruction,—how the bruised mass from the rollers was made the instrument of drawing in a continual succession of fresh, sweet cane, to be likewise crushed, mangled, and cast out, fit only for burning,—a thing which has its mournful counterparts in the social world. The negroes grew, after a time, to signalize my comings and goings with a smile, and were assiduous in doing me small services; but I do not remember that I ever elicited the slightest mark of interest or attention from a Chinese. These men appeared to be in a state of chronic sullenness; they persistently avoided meeting my eye, and emulated the hardness, inflexibility, and soullessness of the implements with which they labored. As they feel the weight and shame of bondage more than the negroes, it is a comfort to think that they can look forward to a day of emancipation; for the coolies are bound for a term of eight years only, during which time their servitude is severe enough, but at the end of which, they are their own masters. It is also a comfort to know that their propensity to suicide operates as some check upon the worst forms of cruelty,—one so often has to be glad, in this world, of things which, in happier circumstances, were fitter subjects for tears.

I observed no absolute cruelty in the treatment of

the hands, but the whole system of sugar-making is one of hard, steady, relentless driving, based upon a nice calculation of the utmost that can be gotten out of human flesh and bones, without immediate exhaustion, deterioration, and consequent loss. One cannot behold it without a sorrowful pity for lives that must run such a round of toilsome motion, yet accomplish no genuine progress. During the grinding season of four months, the engine rests not, night nor day, nor Sunday; the procession of sugar-cane stops not; the furnaces are always red, and the caldrons ever boiling, bubbling, and emitting dense clouds of vapor. The women work in the fields, and at the carts and rollers, but not at the engine, furnaces, or caldrons.

At dusk the large plantation bell rings the *Oracion*, which in times of greater religious strictness, was the signal for a prayer to be said, in house or a-field, but is now merely used to call in the field-hands. The *mayordomo*, whose office resembles that of a purser, now makes the daily distribution of provisions,—generally consisting of jerked beef, rice, and plaintains, or bananas,—and the negroes then file into quarters. At another time we will visit them there.

We return to the piazza, to watch the twilight dusk steal over the fair, tropical landscape. The little enclosure in front is filled with rare and brilliant flowers, and the *receda*, or tree-mignonette, growing twenty or thirty feet high, sends forth its richest odor. The sunset-hues deepen in the west, they swim and flash and fade in exquisite, tender tints, and a golden gloom begins the night.

And wondrously fair is the evening picture in this delicious climate! The large, tropical moon fills it with charmed light, the lustrous leaves of the palms soften it with trembling shadows. The long, level reaches of the cane stir lightly, but soundlessly, under the stealing steps of light-footed zephyrs; the huge canopy of the ceiba hangs motionless in the starry arch of the sky; the purple, distant hills, and the dusky-browed forest, dream soft in the moon-tranced air. Doña Angela brings out some poems of Espronceda's—Spain's last and sweetest singer—and the soft modulations of her tender voice, and the liquid ripple of the Spanish vowels, flow out harmoniously over the scene, with frequent lapses into silence, which are sweeter than any sound. For, whether at noon or night, silence seems most natural to the tropics. They pant and flush with feeling, but it is inarticulate. The landscape is always a poem, but it is seen and felt only, never heard. Bright-plumaged birds swing in the verdant gloom of the palm boughs, but they have no song, only a cry. Yet sweeter and sadder is it than the song of any nightingale, heart-breaking in its sharp pain of helplessness and longing!

Suddenly, a monotonous, minor-keyed murmur of African song rose from the negro-quarters,—first, a high, shrill recitative, and then a wild chorus, sung in unison; both words and music being clearly the product of a race just a little higher than the brutes. If the pathetic, pleading look of a dog's face could be expressed in music, it would sound just so. Yet the strain was sad to me only,—the singers broke into shouts of laughter and clapping of hands! And that touched me most of all;—there is something inexpressibly mournful about the mirth of an enslaved and degraded race. Its very boisterousness and utter abandonment show how great is the reaction from the heavy pressure of forced toil and weary pain.

With the evening, the *cocullus* gleamed out over the cane-fields, like a new creation of terrestrial stars. Yet, beautiful as they were in the distance, and despite the reassuring memory of my two caged pets in Matanzas, I could scarcely repress a thrill of terror when I first beheld the great, fiery eyes and flaming breastplate coming toward me, straight and swift, through the darkness, and only turning aside within two or three inches of my face. It was hard to believe that so much blaze would not burn, or that it could emanate from a creature of less size than a bat. The *cocullus* are easily caught by placing a live coal or two in the grass, and throwing a handkerchief over them as they approach what they mistake for a friendly signal. The little *Cito* brought me one thus ensnared; and told me gravely that it was "*uno de los serenos de los insectos*" (one of the watchmen of the insects). Those who recall the description of the lantern-bearing *serenos* of Havana, in a former chapter, will recognize the appropriateness of the name.

At bedtime, I was shown to an apartment more spacious than it was ever my fortune to occupy, except once, when, in a crowded Southern hotel, the ball-room was assigned me as a dormitory! Yet I think that might have been put inside of this, and still have left

10*

sufficient margin for a chain of contra-dances. The few pieces of furniture were quite lost in its vastness, and a single candle made but feeble encroachments upon its heavy masses of shadow. In one corner was a bed, in nicest order and daintiest array, but of the most immitigable Cuban variety—a wonderful invention for keeping foreigners awake. Through the broad, iron-grated window opposite, I could look straight into the sugar-house, with its vapor-charged atmosphere, its lurid glow, its seething caldrons, its half-naked wretches of attendants, its wild screeching and monotonous chant; and the Inferno of Dante, the Hell of Milton, and the Witches' Cave of Macbeth, met and mingled wildly in my dreams. Not till near dawn did I escape from these into Slumber's undisputed land.

## CHAPTER XXIII.

#### PLANTATION PICTURES.

A SUGAR plantation is a little village within itself, containing church, dwellings, hospital, workshops, storehouses, water-works, and whatever is necessary to its daily economy. That of Santa Sofía numbers about four hundred souls, of whom not more than a dozen or fifteen are contained in white skins; a disproportion which seems to justify, in a measure, the firearms, whips, chains, locks, gratings, etc., which are so prominent a part of its system. How justly these fifteen have acquired the right to dominate over the three hundred and seventy-five, is a question for moralists; but while they exercise it, it behooves them to take measures for their personal safety. The negroes are said to be, in gross, coarse and brutal, the Chinese sly and cruel; if it were not for those same locks, pistols, and other safeguards, I can well understand that my first night at Santa Sofía might have been memorable for worse horrors than the lurid phantasmagoria of my dreams.

Day broke over the plantation as freshly fair as if whips and slave gangs and wearisome toil were also but visions of the night;—and other days followed, full of mellow sunshine and a subtle sweetness of luminous air, wherein to bask and breathe was quite enough for happiness. A half-dozen of such days, in our climate, are counted sufficient atonement for the atmospheric delinquencies of a whole season; here, they were the rule—slowly ripening from golden morn to fervid noon, and thenceforward growing ever sweeter and sweeter, until they departed through a gorgeous sunset arch, crowned with gladness, and leaving on the mind a beatific impression of rare concords of lustrous color, and calm floods of iridescent light, but no distinct record of individuality. Possibly their very eventlessness was their subtlest charm; in such an air, at such a temperature, the mind craved neither the excitement of stirring events, nor the labor of thought—only the calm enjoyment of observation, and the soft play of fancy. Sufficient unto each day was the evil of that dark shadow of bondage and forced labor, brooding over the cane-fields and under the vast roof of the sugar-house; sufficient for its joy to watch the slow-moving panorama of radiant dawns, and prismatic sunsets, and moon-silvered eves, seen across a billowy luxuriance of rustling cane, and through green arches of great boughs of ceiba, palm, and tamarind.

On this pleasant background, the quiet incidents of the dreamy, leisurely plantation-life were softly pencilled;—among them a few scenes stand out sharply in my memory, as more brilliantly or sombrely tinted than the rest, of which I give faint sketches.

First, the *barracon*, or negro-quarter. A quadrangular structure, whose exterior presents to view only a high wall, without other opening than a massive and sombre archway, closed by an iron gate. The *mayoral* turns key, draws bolt, and ushers us into a large court, covered with a scanty growth of coarse, wiry grass. In the middle is a stone fire-place and huge boiler, wherein certain kinds of cookery are done, in the lump, for the entire tenantry. Around us is a hollow square of two-story dwellings, in as close contiguity as the cells of a honeycomb; the second floor being reached by means of exterior galleries and staircases, and each room serving for home to a limited family. The place is wholly deserted and silent; the adult occupants are at work, and the children are cared for elsewhere, during their absence. We look into some of the rooms, and wonder if life is worth living at such a scanty measure of comfort or attainment. There is a bed of rude plank with a blanket on it, a stool or two, a few pots and pans, two or three coarse garments hanging on the wall, occasionally a little crucifix or an image of the Virgin,—and that is all! No pleasantness within, no verdure without, no breadth of scope, no wholesome retirement—merely a place for eating and sleeping, where the slaves and coolies are driven nightly, like sheep to a pen, and locked in, until the morning's call to labor. Over the gateway is the apartment of the *mayoral*, with the door in the side of the arch, anterior to the gate, and a window opening on the court. It has a grim provision of fire-arms, and is evidently a small fortress, commanding the whole interior, from which it would be easy to shoot down the leaders in any disturbance, and reduce insurgents to terms.

Secondly, the hospital. Its exterior and approach are similar to those of the *barracon*. Entering the court, we find forty or fifty naked negro children at play, who undergo a sudden transformation into so many staring ebony statues, at sight of strange visitors; and are immediately ordered off by Doña Angela, with injunctions not to reappear until they have found somewhat wherewith to cover their nakedness. The gentlemen enter a goodnatured plea for the " *negritos*" (Anglicè; little niggers), so summarily dismissed to retirement or the unwonted thraldom of garments; but the mistress, scandalized by their appearance—vicariously, I imagine—maintains that it is "*una cosa indecenta*," and carries her point. One side of the court is occupied by the nursery, where all the babes of the plantation are gathered, in charge of girls eight years old and upwards, overseen by two or three superannuated negro women, too old to be of use elsewhere. Some are wrapped in old shawls, or a bit of ragged blanket, others are muffled in all sorts of nondescript garments, and one small morsel of femininity lies curled up on the floor, quite nude, but with a dingy muslin cap on her tiny, woolly head, which gives her an indescribably elfin and wizened aspect. They are all preternaturally quiet and docile, as I have found slave babies to be everywhere. Is it that they come thus early to a perception of their lot in life, or because they are not indulged and pampered into ill-humor and exaction?"

In an adjacent room, we found the small people just banished from the court, all tangled and snarled together in a rapid process of toilet-making, and a chaotic confusion of ill-assorted and impromptu raiment. A few, who were already dressed, came forward, and knelt down around me, with crossed hands and bended heads, waiting for something—what? " *Una benedicion, señora*," said the kindly-eyed woman who was superintending their operations, seeing my perplexity. Somewhat taken aback by so unusual a request, I yet managed to give them the desired "blessing," according to the sweet Spanish formula, "*Dios os haga bueno!*" and went on my way wondering. I learned, later, that it is an African superstition that the benediction of a stranger, from over the ocean, has a Divine efficacy to brighten the future of the recipient,—a relic, doubtless, of those remote times when all such visitors were welcomed as messengers from the gods. But it needs more of that faith which is potent to remove mountains than I possess, to believe that any one's blessing can work much temporal good to these outcasts of civilization, whose place in the world is so vexing a problem. To be sure the civil law of Cuba is kinder to the slave than ever our own was. It gives him his time on Sundays, to enable him to work out his freedom, if he is so minded. It obliges the master to sell any dissatisfied slave, who can find another person willing to buy him; his value being fixed by a government official at the current market price, rarely taking into account extraordinary capacity or qualifications, so that a really good slave finds little difficulty in changing owners. It does not prohibit him the use of whatever educational advantages he can command; though it may readily be inferred that these are not many, among a people not over solicitous of such privileges for themselves. But how is a plantation negro, working all day long under the eye and whip of a driver, and locked into quarters at night, to bring these laws to bear on his own case, however much it may need them? In the cities and towns, no doubt, they do something to lighten the yoke.

The remainder of the building is the hospital proper, divided into a dispensary, male and female wards, and a lying-in room. The apartments were all large and lofty, even grand in their proportions, like almost everything else on the estate. They were scrupulously clean also, but their extreme barrenness, the absence of all adornment, or of aught to stimulate thought or gratify taste, made them undelightful enough. There was no furniture whatever, except a row of beds on either side; and these were merely oblong forms of thick, heavy plank, about the size and height of an ordinary cot. On these lay the patients, in their usual working garments, with a blanket over them if they liked. At first, it gave me a shock to notice the comfortlessness of the whole; it seemed actual cruelty to put sick people on such beds— tables, rather, where, I thought, the poor, worn-out body might have been dissected as soon as the breath was out of it, without any very harsh violation of the decencies of the place. But I was self-convicted of unreasonableness, after a little, since the idolized darling of the wealthiest Cuban house is scarcely more luxuriously lodged,—the degree of comfort between the side of a plank and a piece of canvas stretched tightly over an iron frame being much too nice to be appreciable to any one not born to it.

But the blank, stolid, utterly unilluminated faces on those beds were pitiful to behold! Perhaps the African face, by reason of its coarse, heavy traits, and sombre coloring, is always more profoundly and haggardly melancholy, in sickness, than any other; and here, that expression seemed intensified by the meagreness and unloveliness of the surroundings. The patients scarcely noticed me, as I paused to look at them; though one or two made a faint attempt at a smile, in response to some kind words from the mistress of the estate. One was already beyond the reach of all sublunary interests; the stupor of death was settling on her face, the fixed, glazed eye might even now catch some bewildering glimpses of the "glory that shall be revealed," even to this hapless, benighted soul. I noted the fact with something very like gladness; the door of death seemed the only effectual escape from a life of such hard and hopeless limitations. What possible happiness or improvement was there in store for any of these forlorn wretches, even if they should manage to struggle through this present misery of sickness? which, to do them justice, not one of them seemed trying for. They had not found life so good or glad as to be unwilling to give it up; they just lay quietly on their hard couches, passive and uncomplaining, and let God and their master do with them as they would. There was neither light, nor hope, nor desire, in their hard-lined faces, nothing but a flaccid and dejected helplessness, in lieu of resignation; as if they were conscious that they were born into the world for this and nothing else, and blindly accepted their hard lot, without being able to understand it. Even in the little children, this characteristic seemed as perfectly developed as in their elders, oppressing one with a sense of something dolefully amiss and out-of-joint in all the conditions of humanity.

Here and there, in strong contrast with these depressed and nerveless Africans, a Chinese glowered like a spark of fire amid gray ashes; his usual expression of sullen insubordination being sharpened by the pressure of physical suffering. One of these sat on the edge of his bed, with a swollen and bandaged limb drawn up beside him—the very incarnation of impotent hate and rage. The mayoral laid a firm, detaining grasp on his shoulder, under which I could see the man wince and shiver, while the official told me how he had run away weeks ago, and hidden in the woods, leading a sort of highwayman's life, and baffling all pursuit, until he cut his foot badly on a sharp stone, in jumping a stream; which wound festered and gangrened, and so disabled him that he could no longer procure food, nor drag his wasted body from one hiding-place to another; when he was found—half-dead, but still untamed in spirit—and brought back to prison. Since which time, he had twice attempted suicide. The Chinese meanwhile regarded us with a look that would have stabbed us both to the heart, if looks were available for such a purpose. Plainly, he felt himself at war with the whole tyrannous universe; and especially resented the indignity of being exhibited and commented upon as if he had been a wild beast.

From a region so suggestive of miserable doubt and questioning of Providence as this, it was good to turn aside into the lying-in room, and see how the goodness of God was vindicated, even here, to our low, human apprehension. Something of that same pride and joy of motherhood, which makes such a light in happier places, was here visible also, helping these poor women through their sufferings, and shining in the faces of those whose babes were held up to view, and patted, and praised—babyhood being a wonderful and beautiful thing everywhere! Nor did this joy appear to be clouded by any misgivings about the future of these small slips of humanity, set to grow in so unkindly a soil. In the sick wards I had found myself uncomfortably face to face with the great problem of life—the presence of sin and misery in the creation of an all-wise and beneficent God,—here, I seemed to have gone a long way toward its solution. Out of the deepest pain is born the extremest pleasure; and the suffering and sorrow of this present time are often but the birth-throes of a joy "unspeakable and full of glory," that shall be brought forth hereafter unto all who love God.

The little chapel next claims our attention, a plain, brown-stuccoed edifice, where occasional services are held by the priests of the neighboring village, and whose square tower is rather a pretty object, rising above the red roofs of the adjacent buildings. Its interior is still gay with the decorations for a recent festival; artificial flowers are wreathed and grouped everywhere, both flowers and arrangement being due to the pretty and skilful fingers of the *señoritas* Engracia, Josifa, and Conchita. In the little sacristy are the priestly vestments, elaborately embroidered by the same agile fingers. Doña Carlota unfolds and exhibits them,—the green for common use, the red for the " Corpus Christi," the white for Christmas, Easter, weddings, and christenings. Last of all, the black for funerals.

"I thank God," says the *señora*, solemnly, and with a slight tremor in her voice, " there has never yet been any need of these; but we have them ready, you see, and none can tell how soon they may be wanted."

She is thinking, doubtless, that, in virtue of ill-health and advanced age, she has a right to expect to need them first, but I read differently the oracles of the future. The youngest child of the house has one of those sweet, rapt, far-seeing faces, never long vouchsafed to any home, save as a tender and beatific memory, linking the trials of earth with the promises of heaven.

A steep staircase leads to the little, square tower-top. The view from thence is extensive but monotonous,— almost any New England landscape would present a more striking and varied outline; yet there is a tropical character about it that makes it richly worth observing. Over all the outer circle—beyond an immediate proximity of rippling reaches of cane, and soft shades of palm, mimosa, and bamboo—are bright, bold billows of foliage, tossed aloft from remote forests; and on one side the blue, flowing outline of distant hills. In truth, if there were nothing else to look at, palms and bamboos alone might well satisfy one's thirst for natural beauty.

Directly behind the house is a large enclosure devoted to vegetables and fruits. Thither, at sunset-time, I prevail upon Engracia to accompany me. She hesitates at first, to be sure, and tells me that she never goes there, the servants will bring me whatever I want; but upon being assured that I desire neither fruits nor vegetables, but only to observe their peculiarities of culture and growth, many of them being known to me hitherto merely as things of bales and bags and boxes, and grocers' counters, she consents,—albeit, not without a certain reluctance, which I set down to Cuban indolence, and pitilessly ignore.

Nearest the house are the vegetable beds, kept orderly enough, but with too strong a likeness to kitchen gardens everywhere, to be deeply interesting. The only unfamiliar forms are the *ñame*, a species of yam, growing to an enormous size; and the *malanga* and *cazabe*, both farinaceous roots, from the latter of which tapioca is made. Next, come stiff battalions of pine-apples, in various stages of maturity; and after them, a large melon-patch covered with a thick tangle of luxuriant vines, among the leaves of which great green and russet rounds are industriously secreting sweets from the tropical sunbeams. To these succeeds a small forest of banana-trees, with their long, fragile leaves gently swaying in the evening breeze, their purple buds nestling close to the parent stalk, and their heavy clusters of green and ripe fruit, here called *manos* (hands), of which each banana is a "finger." We next plunge into a grove of orange trees, alike fragrant with dark green foliage, bridal blossoms, and golden fruit; and we finally lose ourselves in a kind of orchard wilderness, for which Art has done what she could, and then handed it over to Nature, for a finishing touch of wildness and grace. Here, the chestnut-like *mango*, with its pear-shaped fruit and dense foliage, stands side by side with the dark-leaved and gray-fruited *mamey*; the elm-like *aguacate*, and the drooping tamarind lean and whisper together; the *sapota* mingles its fruit of brown with the green and yellow balls of the *calabazo*; the bright scarlet of the pomegranate's blossoms touches the delicate pink of those of the almond; and the bindweed and the love-vine marry them all together, and wreathe their topmost boughs with graceful coronals of leaves and filaments. Here and there, a tall palm has joined itself to the pleasant company, a magnolia has also found room for its smooth trunk and shining leaves, and a group of young acacias have stolen into an unguarded corner. The whole scene glows with brilliant coloring;—the sky is roseate; the leaves above and around are reddened by the sunset beams; the crimson and scarlet, the orange and gold, of the fruits and blossoms are like flame; even the earth is red, where it shows through the undergrowth. The autumnal glories of New England are not brighter. And there, perchance, we touch upon the the secret of the sadness always latent in the tropical landscape. Perfection of any kind, in this world, is near its opposite; and amid the abounding life of the tropics there is continual decay. Perpetual summer implies perpetual autumn : some plants must needs be ever dying, some trees shedding their foliage. In many cases, the new growth pushes off the old, and under the boughs that are at once thick-clad with verdure, white with blossoms, and golden with fruit, one hears beneath his tread the rustle of fallen leaves.

The boundary wall of the enclosure is covered with mosses and creeping things. A wild convolvulus and passion-vine have so tangled themselves together that no mortal hand can separate them ; and a night-blooming cereus has climbed to the topmost stone, to look out over the adjacent fields at the sunset, or at the negroes and coolies cutting cane by the latest beams. The nearest of these—a gigantic African—no sooner spies us than he breaks out into a strain of fulsome compliment, —"*Dios mio!* what beauty! *Santa Maria!* what grace! *Ay!* what pretty little feet! *Ay!* what beautiful little hands!" and so on, *ad nauseam*, and not without a vicious leer. If I open my eyes only a trifle wider at the creature's impudence, it is because I have learned that the most courteous Don of the district would probably do the very same thing in similar circumstances; and I really do not see that it is worse in the slave than in the master. But I *am* amazed, when I discover that this flowery discourse has sent Engracia flying toward the house like a startled deer. Her white dress is already disappearing among the trunks of the trees; and nothing remains but for me to follow more slowly, reflecting upon the anomalies of a system under which the daughter of the house flees in terror from the sight of one of its dependents. Halfway to the mansion, I meet a servant sent after me in hot haste; and on the piazza I find Engracia trembling with fear, and recounting our adventure to her excited sisters. It is my first and last independent ramble in Cuba.

An invitation to dine at the neighboring plantation of San Benito, adds some queer, crowded pictures of the Flemish school to our gallery. First, there is the transit thither,—a complete *melée* of *volantes*, saddle-horses, mules, negroes, and dogs, fifteen or twenty in all, tearing across the cane-fields, or through the grand palm-avenues, in the amber glory of the late afternoon, at a rate and with an amount of noise that would have befitted well a fox-chase. The *volantes* have each three horses,—a prodigality of motive power only to be seen in the rural districts, and apparently subserving no end but that of picturesqueness, since the extra horse occupies himself mainly in tumbling into ditches, entangling himself in wayside shrubbery, and jerking and jostling the shaft-horse; which latter endures the infliction with the stoicism appropriate to the inevitable. The ladies wear no shawls nor bonnets, only fluttering scarfs and ribbons, that vie with the tropical landscape in color. The road is everywhere beautiful, and often picturesque; on either side are the billowy canefields, while the palms, of which one never tires, meet above our heads, and stretch away before us in long, temple-like vistas. Crossing a bridge, we are wrapped, for a moment, in a thicket of willow-like bamboos. Reaching the top of a slight eminence, we discover afar the rolling outline of purple hills. Passing along the edge of a forest, we are charmed with the exuberance and diversity of its flowery undergrowth,—the pink, white, and purple convolvuli, the flaming fever-flower, the sunny-eyed and sweet-breathed jessamine, the many varieties of the wild passion-vine, the white-chaliced mangrove, the richly perfumed heliotrope, and divers others, which I do not recognize individually, but all of which help to fill me with a vague sense of inexhaustible beauty and abounding fragrance. And never was there sunshine so rich, so soft, and so dream-like, as that through which gallops our straggling party, waking the drowsy echoes with noisy clatter of *volantes* and hoofs, shrill chorus of talk and laughter, chattering of negroes and barking of dogs.

The dining-room of San Benito is entirely open, on one side, to the court, at the farther end of which are grouped, not unpicturesquely, our own servants and horses. The guests at table number twenty-two, —not including the dogs underneath the board, nor the parrots, pigeons, and chickens, that hover above and around, to pick up the crumbs. Neither do I take into the account a small army of cadaverous, squealing pigs, nor a scorpion that suddenly appears on a rough rafter, over Conchita's head, and is despatched with some difficulty by the joint forces of three of the gentlemen, two of the servants, a cane, a riding-whip, an umbrella, and two brooms, in the midst of general confusion and dismay. However, this little digression only serves to stimulate conversation; everybody talks, laughs, expletizes, and gesticulates, at the same moment, only screaming louder as the chorus swells higher,—the pigeons and chickens taking their full shares in the talk, and the parrots adding their shrill laughter to the merriment. Notwithstanding these oddities, the dinner is served with a sufficient amount of Cuban state and ceremony. There is a deal of cut-glass and silver plate; the courses are many, the viands excellent, the attendance adequate. I sit at the right of our host; and never was the English language so broken into inch pieces, so deftly cemented together again with pantomimic gesture, and so artfully twisted into elaborate compliment, as by that dark, smiling, low-voiced, and gray-haired Don Diego. A dinner whereat he presides must needs have a stronger flavor of the court than of the country, despite pigs, parrots, chickens, and scorpions.

The feast being ended, there is an almost unanimous withdrawal to the broad, airy piazza. The two elder gentlemen, only, remain behind with their cigars; the younger ones composedly light theirs outside. The practice of smoking is so universal in Cuba, it is considered so much a matter of course, that ladies are seldom asked if it is disagreeable to them,—never, except as the merest formality, the reply being taken for granted. I am not a little surprised, therefore, when Don Diego joins our party, to see his son Casimiro remove his cigar from his mouth, and, holding it on the side remote from the elder gentleman, quietly slip away to the farther end of the piazza to finish it. I am so struck by the oddity of the circumstance, that I venture to ask Engracia, in an aside, what it means. She replies that it is an act of disrespect for a son to smoke in the presence of his parents.

"Why?" I ask, with pardonable obtuseness, seeing that the parents all smoke, to a man (and sometimes to a woman), and cannot well help knowing that their sons unhesitatingly follow their example

"*Es un vicio, V. sabe!*" (It is a vice, you know), she answers, with a little grimace, and a most expressive shrug of the shoulders.

The evening lets us into the mysteries of Cuban courtship,—if there can be said to be any mystery about a thing which must needs be carried on so openly. In one corner of the *sala*, the eldest son of the house is pouring soft whispers into the willing ear of his cousin Caterina, who is formally betrothed to him; at one end of the double row of chairs, the second son is doing the very same thing to the beautiful Conchita, of Santa Sofía; farther on, the third, a round, stolid, good-natured youth of nineteen, is by the side of his fair *fiancée* of twenty-two, who is also his mother's sister, and consequently his *aunt;* and the younger members of both households are likewise arranged in cooing pairs; all of which goes to show that love is early fledged in Cuba, and often flies in strange directions.

Into this soft concert of wooing somebody sends a proposition for a dance. Josifa goes to the piano, the party quickly resolves itself into couples (where it is not already done), and begins the slow, dreamy, circling measures of the favorite *contra-danza*. Old and young join, even to the grandmother; and round and round they go, solemn, stately, and deliberate, as the planets in their courses,—now and then facing each other for a right and left, and then going round and round again,— till one's brain reels with the sight, and the chairs and tables, the pictures and the lights, seem to be going round and round, too. There is no doubt at all about the negroes in the court,—their low laughter and the rhythm of their feet, as they whirl and stamp to the sound of the music, are plainly to be heard; and very likely I might see the pigs and the chickens, the parrots and the pigeons, amicably revolving and balancing in company, if I were not too sleepy to look out. For it is getting fearfully late; that slow, dreamy, tireless dance was certainly meant for eternity rather than time, —people who have only an earthly afternoon or evening before them ought never to engage in it. However, it is finally brought to an end, the *volantes* and saddle-horses are ordered round, there is a pleasant tangle of kissing and leave-taking on the piazza, a rapid mounting of seats and saddles, a clear-toned "*Vamos!*" from Don Gervasio, and we are *en route* for Santa Sofía.

I came in a *volante*, but I return on horseback, having exchanged places with Josifa, for reasons of no value to anybody but the owner. It is my first trial of a Cuban saddle, but having been early accustomed to ride on any saddle—or none, at a pinch—it gives me no trouble. Especially, as my pony's gait is scarcely less light, stealthy, and swift, than that of a phantom-horse.

It stirs me not in the saddle, it makes a seeming dead level of all the ruts and roughnesses of the road,—I might carry a brimming cup in my hand, and spill no drop of its contents. Our way is a combination of tropical light, warmth, stillness, and fragrance, too delectable to be fully enjoyed otherwise than slowly and silently, drop by drop; so Juan and I quietly fall into the rear, and let the noise and confusion of our miscellaneous party gradually die away in the forward distance. The moonlight (have I ever before mentioned Cuban moonlight?) is like a spell of enchantment; it seems to set the scene entirely apart from the every-day world. It glorifies the palm-groups with a grace too fair for aught but the banks of the River of Life; it transfigures the canefields into a shining sea of glass; it makes of the forest an enchanted ground of rippling lights and tremulous shadows; it breathes through the long, arched, and columned vistas of the grand old palm avenues the very spirit of consecration. The air is full of the incense of unseen flowers,—unseen, save where the light finger of a moonbeam touches some white or yellow chalice into unearthly beauty and delicacy. We recognize the mangrove, the jessamine, the lime, the heliotrope, and the wild grapevine, by their fragrant breath; and we are caught and held entranced by the odorous blossoms of a bitter orange-tree, that lean far over the road and touch our cheeks with their dewy lips.

Suddenly, a song, faint but lusciously sweet, rises from a remote thicket. Spellbound we listen, as it slowly draws near,—swelling higher and higher, till the boughs overhead seem possessed with the very soul of melody, as well as of fragrance,—and breaks off abruptly, at last, as if the singer might have been startled by the sight of our statuesque figures.

"What is it?" I ask Juan, drawing a long breath.

"It is a nightingale," he answers, absently.

Is he dreaming of the orange groves of Andalusia? or are there nightingales in Cuba? But I will not break the silence by a sound. Be it a nightingale forevermore!

## CHAPTER XXIV.

#### FIRE IN THE CANE!

BUT the latter days of my stay at Santa Sofía were to be made memorable by more stirring pictures. We were sitting on the piazza, one morning—Doña Angela, Engracia, and I—when I noticed a light, fleecy cloud rising slowly over the fruit gardens in the rear; which gradually increased in volume, and deepened in color, until a faint odor of smoke began to pervade the atmosphere. Then my companions suddenly started up with alarmed faces, and rapid exclamations and questions. Presently, an unusual stir and excitement became apparent in the sugar-house—the engineer, and others came out and stood in knots, discussing the smoke and its possibilities. Don Julio quickly joined them, and messengers were sent forth in hot haste. There was a short interval of seething suspense and expectation; and then a panic-stricken negro came flying up the road, calling out breathlessly those words most appalling to a planter's ears, "*El fuego en la caña!*" (Fire in the cane!) The adjacent plantation, La Bellorita, was on fire!

Then ensued a scene of such terror and confusion as seemed to me quite disproportioned to the occasion.

The *señoritas* wept and wrung their hands, Doña Angela gathered her three children in her arms and held them tight, with an expression that seemed to say that no fire should break through that loving barrier, and the elder lady strove vainly to control her trembling hands and quivering lips. I knew, of course, that destruction of the cane meant pecuniary loss to the planter, but I did not then know that these fires frequently swallow up dwellings, negro-quarters, sugar-houses, cattle, and even human life, in their progress, leaving nothing behind but a black, smoking desolation.

Don Julio mounts his horse and rides off to the scene of the conflagration, to offer his assistance to his suffering friend. The field-hands are called in, formed into gangs, under drivers, and sent off after him. Later in the day, the engine is stopped, for the first and only time in the season, and all the resources of the estate are strained to the utmost to meet and conquer the terrible foe. Meanwhile, the black cloud of smoke spreads and rises, hanging a veil over the face of the sun, which shoots through it only feeble, yellowish rays; and we women watch and wait, under the constant excitement of bulletins from the fire. Now it spreads—now it is stayed—now it breaks from all control and marches triumphantly over the estate, burning carts and oxen where they stand, and driving the frightened negroes before it! Now it has reached the sugar-house, and machinery, furnaces, and boilers, are wrapped in a sheet of wrathful flame! Now it attacks the *barracon*, and the poor homes and possessions of the negroes are quickly laid in ashes! Now, the patients are brought out of the hospital, and that becomes a savory morsel for the tooth of the destroyer. Must the mansion burn, too? For a time, its fate trembles in the balance. Fortunately there was but little shade or verdure around it, and that little was cut down and borne off in the first alarm; moreover, it is girdled with a host of negroes and coolies, armed with bushes, blankets, buckets of water, and whatever may arrest the flames,—and so, it escapes!

But the fire is spreading rapidly in the direction of Santa Sofía, and Don Julio finds that, in order to save one part of his plantation, he must sacrifice another. Several acres of cane are quickly isolated from the rest, by clearing a broad belt all around them, and the torch is set to the doomed fields. Slowly, light wreaths of smoke curl upward, and spread and darken, red tongues of fire fork and flare among them; then a black, dense cloud sweeps grandly over the field, with lurid banners of flame in the midst, and a sound like the surging of a stormy sea. It rushes, red and angry, toward the advancing fire beyond—the columns of smoke meet and mingle—the flames grapple each other with a fierce, exultant roar—they rise, and fall, and leap, and wrestle together—they wreathe and twist, and flash and flare, in the death-struggle—they rise again, and quiver, and flicker, and fall to rise no more. On this side, the fire is arrested, and Santa Sofía is saved!

But on our neighbor's ground, the fight still goes on, and not until evening does Don Julio ride back to say that all is over. Then the negroes come slowly and wearily homeward,—a forlorn, haggard, begrimed, utterly exhausted company, with some burned limbs and blistered faces among them. These are ordered to the hospital, and the rest are locked into quarters, with an intimation that two or three days of entire rest will be given them before they are remanded to labor—which brings a little light into their stolid faces. Some of the least exhausted of them, however, after a brief season of rest and refreshment, must needs be detailed as a night-watch, under the supervision of the *contra-mayorales;* for sparks are still rising from the late scene of conflagration, and may be wafted into neighboring canefields.

Sweet, after this exciting day, is the serenity of the tropical night, with its coronet of stars, its mellow effulgence of moonlight, its breath of coolness and balm. We draw together on the piazza, and rehearse the incidents of the fire, discovering new touches of the comic or the pathetic; or we discuss its origin, wondering whether the incendiary spark fell from the furtive cigar of a slave, transgressing the order not to smoke in the cane, or was flung abroad by the railway engine this morning, as it steamed across a corner of La Bellorita, half a mile distant. And as we talk, the breeze comes to us across the flower-beds of the little front enclosure, and its perfume changes from rose to geranium, from violet to heliotrope, from orange to verbena and mignonette. And our sleep is undisturbed, for the *ingenio* is dark and silent, and nought is heard save the faint, hourly cry of the nightwatch, echoing across distant canefields.

The next morning we ride over to the ruins. Acres upon acres of blackened stalks of cane, with red sparks of fire in them, and slender columns of gray smoke over them; charred frames of carts, and blistered bodies of oxen; heaps of ashes and embers to mark the sites of the *barracon* and hospital, and woe-begone, homeless wretches crawling over them; the huge, black skeleton of the engine grimly overlooking the dingy *débris* of the sugar-house; and in the midst, the white colonnaded mansion staring out, still and ghostly, over the dreary waste!

I am amazed to learn that those prostrate, grimy stalks are still available for a dark, heavy, most inferior quality of sugar, if quickly worked up; and my host has already sent his neighbor an elaborately worded message, which, however, is as full of genuine kindness as of Cuban courtesy, since it places his own sugar-house, and all the accessories, at his immediate disposal.

"It will leave the boilers and vats in such a state that my own sugar will be dingy for days afterward," he says to me, "but there is no telling how soon I may need the same favor, and we planters always do it for each other. I presume that Don Hernandez has his choice of half the *ingenios* in the vicinity. When all is done, his loss will not be less than three hundred thousand dollars."

## CHAPTER XXV.

#### A CAFETAL.

THE eyes of the morning were not yet opened when Chiquita—the pretty, soft-voiced lady's maid of Santa Sofía—stood at my bedside. "The compliments of Don Juan, *señora*, and he kisses your adorable little hands, and throws himself at your beautiful little feet, and would it please you to take an early drive this morning."

Perhaps it would be too much to say that a long sojourn in the United States has taken the fine edge off from Juan's native courtesy, yet certain it is that he would not send those flowers of Spanish rhetoric to an American market. But Chiquita, doubtless, thought the omission accidental rather than deliberate, and so made over his simple message into something more accordant with her own notions of fitness, before she delivered it into my amused ears. There is never any doubt that a Cuban servant will do full justice to the most elaborately complimentary message you choose to send; the chances are that she will "better the instruction."

When our *volante* came to the door, the day had just gotten its eyes open, and its roseate smile brightened the hilltops. At first, our way lay through green levels of dew-gemmed sugar-cane, and was frequently bordered by stately old palms, whose boughs shone and rustled like satin in the sweet, fresh breeze of the tropical morning. I also noticed with interest hedges of aloe,—better known to us as the century plant,—with tall, tree-like stems, from which the crimson or yellow blossoms had lately fallen, rising from them here and there; and I inquired of our old, white-headed *calesero* if it was true that they flowered but once in a hundred years? "I think not, *señora*," he answered, smiling. "I am certain that some of those plants have bloomed twice in my remembrance. Others, to be sure, have not bloomed at all."

The soil of these plantations is noticeably red in color, resembling nothing so much as moist brickdust, but it is exceedingly fertile. The sugar-cane grows to the height of eight or ten feet, and the stalks are thick and succulent. In it we saw negroes and coolies at work, each gang being supervised by a driver—or *contra-mayoral*, as he is termed here,—with a whip in his hand, as a badge of office. Every laborer had a bright, sharp *machete*,—an instrument which is half a sword and half a sickle; two strokes of this stripped the upright stalk of its long leaves, and a third laid it on the ground. They worked silently and swiftly, and the dense, waving cane fell fast before them. After them came ox-carts, with frames in them, which were quickly loaded with the stalks, and driven off to the sugarhouse. The leaves serve as food for the cattle.

On the outskirts of the plantation, dividing the cultivated fields from those where Nature still had everything her own way, we found stone walls, similar in construction to those of New England, but far prettier in general effect; since the Great Mother, being unable to get rid of them, had kindly taken them in hand, and done her best to make them beautiful with rich brown of weather-stains, and soft greenery of mosses, and close-clinging drapery of flowering vines, and a dense border of luxuriant ferns and other accumulated tropical vegetation; among which, growing wild, were many of the plants that we cultivate in gardens at home. In the thickets, I frequently beheld the dreary spectacle of some fine forest tree, strangling in the embrace of the *jaguey-marcho*, the most deadly of parasites. It commences its insidious work indiscriminately among the branches or on the trunk of the tree, and in a few years, the body of its victim is almost, or wholly, covered with a curious, gnarled, twisted, and interlaced overgrowth, varying from an inch to two or three inches in thickness; and its stiff, yellowish green foliage mixes with the richer and more graceful verdure which it is its purpose to destroy. By and by, the throttled tree pales and droops, the trunk seems to heave and strain with a vain effort to burst its fetters, then it slowly withers, dies, and crumbles away; and the miserable parasite is left standing alone, for a time, flaunting its fetid, yellow flowers over the grave of its late companion. But retribution is at hand. At the first touch of the hurricane, sweeping up from the south—the first onset of the tempest marching down from the north—the hollow mockery of a tree falls with a crash, to mingle its ashes with those of its betrayed friend, by whose help it lived its heartless life, and reached its temporary elevation. *El cupey* belongs to the same order as the *jaguey-marcho*, and strongly resembles it in its habits and appearance; but the smaller parasitical plants, of which there are many, are often graceful of form, and beautiful with every hue of blossoms.

We might have spent the entire morning pleasantly in the lanes and avenues of Santa Sofía, had we chosen, so large an area does it cover; but Juan designed to show me a *cafetal;* and after crossing one or two adjacent plantations, we came upon a pleasant tract of hill-country, and were soon in the midst of a sylvan scene that seemed to take the Garden of Eden out of the mists of tradition, and make it a matter of visual experience. The coffee-plant needs to grow under shade; therefore the estate is first planted with whatever fruit and shade trees are most to the owner's taste, and becomes a vast grove of cocoa, tamarind, mango, cedar, guava, plantain, cacao, magnolia, mimosa, guanabana, etc. Under these grows the coffee plant, an evergreen shrub, covered with snowy, fragrant blossoms, greatly similar to the white jessamine, and a round, cherry-like fruit, of changeful hues of green, white, yellow, and red, according to its degree of maturity,—both fruit and flowers being found on the shrub at the same time. It grows naturally to a height of sixteen or eighteen feet, but is kept pruned down to five or six, for greater convenience in picking.

These groves are permeated by shady, winding paths, in which it would be a delight to lose one's self, and divided into regular squares by broad avenues of palms, and narrower alleys of orange, mango, and other beautiful tropical trees. Interspersed everywhere are flowering shrubs and vines,—the oleander, the pomegranate, the allspice, the lemon, the lime, the yellow elder, roses, jessamines, the tree mignonette, the scarlet *penon*, and a hundred others, with blossoms of every hue and odor. The cactus family is largely represented, the most highly prized variety being the night-blooming cereus, which seems an aspiring plant, climbing walls and gateways, and catching hold of the boughs of trees, the better to mount into a region of purer air and clearer light. And everywhere, amid the sunshine and the flowers, are butterflies and humming-birds, and innumerable insects, some changefully gleaming with prismatic tints, others flashing like animated gems.

Thus, it will be seen, the *cafetal* becomes an immense pleasure garden,—full of flowers and fruit—rich canopies of verdure and soft glooms of shade—pleasant, meandering walks—and green archways of interlacing boughs, through which the sunshine seems to drip more goldenly than elsewhere. The Cubans call it "Paradise," and I thought it the loveliest, peacefullest, most sylvan and flowery abode that ever the taste or thrift of man devised for himself. How safe, good, and happy, life ought to be in such a lovely environment! If it is not so, if the weakness and wickedness of human nature are fostered even here, one may as well give over, once for all, waiting for the good time and favorable circumstances which seem so essential to the work of self-amendment, and straightway set about it, in whatever narrow path and meagre outlook are open to him.

In one of the avenues we came upon a dark, middle-aged gentleman, leaning upon a cane, who, recognizing our *volante* and *calesero* as the property of a neighbor and friend, lifted his hat to us, introduced himself as the proprietor of the estate, and besought us to taste of his fruit. A lithe mulatto boy was forthwith set to climbing trees; and the fruits thereof, with the morning-dew still on them, were showered into the *volante;* while our new acquaintance amused himself with preparing various unfamiliar varieties for me to try, and watching the effect. One sort was handed to me with so transparently mischievous a smile, that I was forewarned of evil at once, and took care not to plunge rashly into its acid depths; but a slight flavor thereof sufficed to set all my teeth on edge.

"What can it possibly be used for?" I ask, shuddering.

"The expressed juice often serves in lieu of vinegar, and we make a good preserve of the ripe fruit," is the answer.

My glance goes back to the specimen in my hand, and rests there meditatively. "Can I afford you any further information?" asks the polite Don.

"No—yes—that is, *señor*, I *should* like to know how many sugar-crops are required to sweeten a jar of that preserve!" Whereat he laughs as heartily as a Spaniard ever deigns to laugh.

Nor did the Don's attentions stop here. He introduced us to a pair of flamingoes in a pen,—odd, long-legged and long-necked birds of the crane family, awkward in movement, but of the most beautiful rose-color, shading into white, and not less than four feet high. He gave me a branch of the *Flor de Pascua*, or Easter Flower, with cream-colored, wax-like blossoms, and foliage of bright scarlet. He exhibited a specimen of the *guana*, or lace-tree, the bark of which, when duly soaked in water, is capable of being separated into innumerable webs, of a delicate, mull-like texture, which are embroidered, and used as a substitute for lace. Seeing a chameleon on a tamarind tree near us, he sent the aforesaid mulatto boy in chase of that, and dissertated learnedly upon its habits and changes of color. Finally, he showed us through the coffee-buildings.

The operations of the *cafetal* present nothing of the hard and repulsive features of the *ingenio*. It is simply an easy and beautiful system of horticulture, on a most extensive scale. The labor is chiefly manual, and the profit is derived directly from the culture and products of the soil, without the intervention of costly machinery, or the necessity of much scientific knowledge and skill. There is no occasion for night labor, and the negroes looked altogether heartier and happier than those of the *ingenio*. During the winter months, they are employed in gathering the various and abundant fruits for market, and in tending the coffee-plants. From August to December, the coffee-berries mostly ripen, when they are about the size and general appearance of our red cherries. The coffee-berry, or grain, of commerce, is the *seed* of this fruit; two of which are contained in each berry, having their flat surfaces together, and a sweet, mucilaginous pulp around them. The ripe berries are picked carefully, by hand, in baskets, and spread on *secaderos*, or driers,—certain large, wooden frames, where they are exposed to the sun by day, and protected from the dew by night, for about three weeks, or until they are quite dry and hard. They are next cracked open, and the seed dislodged, by means of a heavy, wooden wheel, moving in a circular trough which is kept filled with the dried fruit. They are then passed through a fanning-mill, which clears them from the dried pulp, and separates the larger grains from the smaller ones, with the help of a wire sieve which allows the latter, with the dirt, to fall through into a receiver, and passes on the former to a different receptacle. The contents of the receiver are then spread out on long tables, at which a company of negroes are seated, who pick out the dirt, and make a separate heap of the broken grains. The coffee is then bagged, and ready for market. Some of the older trees produce a small, well rounded berry, which is reckoned equal to the finest Mocha.

The coffee-culture, however, is fast declining in Cuba, on account of the little encouragement it receives from the Home Government, the successful competition of Brazil and the French Antilles, and the greater profits of sugar-making. Year by year, therefore, these lovely gardens and groves are cleared, and transformed, as far as the nature of the ground will admit, into a vast monotony of sun-steeped cane-fields. For the cane loves sun, not shade, and wherever it appears, the trees fall,—except in the few palm-avenues which are retained for boundaries and roadways, and the shade trees of the *casa de vivienda*.

It was with difficulty that our new friend was constrained to limit his favors to the bestowal of flowers and fruit, and the exhibition of natural curiosities and coffee-buildings. He invited us to take coffee, to take wine, to stay and dine with him, to spend the night, and make a more thorough investigation of the premises; all of which hospitalities we were obliged steadfastly to decline, and set our faces toward Santa Sofía. For, this being my last day in that delightful precinct, I was unwilling to lose so much of the society of its inmates, between whom and myself there had sprung up one of those wayside friendships—rapid in growth as Jonah's gourd, but not necessarily so transitory—which contribute so much to the pleasure of travel. Hitherto, I frankly confess, I had not found the Cuban ladies and myself entirely in harmony; our education, religion, habits of life and thought, were so dissimilar that the maintenance of a certain degree of reserve had seemed a wise precaution against uncomfortable jarring of sentiment. But Doña Angela and I suited to the core of our hearts; nor was this consonance anywise disturbed by her frank avowal of all manner of Spanish prejudice and misconception, nor the many rude Americanisms with which I parried them. She was very severe on our civil war, had a holy horror of "*filibusteros*," and could be especially eloquent about the length of our tax-list.* I predicted the speedy adoption of republican institutions in Spain, the ultimate absorption of Cuba by the United States, and produced my "ticket of disembarkation" and my subsequent "permits" for travel and for residence. She ridiculed the squeamishness of American women, alleging that it was currently reported in Cuba that they never confessed to a pain in any organ lower than the throat, even to their family physician. I retorted that it was as universally believed in the United States that all Cuban ladies smoked. She animadverted upon the flippancy, free manners and flirtations of our young ladies; and I commented on the vacuity and inefficiency of her countrywomen. Privately, how-

---

* It may not be amiss to mention some items of Cuban taxation. There is a poll-tax, an income-tax, a tax upon industry, property, and commerce. All crops pay a per centage. All contracts must be made upon stamped paper, furnished by the government at (if I remember correctly) eight dollars per sheet. Permits, or licenses, must be obtained for opening a school, store, market, place of public amusement or entertainment, for street-vending, for entering a profession, for building or repairing, for changing residence (whether from house to house, or town to town), for giving a party, for keeping a carriage, for hiring out a slave, for issuing a paper or pamphlet, and for travelling in the island, and a passport must be obtained for leaving it,—any failure to obtain which permits is punishable by a fine. Less than half the revenue thus obtained is required for the governmental expenses of the island, the remainder is remitted to the Home Government. No wonder that Cuba has received the expressive, if inelegant, nickname of "*La vaca de leche de España*"—the milch cow of Spain!

ever, I more than half concurred with Doña Angela in her last stricture. Not that I would willingly see the rigid Cuban code of propriety adopted in my own land, since a little more freedom of action is quite compatible with true delicacy; and fosters, moreover, that courage and self-reliance which may be purity's best safeguards. But it must be acknowledged that, in our society, the liberty of young people is fast degenerating into a license that must needs be as pernicious in its effects, as it is unlovely in its manifestations. Very few American girls, nowadays, possess that tender grace of budding womanhood, folded about with soft veilings of gentle humility and maidenly reserve, which is, nevertheless, girlhood's most potent charm.

We returned to Santa Sofía by a different road, taking in our way several small farms, variously termed *vegas, potreros, sitios, estancias,* and *fincas,* according as they made a specialty of tobacco, cattle, fruits, and vegetables, or bees. The houses were generally rude in make and material, though sometimes roomy, and with numerous outbuildings; the most usual pattern being a rough construction of bamboo poles, sided with palm-boards and thatched with palm-leaves, consisting of a living-room and a sleeping-room or two, all on one floor; connected with which, by a simple roof, was a small kitchen. Here we saw the *guajiro,* or countryman, at home. He was at once simple and astute, active and lazy, brave and boastful, superstitious and irreligious, domestic and vagabond. He did no regular work, but divided his time about equally between overseeing the handful of negroes, or other laborers, employed on his place, and in gambling, cock-fighting, and loafing. He was not unintelligent, at least, as regarded his own business; and he had the innate Cuban courtesy of manner. He gladly showed us all that we cared to see, politely answered our questions, and did not suffer us to depart without a pressing invitation to take coffee—the universal Cuban beverage.

# CHAPTER XXVI.

### BEMBA AND LIMONAR.

ON the following morning the *volante* was at the door at daybreak, and I took leave of Santa Sofía with genuine regret, knowing that henceforth it was lost from my actual life, however greenly its memories might cling to my heart. We were to return to Matanzas by a different route, and a drive of three or four miles brought us to Bemba, a small town where we were to take the cars. The train had not arrived when we alighted at the depot,—a most uninviting spot for even a temporary sojourn. So dismissing the *calesero*, we began, with our restless American habit, to promenade up and down the principal street, followed by the gaze of half the population. Nothing more unlike an American town can well be imagined. It consisted of two or three narrow streets, irregularly paved with small round stones, and bordered by rows of contiguous houses, of different heights and dates, but all run in the inevitable one-storied, massive-walled, red-tiled mould; and all apparently of an antiquity that might be called venerable, but which was possibly owing as much to the ageing influences of the climate as to the lapse of years. Their interiors were correspondingly shabby and dingy, with the usual paucity of furniture, and looked as if they might have been inhabited by a long succession of unthrifty generations. Turning a corner, we found a row of still poorer houses, very coarsely and clumsily built, and stuck so close together as to give a dismal impression of a sombre, stifled, festering, unwholesome atmosphere for the occupants. This fashion of paving village streets, and building village houses in such close proximity, shuts out every rural charm,— all those soft depths of verdure and shade, and pleasant mosaics of grass-plot and garden, which make a New England village so picturesque an object. Not a tree, nor shrub, nor blade of grass, brightened the scene; and the sky was merely a narrow, shimmering strip overhead.

The town was so small that I had twice traversed its entire length, within a few minutes; passing each time a little coffee-house, whose stone floor joined the street pavement, and whose small round tables encroached upon that narrow pathway to an inconvenient extent. At one of these sat a handsome, portly gentleman, with a cheerful twinkle in his eye; whose table service narrowly escaped being swept off by my garments at every turn. On my third appearance this personage rose, bowed low, and said, with inimitable grace of phrase and manner, "As there was yet some time before the train was due, and the village offered little to interest strangers, and the sun was exceeding hot, perhaps we would do him the honor to take a cup of coffee with him, while we waited. Otherwise" (auother low bow) "his unhappy table must beg pardon for being so much in our way."

It was good to find so fair a flower of the generous, old-time hospitality springing up in the midst of the selfish modern civilization, and I could not find it in my heart to leave it unplucked. So I nodded to Juan, and we sat down opposite the courtly stranger, in the narrow street of the quaint little town, and partook of his coffee and rolls, and listened to his humorous, meandering talk, and answered his questions about those United States which he had always meant to visit for himself, but would never now behold, it was plain to see. For the sluggish spell of the fervid Cuban sky was strong upon him, and he would dream away his life in that quiet, queer old town, brightening its memory to strangers with the amaranthine flower of an unsurpassed and unsurpassable courtesy, knowing nothing of the outside world save what the train and the newspaper brought him, and wondering, by and by, when it was that he grew so old!

We also made a brief stop at the little village of Limonar, highly recommended to invalids as a place of residence for the spring months, on account of its pure and invigorating air. It lies in the midst of a gently undulating and deeply fertile country, with here and there a wooded hill, and on one side, a blue chain of mountains. Its outward aspect is that of all Cuban villages,—a small *plaza*, planted with palms, a church, two or three *posadas*, or inns, a few shops, and a cluster of red-tiled roofs. Its inhabitants seemed very idle in the warm, summery day, they were seated at their open doors and windows, or gathered in little groups on the sidewalks, leisurely chatting together, and coolly observant of the passing stranger. It was all very dreamy, and very picturesque,—the idle groups, the little *plaza* steeped in warmth and languor, the distant mountains wrapped in slumbrous folds of haze, and, on the green, breeze-kissed hillsides, the plumy cocoa-nut trees rocking themselves to sleep.

I saw nothing worth noting, in the matter of scenery, on my homeward journey; there was only the old material of hills and valleys, palms, ceibas and cane-fields, kaleidoscopically wrought into new pictures, which one would never tire of gazing upon, but which may well become wearisome in my feeble sketches. But I did find an order of beings in those cars, that, to my long unwonted eyes, seemed now to be seen for the first time. Certain commercial agents, from the United States, were on board, making a tour of the plantations, with designs upon the forthcoming sugar crops. Their figures did not appear to advantage, drawn in strong light and shade on a background of grave Spanish courteousness and dignity. They put their feet on the seats, they yawned and stretched, they roamed restlessly up and down the passage way, they shouted bad witticisms to each other from opposite ends of the cars, they badgered the conductor, and they smoked as vigorously as the Spaniards, but with far greater and more reckless expenditure of saliva. They seemed to have left all the decent restraints of life at home, to roam lawlessly among a people whereof the ceremonious politeness has passed into a proverb. Yet·no doubt any one of them would have resigned his seat to me instantly, if the cars had been crowded, and taken it quite as a matter of course, if I had omitted to say "thank you." Verily, we are at once the worst and the best mannered people in the world!

And once again I was startled to find how things once familiar had grown strange to me. On a little elevation near the railway, with a barren monotony of low, wild shrubbery around it, stood one of those brown-painted, many-windowed, ornate villas, which are growing up everywhere in my own country, but of which there is not, I presume, another specimen in all Cuba. I used to think them pretty, and should find them so still, doubtless, in surroundings better adapted to them; but beside the grand, simple sweep of the tropical landscape, the toy-like dwelling was insufferably petty and finical. I comprehended, then, that architecture must necessarily be a growth and not a creation, and that every style has some subtle relation to the climate where it was born, and does not bear transplanting. The straight, simple lines, broad colonnades, and massive cornice of Santa Sofía came back to me now as the ideal perfection of a Cuban dwelling, though I had not thought of it before.

By and by, the lofty head of the *Monte del Pan* rose over the hill ranges, and welcomed me back to Matanzas; which was all the more homelike that I had lived there long enough to get a little tired of it before

I went away. I suspect that much of the charm of home and friends is due to this same placid wontedness, verging on tedium; without it there may be gayety, excitement, tumultuous alternations of exhilaration and depression, but no tranquil, peaceful happiness, "flowing like a river." Certain it is that the four walls of my little room, of which I had grown immensely weary before I left them, now took on the most genial, comfortable, restful aspect, making me feel and say from my heart, "How good it is to be at home!"

## CHAPTER XXVII.

### SHADOW.

THOUGH Cuba is justly called a paradise, yet it is an earthly one, and subject to earthly conditions. Disease and death have their sombre part in its life. And, for a brief space, I came just enough within their shadow to be able to acquaint my readers with some peculiarities of Cuban sick-rooms and Cuban funerals,—though not enough to make the task difficult, by reason of recollections personally painful.

I should have said, at the end of the last chapter, that I did not enter those four familiar walls without some difficulty. The arrival of our *volante* before the Sámano threshold being duly announced within, Doña Coloma appeared in the door, with a welcoming smile, but a warning gesture. There was sickness in the house, she said. Dolorita had been seized with doubtful symptoms two days before; the nature of her disease was still uncertain. But the rest of the children had been sent to their grandmother, until further developments. Nor must I be exposed to danger. Her mother would be happy to receive me also. So would her sister Lolita. Both had placed their houses unreservedly at my disposal. I had but to choose, and let the *volante* convey me forthwith to the preferred haven.

"What is the disease supposed to be?" I asked, going straight at the point hidden under all this careful discourse.

Evidently Doña Coloma found it hard to put her fear into plain words. She could not tell—she hoped—it might be nothing serious—but—there had been a case of small-pox next door—and—

"Is that all?" I responded, cheerfully. "Then, if you do not absolutely shut your doors against me, I shall come in. Did we all pass unhurt and undismayed through the small-pox epidemic of two months ago, to run away from a sporadic case or two, now?"

The *señora's* face brightened visibly. Courage is contagious, as well as fear. Nevertheless, the atmosphere of the house was far from cheerful. Dolorita was quarantined at the farther end of one of the wings. The servants moved about stealthily, with panic-shadowed faces. There was an unnatural silence and orderliness throughout the large rooms and long galleries—no scurrying to and fro of children's feet, no shouting and laughter, no litter of play-things. Especially did I miss Odila's comical pranks and wild flow of spirits.

At dusk, the doctor made one of his semi-daily visits. Watching him closely, it struck me that he did not look like a man in doubt, nor one burdened with a disagreeable certainty, though he still declined to speak positively with regard to the disease. But he might have reasons of his own for keeping others in suspense. In a house of so many inmates, a certain degree of anxiety and dread was, no doubt, conducive to the quiet and regularity of the sick-room. And, in the confidence thus inspired, I ventured to pay it a visit.

But, upon my first glance at the patient, I half repented of my temerity. Certainly, nothing but small-pox could be answerable for a skin like that! Always very dark of complexion, Dolorita was now a perfect little blackamoor. Her small countenance was positively elfish in its dinginess and its sharpness. This effect was enhanced by a large blue cotton handkerchief wound round her head, turban-fashion. "What for?" I could not help asking. "To keep her from taking cold," responded her mother. A most unnecessary precaution, it seemed to me, with the thermometer ranging from eighty-four to ninety!

Observing the dingy face more narrowly, I was somewhat reassured to notice that it still had a very natural expression—Dolorita's own habitual self-complacence, rather intensified than otherwise under the favorable influences consequent upon being the centre of interest,—a position always congenial to the tastes of the little maiden. She responded to my polite inquiries in a tone wherein a certain satisfaction was so thinly masked by a doleful whine, that I was made tolerably easy about her, at once. It was plain that her situation was neither so dangerous nor so painful but that she was able to extract a considerable degree of enjoyment from it. And, gradually, a suspicion arose within me that the duskiness of her complexion was possibly owing to another cause than disease, that a plentiful application of soap and water would produce a more magical effect than was ever wrought by the artfullest cosmetic. As delicately as might be, I ventured to hint this possibility to her mother. She replied, composedly, that Dolorita was, without doubt, frightfully dirty; but, inasmuch as she had a little fever, it was impossible to wash her with water; and as she had an insurmountable antipathy to *aguardiente* (cane-rum), and would not allow them to touch her with it, there was nothing to be done but to let her go unwashed till the fever left her!

This dread of water, and the belief in the necessity of bundling up a patient's head, seem to be common to all Cuban nurses. A medicamental peculiarity is the free use of olive oil and garlic, both in professional and domestic practice. A favorite article of sick-diet is a certain *sopa de pan*, prepared by laying a slice of bread (toasted or not, at discretion) in a deep plate, breaking a raw egg upon it, and pouring a weak beef or chicken broth, boiling hot, over the whole. I remember nothing else that was noteworthy in the regimen of the sick-room.

At breakfast, next morning, considerable excitement was caused by the sudden appearance of Odila, somewhat scantily clad in a chemise and an apron. The news of my return being the one drop too much in the poor child's cup of homesickness, she had eluded the vigilance of grandmother and nurse, snatched the nearest garments, and made the best of her way home. She now threw herself upon my neck in a kind of insane rapture, showered me with kisses, choked me with hugs, and finally fell to chewing my hair, by way of outlet to her overflowing gladness. From this whimsical occupation she was torn, perforce, by Atanasia, and, despite her frantic struggles and puny wrath, dragged back to exile.

However, it was soon over. That very afternoon, the doctor favored us with his professional conclusions. Dolorita had been threatened with a fever, but it had gracefully yielded to timely and efficient remedies. There was no longer any cause for apprehension. Thus the shadow—never very deep, except for the possibilities that seemed to lurk within it—was lifted from our dwelling.

Scarce a week after, a near neighbor and familiar friend died suddenly, of apoplexy. Immediately Doña Coloma sent a message of condolence to the afflicted family, placed a man-servant at their disposal, and offered her own assistance in the preparation of mourning garments,—the latter friendly office being of special avail in a country where the interval between death and interment seldom exceeds twenty-four hours. Her offer being gratefully accepted, she straightway set to work upon certain black material sent her, and scarce intermitted her labors till the time of the funeral.

Meanwhile the corpse was laid in state. A platform, covered with black cloth, was erected in the middle of the *sala*, upon which the coffin was placed, resting upon three large cushions. Around this platform were twelve candlesticks, not less than five or six feet high, containing lighted wax candles of about the same height; and between these, were smaller ones,—all of which were to be kept burning until the removal of the corpse. The walls, doors, and windows, were lugubriously draped with black; as was also an adjoining room, for the use of the mourners. A guard of honor kept watch over the corpse, composed of servants in livery, furnished by friends and neighbors; to which, as aforementioned, Doña Coloma had contributed her quota. The final effect of these arrangements was both sombre and imposing.

At night, it being supposed that the grief of the near relatives was too acute to admit of sleep, many of the friends of the family, both male and female, joined them, to form a *velada*,—a word corresponding very nearly, in this sense, to the Irish " wake." At midnight, a supper was served; at which time, the gathering might almost have been mistaken for a pleasure-party. On the following day, too, just before the funeral, a dinner was provided for all present who cared to partake of it.

At two o'clock, P.M., the funeral rites began with the recital of prayers, three or four priests being present, each of whom would receive a fee for his trouble. The procession was then formed: the priests led the way, on foot, and in their robes, followed by three acolyths bearing long silver rods surmounted by crosses and lighted tapers; next, came the hearse, with glass sides and top, surrounded by the aforesaid guard of honor; then a long double file of the male friends and acquaintances of the deceased; and after them, their own empty *volantes* and carriages, and as many others as had been sent for the purpose, making a long line of unoccupied vehicles and liveried coachmen. No females joined in the procession,—neither did the nearest male relatives of the deceased,—to do so would be deemed inconsistent with their grief. All persons in the streets stopped and lifted their hats, as the procession passed.

At the cathedral, there were more candles and more prayers, a responsory was sung, and the coffin was sprinkled with holy water. The procession then moved to the *Campo Santo* (literally, "holy ground"—otherwise, cemetery)—a barren and repulsive spot enough. It is surrounded by high walls, and traversed by others, all eight or ten feet thick, and honeycombed with row upon row of niches for the reception of coffins,—some open, some closed with marble slabs bearing the name, date of death, etc., of the occupant. The open ground between the walls is filled by the graves of the humbler classes, all level with the ground, and marked by a small horizontal slab;—here also are a few family vaults. There is no ostentation, neither is there any beauty;—the whole is hard, bare, cheerless.

The coffin, which we have followed thus far, was deposited in one of the above-named niches, during the recital of prayers; and the opening was closed. The members of the funeral suite then entered their carriages, and drove back to the desolate dwelling. Here, the *sala* had been cleared of the funeral apparatus, and filled with rows of chairs, in one of which rows sat the bereaved family. The returned suite took seats, and remained in profound silence for about half an hour. Then, one by one, they rose, shook hands with the mourners, and took their leave. Other visits of condolence filled up the day.

One of these was made by Doña Coloma, in the evening. Left at home, alone, I turned to the piano for amusement. Very soon, Francisca appeared, with an extremely troubled face. Being asked the cause thereof, she found courage to inform me, with many excuses and much begging of pardon, that Doña Coloma would be greatly distressed to have the sound of a piano heard in the house, so soon after the funeral of an acquaintance. Of course, I closed the instrument at once, and thus it remained until the following Sunday, when Dolorita broke the spell of silence by a spirited waltz.

It is scarcely necessary to say, after this, that the customs of mourning are very strict. Black garments are scrupulously worn, society is eschewed, and the windows of the bereaved house, opening on the street, are kept closed—or partially so, at least—for six months.

## CHAPTER XXVIII.

#### WAITING IN HAVANA.

THUS far, my story's movement has been progressive, now it takes a backward curve. And there is a certain sadness always inseparable from return. Onward—ever onward—is the rule of life, and to turn back on the old paths to the old places and the old pursuits, seems, at the first glance, to involve some corresponding inward retrogradation. Not till the return is consummated do we learn (and sadly still!) that the soul never goes back to the old standpoint, nor the mind to the cast-off habit of thought. Nor are the places and the faces to which we recur ever quite the same. Time has carried them along also; and so we come to understand, finally, that whichever way our footsteps turn, according to human vision and nomenclature, we are ever going forward. Life has no absolute retrograde.

I did not know how many rootlets I had sent down into the kindly soil of Matanzas, till the time of leave-taking came. Although its name is of dismal import enough—meaning literally "The place of slaughter," and earned honestly by a wholesale massacre of the crew of a Spanish ship by the Indians, in the time of Diego Velasquez—it had been a place of renewing of life to me. And I had gratefully learned it by heart. Few of its inhabitants, I fancied, knew more of its ins and outs than I did. Day after day I had traversed its narrow streets, its bay-kissed *paseo*, its flower-embroidered *plaza;* and, evening after evening, I had watched the twilight-gray creep up the Cumbre, and the stars smile down into the clear depths of the rivers San Juan and Yumurí. I was familiar with the gay little shops and queer old houses of Versailles, and the narrow crowded life and shabby, evil-odored dwellings of Puebla Nueva. I had had nothing to do with its work-a-day life, and little enough with its social one; my business and pleasure had been chiefly to observe; and I had done that so thoroughly *con amore*, that the things upon which I had looked so long seemed to have become a part of me, and separation was difficult and painful. Some of the roots came up slowly, with the earth still clinging to them; others broke off short, with a wrench; a few refused to do either, and subjected their tough and elastic fibre to the strain of a voyage over the sea, and the long tension, and possible attenuation and decay, of a term of slow-rolling years. Nevertheless, I realized that this indestructible tendency of the human heart to send forth roots and tendrils, wherever it is transplanted, is a comfortable endowment. For Life separates friends and exiles patriots. And what were the stress of homesickness, if the affections had no inalienable faculty of continuous reproduction and growth!

We left Matanzas at ten o'clock, A.M. We have it on the authority of Rob Roy McGregor that no wise man returns by the same road he came, provided another be open to him; and although we have not the same excellent reasons for preferring a different route as the Scotch freebooter (who doubtless found inconvenient reckonings to settle on any twice-trod path), there is a deep philosophy in his maxim to which we are not insensible. So we take the nearer and shorter route to Havana, by Regla. The road is not so picturesque as the other, nor yet wholly devoid of interest. Everywhere there is a wide, unwavering level of flower-paven valley, or silent, sun-parched plain, stretching away to a rugged outline of distant hills, on which the blue arch of the sky rests tremulously. And such a blue! the delicate depths of which seem evermore opening before our fascinated gaze, until we are ready to believe that, if we could only look long enough, and purely enough, we might behold the jasper foundations and pearly gates of the heavenly city.

The railroad was as straight as a bird's homeward flight, involving no triumphs of engineering skill in its construction. Looking from the rear car, we saw two lines of rail run back, perfectly straight and level, for miles, until they met in the distant vanishing point of the perspective. Only once did we pass through any considerable cutting; but that keeps fast hold of my memory in virtue of the profusion of delicate ferns that clung to every nook and cleft of its rough sides,—the loveliest, I thought, in the fleeting glimpse I had of them, that I had ever seen. And since it was impossible to subject them to the disenchantment of actual touch and inspection, they are still preserved in the intangible and ineffaceable beauty of a passing, poetic vision.

Regla, the terminus of the railway, is a quaint, slovenly suburb of Havana, on the opposite bank of the harbor. Passing through it, we saw a swift panorama of ill-paven streets, and shabby, old houses, with a picturesque chronology of stain and patch on their stuccoed walls; and through their open doorways we caught glimpses of half-naked children rolling on the stone floors, gambolling and quarrelling, and of untidy mothers, lolling in rocking-chairs. Its chief objects of interest are found on the water-front,—certain immense warehouses of stone and iron, for the storage of sugar, molasses, coffee, etc. They are built in a continuous range, fifty-eight in number, with a depth of over three hundred feet. A statue of their designer, an enterprising Cuban, Don Eduardo Fesser by name, is one of the chief ornaments of the place.

We crossed from Regla to Havana by a steam ferry. On the landing we were beset by a band of brigands (commonly termed "hackmen"), one of whom succeeded in forcing us into a nondescript vehicle, yclept a "victoria," tumbled my trunks upon the box, climbed atop of them, and rattled off at a reckless rate to a building that looked like a stronghold of the Middle Ages, but was really the "Hotel Santa Ysabel," once the residence of a Spanish nobleman. The street-front was penetrated by a heavy archway, leading to a central court. It was impossible not to notice the thickness of the walls, and the care taken to render the place inaccessible from the street. The stout folding doors at the entrance looked fitter for a fortress than a peaceable dwelling, and the windows were defended by thick iron bars.

The court had been roofed over and made to serve as a public dining-room. It was filled with small tables, and in its centre was a pretty piece of rock-work, with ferns and flowers growing out of it, and jets of water falling into a basin, where I caught the glancing gleams of gold-fish. The rooms on the ground-floor, opening on the court, were used for storerooms and offices. On the right of the entrance, a broad stone staircase led to the second floor. A large parlor extended across the front, with a balcony overhanging the street. A gallery ran around the court, upon which the sleeping-rooms opened. These were originally spacious, but had each been divided, to suit hotel purposes, into four small rooms, by partitions eight or nine feet high; so that the occupants of contiguous rooms could not avoid hearing each other's movements and conversation. It mattered little now, however, as the hotel was well-nigh deserted. Yellow fever had appeared in the city two weeks before, and was followed by the usual stampede of foreigners.

No bells, but, in lieu thereof, the privilege of leaning over the gallery rails and shouting, "*Criado!*" "*muchacho!*" or anything you like, until somebody comes. Doing this, I evoke from the depth below a certain idiotic negro, who tells me he is called "Pablo," but whom I shall denominate "Stupido," out of respect to the Apostle to the Gentiles, and a preference for giving things their right names. I explain to him, with great circumstantiality, to prevent mistakes, that I want my small trunk brought immediately to my room, and the large one stored until my departure. After a long interval, there is great confusion and turmoil in the gallery,—a sound of thumping, and scratching, and scraping, that seems to threaten the speedy demolition of something,— and looking out, I discover my ark of a travelling trunk slowly approaching on Stupido's head; albeit doing its best to meet its owner's wishes by thrusting a corner into every doorway, and catching on every projection. I confront the bearer and reiterate my directions. The trunk retrogrades; but in course of time I hear it advancing up the opposite gallery, in the same unwilling manner. I bar the passage, and request to know what is to be done with it now. Stupido opines that if the *señora* does not want it, the *señor* must, and is taking it to Juan's room. "Put it in the baggage room," I repeat. "But, *señora*, there is no baggage room." "Put it where you like then," I exclaim, in a rage, "but do not let me see it above stairs again, or you'll not get so much as a *media* for your trouble." The trunk wheels about, and recedes. Ten minutes later, Stupido brings me an unknown valise. I remand that, and the right thing comes at last,—chiefly, I suspect, because there is nothing else to bring.

On the broad landing, at the head of the grand staircase, a Spanish Don is reading the "Diario," with that air of owning, not only the hotel and the city, but the whole island, and a considerable part of the universe besides, which is characteristic of most of the "*peninsulanos*" (natives of Old Spain) in Cuba. His wife is in the parlor,—"fat and forty," certainly,—but not the most inveterately idealistic mind could think her "fair." Her son Pepito, a little man of four or five years of age, and of preternatural grimness and gravity of aspect, prowls about with one corner of his small "*capa*" thrown over his shoulder, after the manner of the traditional stage-bandit, and with the air of being continually on the watch for a foe. These, and a half-dozen commercial agents, make up the sum total of the hotel's guests.

The Doña intermits her contemplation of the opposite wall, on my entrance, and enters languidly into conversation. She thinks the Americans a charming people, but confesses that the spectacle of their activity and energy is almost too much for her nerves. She reports the hotel intolerably dull, and emphasizes the statement with a yawn. She complains that Stupido is seldom in the way of her orders, and systematically misunderstands them, when he is. Finally, she discovers that Pepito has slipped out, and is moved to utter a Jeremiade on his account. "That child," she says dolefully, "has the most incredible faculty for getting into mischief; he keeps my nerves continually on the stretch. If you should encounter him on your way, will you do me the inestimable favor to send him back?"

At the farther end of the gallery a bedroom door is suddenly flung open, Pepito is somehow ejected, a momentary vision of a wrathful hand and boot appears on the threshold, and the door closes with a bang. Seeing me on the scene, Pepito heroically resists his inclination to cry, picks himself up, folds his *capa* majestically around him, and makes a dignified retreat. Soon after, a smothered sound of sobs and cries attests that he has found his mother's bosom, and given a natural vent to his wounded feelings.

There was as yet no sign of the American steamer which was to bear me and my fortunes from Cuba, nor for the two following days; meanwhile, we killed time by visiting such places of interest as we had not seen before, or desired to see again. The weather was fearfully hot; nevertheless, we sturdily adventured through the close streets and fervid sunshine, in the face of much good-natured remonstrance from people who believe that all Americans who put foot out of doors before four o'clock, at this season, deliberately offer themselves as candidates for the yellow fever. We spent hours among the exuberant verdure and brilliant bloom of the Botanic Garden,—steadily declining, however, to make any acquaintance with the stiff, unwieldly Latin names, whereby the gardener would have introduced them to us,—and noting how difficult it is to keep tropical nature pruned and trimmed to any semblance of order. We painfully toiled up the winding stair of the Cathedral's bell-tower, and deciphered the dates and legends of the bells; one of which is hundreds of years old, and as divinely sweet of tone as if it had continually fed and ripened on the echoes of its own melody. We invaded the quarters of the bell-ringer, opening on the leads, and with a magnificent outlook over city and bay—a delightful *sanctum* for a bookish man or woman,—and found that personage employing his leisure, and eking out his income, with the manufacture of cigars. We descried the mural tablet at the corner of the "*Calle del Obispo*," and learned that, just one hundred years ago, Doña Maria Cepero, daughter of the then Governor, was killed by the accidental discharge of a gun, while kneeling at her devotions near this spot,—a record from which the lapse of a century had stolen all the sadness, and made it read like a song of triumph. We stormed the Morro with the magic words "An American lady who desires to see the interior," were admitted without the required official permit, and introduced to a dozen huge guns, collectively known as the "Twelve Apostles," and individually as "*San Matéo*," "*San Marcos*," "*San Lucas*," etc.; also to much solid, Cyclopean masonry; also to the view of city, shipping, and ocean, from the parapet; also to the quarters of the garrison, cool as a cave (and almost as dark), by reason of the thickness of the walls; also to "The Lantern," a little room where the signals, flags, telescopes, etc., are kept, and just above which is the beacon, visible forty miles at sea. Here, an official in shoulder straps, with a cigar in his mouth, graciously exhibited what little there was to be seen; but his eyes nearly jumped out of his head when he saw me take out my note-book. "Do you know what you are doing?" said he. "All writing and sketching are strictly forbidden in and about the Morro, on pain of fine and imprisonment." Finally, we climbed the long slope to the *Cabaña* fortress, where we saw more masonry, more guns, more soldiers, and more views. This is the great stronghold of the island, and is said to be one of the finest fortifications in the world. The officer of the guard obligingly furnished us with an intelligent guide, who showed us through quarters, barracks, storehouses, casemates, and water-batteries, made us note the exceeding thickness of the walls, pointed out the many fine views from the parapets, informed us that the fortification was completed in 1771, at a cost of forty millions,— in those days an incredible sum,—and related an anecdote in point. Charles III., being then king of Spain, no sooner received the report of this enormous expenditure, than he seized a spy-glass, and began to scan the western horizon. "May I ask what your Majesty is looking for?" inquired his wondering minister. "For the *Cabañas*," quietly replied the monarch;—"if it cost as much as that, it ought to be large enough to be seen at any distance."

Then we proceeded to the "*Universidad de Belen*," formerly a Franciscan monastery, but since 1854 the Royal College of Havana, under the direction of the "Society of Jesus." It is a fine group of buildings, in the form of a hollow square, built of tawny yellow stone. The inmates consist of a rector, sixty or seventy clerical and lay brethren, and above three hundred pupils. The entire labor of the institution is performed by the brethren,—from the celebration of a mass in the chapel and the giving of instruction in the scientific and classic departments, down to the cooking of food and the sweeping of corridors. One of them acted as guide. He was a dark, slight, low-voiced man, speaking English fluently, with an aspect of gentle scholarliness, and refined, courteous manners. His head was shaven, and fringed with short, black hair, and he was habited in the dress of the order,—a long cassock of coarse black cloth, with a cape, buttoned close to the throat, and not a line of white about it anywhere;—all of which produced a singularly illusive and spectral effect, making me feel, while conversing with him, that I was talking across a gulf not less wide than the one which divides our age from that of Ignatius Loyola.

First, he showed us the Cabinet of Natural History, containing collections of minerals, shells, fossils, birds, insects, native woods, coins, etc., etc.; apologizing—very unnecessarily—for their incompleteness, on the score of their comparative youth. For there was much more of them than my receptivity could take in and assimilate, in the short examination we gave them; and I felt so fearfully overgorged at the end, as to excite a profound pity for visitors to the cabinets and museums of the twentieth century. It is to be hoped that the working of the inevitable law of decay may clear out some of the rubbish, even from these cherished accumulations, and so lighten their labor! Then he led us solemnly through the library, the books being all under lock and key,—a discreet measure, I concluded, to prevent the minds of the younger brethren from going astray among such profane authors as Voltaire, Rousseau, Boccacio, and Byron, whose names I saw on the imprisoned volumes. Next, we inspected the laboratory, the observatory, and the philosophic apparatus; and our guide lingered over the exhibition of a fine telescope with a kind of fatherly tenderness, indicative of great familiarity with its use. So I said to him, out of pure mischief, desiring to see if the settled gravity of his face was altogether imperturbable,—" I forget, just now, whether the Jesuits had anything to do with the sentence and imprisonment of Galileo ?"

"My memory is much too modest to presume to prompt yours," he answered, with a keen glance, an amused quiver of the corners of the mouth, and a bow so much better suited to the court of Louis Fourteenth than to the bare scientific sanctum of a Jesuit College, that it silenced me forthwith.

Then we examined the dormitories,—a vast and lofty hall, divided by low partitions into spaces just large enough to admit an iron bedstead, a chair, and a table. The whole place might have been the headquarters of the fairy Order for neatness and regularity; but there was also a bareness and rigidity about it which spoke powerfully of the severity and asceticism of a monastic institution. Finally, we saw the chapel. It is not large, has an open floor of marble, a gallery, a small organ, a high altar of colored marbles, decorated with flowers, images, crosses, and relics, and a smaller altar in the sacristy behind, where an undying lamp burns before the place where the Host is kept. In the vestry, we were shown some gorgeous priestly vestments, adorned with jewels. The lace on one of these is said to have cost three

13

thousand dollars, and was the gift of a Spanish lady of rank.

Toward sunset, we drove on the *Paseo de Tacon*, and found the same stream of *volantes* and black eyes and gay dresses flowing through it, that was described in an early chapter. At least, if not made up of the same individual waves, there was precisely the same general form of flood. The spectacle was too familiar to have any potent attraction for us, so we extended our drive beyond it, to a little eminence where we could look out upon the ocean, over a sunset-reddened plain, sprinkled with the soft glooms and columnar trunks of palm-trees. Forgive me if my eyes and my imagination linger among them. For the palm is the concrete tropic, and the essence of the Orient. Over it the sky has a bluer depth and more velvet softness than elsewhere; under it waters lapse more dreamily musical. All the sweet old Bible pictures have it for a back-ground; and wherever it grows, Cleopatra, and Memnon, and the Nile, seem not afar off. Moreover, it is the symbol of peace—that gentle gift of God which, when we have tried love and joy, and found them wanting, solaces our aching hearts, and leads us up to the very gate of Heaven.

Furthermore, Humboldt, whose authority is final in such matters, names the palm the "crown of the vegetable creation." On the island of Cuba alone, there are over sixty varieties; furnishing fruit, wine, oil, thatch, drinking-cups, hats, fans, firewood, and fibre for coarse cloth and matting, to the inhabitants; and, I doubt not, a hundred other uses lie dormant in their stately trunks and graceful boughs, waiting for a more enterprising race to find them out.

We devoted the following day to getting an idea of the suburbs of Havana. Marinao is a pretty, airy village, much resorted to by the wealthy *Habaneros*, during the summer months. It has a close-built main street, with the usual variety of shops, inns, and restaurants; it has several pleasant, bowery lanes, and many handsome country seats, half-hidden in tropical foliage and flowers; and it has a palmy hill-top, commanding a fine view of the adjacent country, the spires of Havana, and the blue sea. It has also a somewhat dilapidated mineral spring, around which we found a nondescript crowd of water-carriers, filling small casks with its cool, but not overclear, flow, to supply their customers in the village.

Puentes Grandes is about halfway between Havana and Marinao, and, though considerably smaller, greatly resembles the latter place in character.

Guanabacoa, on the eastern side of the bay, is one of the oldest towns on the island, and is proportionably solid, squalid, and antiquated. Its population numbers eight thousand, it has a cathedral (so called), a convent, two markets, a *plaza*, and a queer old cemetery and church. Its chief attraction is found, however, in the mineral baths of Santa Rita, which enjoy a high reputation for curative power in various nervous and bilious disorders. The buildings are of stone, with tiled floors and stone basins, are tolerably well arranged, and are kept in good order. A noticeable feature, to a foreigner, is the number of shrines, appropriately decorated with images and flowers, prepared for the devotions and offerings of the patients.

In all these towns, and particularly in ancient Guanabacoa, I saw much that would delight the soul of an artist, — quaint balconied windows, — odd, lumbering doors, — bowed and crumbling cornices, lintels, and door-posts, — a great deal of picturesque dirt, in the shape of richly embrowned and blackened walls, beautifully besmooched roofs, and grimy interiors, — also, a sparkling stream, a rustic bridge, a winding, shady path, — and everywhere, palms! But I had only a little time to look at these things, and none at all to describe them; for which, the reader, remembering that most of them (or something similar) have already appeared in these pages, will not forget to be grateful.

## CHAPTER XXIX.

#### DEPARTURE.

EARLY the next morning, the arrival of the American steamer was reported; and indubitable evidence thereof was to be found in the parlor, 'in the persons of two lively ladies in round hats and short dresses, and with a general air of capability and self-reliance that has no place among the belongings of a *Cubanera.* My heart warmed to the sight,—I had not seen a countrywoman's face for months,—straightway I went and introduced myself to them. I was received most kindly, and we were presently in possession of such facts, relative to each other's history and destination, as were necessary to a good understanding and pleasant intercourse. My countrywomen were on their way to New Orleans, and had taken advantage of the steamer's touching at Havana to snatch a glimpse of a foreign country and foreign ways. Already they had explored half the city, on foot and unattended, and had accomplished a wonderful amount of shopping. "How ever did you manage it," I asked, seeing that Spanish was an unknown tongue to them.

"We pointed to the goods that we wanted," replied one, "and held out our purses to the shopman. He counted out the price if it was too much, we shook our heads, and took back our money. If it was reasonable, we nodded, and he kept the money and wrapped up the goods."

Strange to say, they had not been cheated; but whether it was due to their own sharpness, or to the shopkeeper's pity for their apparent helplessness, is more than I can tell. In the streets, they had met with less consideration. "I have heard a deal about Spanish courtesy, but I believe it is all a fable," said one of them, indignantly. "The men and boys stared, and ran after us; and some of them shouted things which, I suspect, we may be glad that we could not understand." They were amazed to learn that their simple and natural proceeding had grievously outraged Cuban notions of propriety.

At three o'clock, the interpreter of the hotel escorted us to the steamer. One victoria accommodated us and him, and another preceded us with the trunks. Once, the latter vehicle got considerably in advance, whereupon our own driver was sharply bidden to "catch up;" and as soon as we were within hailing distance, the interpreter hurled at his colleague an oath, an injunction to keep in sight, and a threat,—a pregnant commentary on the honesty of his class. This personage also procured the "permits to leave,"—certain bits of printed paper whereby the government makes a final four dollars out of foreigners. Looking at mine, I was amused to see, among other provisions, that a traveller who brings his wife hither, is not permitted to leave without her, unless he presents her written consent at the Passport Bureau. It must be conceded that despotism has its good side.

We find the deck of the "Cuba" piled with crates of oranges, and every empty state-room and corner stuffed with bananas, now green, but expected to make some advance in maturity ere we make our port. Fruit-boats surround the steamer, from which the passengers lay in riper stores for their own use, during the voyage. A forest of masts is about us, with flags of every nation flying; and one Spanish man-of-war, long, black, and villainous-looking, is moored just beyond us. The western sky is radiant; on one side, a shimmer of sunset gold is on the water, on the other, a line of silver from the rising moon. The last trunk is lifted on board, the revenue officer departs, the anchor is up, and the vessel moves. Slowly we leave the fair city behind; more swiftly we pass the Cabaña, the Morro, and the Punta fortresses, and slide out upon the open sea, followed by the sound of the evening drum-beat from their walls. Behind us, is a wavy, hazy outline of green and gold; before, the wide expanse of the heaving ocean. On a neck of land, a tall palm comes out to look at us, and bends its plumy crest as with a last adieu. Farewell, tree beautiful and beloved! Farewell! sweet "Island of Flowers!" Farewell, dear, hospitable, indolent, kindly, courteous people!

And now, O, Home-Faces! vessel and heart beat steadily toward you!

---

Go to Cuba, friends and readers mine, all of you who

can. There are only four days—five, at most—between you and its greenness, its goldenness, its grace, and its grotesqueness. A much longer journey would not take you into a land richer in all that is contained in that pregnant word—*foreign*. If you go to England, you find a country teeming with historic interest, and full of a gentle picturesqueness, it is true; but far from unhomelike in its English tongue and ways, and whereof the scenes and images have been familiar, through study or by report, from childhood. But in Cuba, language, architecture, landscape, flora, manners,—all are new, strange, and suggestive. Life becomes continuous picture and poem, through which you drift so inevitably into dreamland, as to make it forever after uncertain how much of what you beheld was of the actual earth, how much of the domain of imagination. Especially is this the case in some of the old eastern and southern towns, where the Andalusian (and through them the Moorish) traits have been less exposed to the modifying influence of the stream of foreign travel. Linger not too long in Havana, therefore; better things—that is to say, things less modish and more picturesque—are to be had, for the seeking. Neither hurry from flower to flower, as if there were never more a to-morrow, but sit down quietly by each, and slowly extract its sweetness and its meaning. So shall Cuba be to you a thing of beauty, in the possession, and in the remembrance, a joy forevermore.

THE END.

www.ingramcontent.com/pod-product-compliance
Lightning Source LLC
Chambersburg PA
CBHW032050230426
43672CB00009B/1541